Daily

and Comfort

*Inspiration for a Meaningful Life While
Living with Chronic Pain and Chronic Illness*

Chronic Pain
Anonymous ®
*"... a fellowship for those with
chronic pain and chronic illness."*

Daily Peace, Joy, and Comfort

Inspiration for a Meaningful Life While Living with Chronic Pain and Chronic Illness

ISBN: 978-1-7353295-0-5

Library of Congress Control Number:

Chronic Pain Anonymous World Services, Inc.
13802 N. Scottsdale Rd.
Ste. 151-10
Scottsdale, AZ 85254-3403

E-mail: inquiry@chronicpainanonymous.org
Website: www.chronicpainanonymous.org
Phone number: 888-561-2220

Pending CPA World Service Conference Approval

Fellowship Review Edition 0

CPA Serenity Prayer

God, grant me the serenity
to accept the things I cannot change,
the courage to change the things I can,
and the wisdom to know the difference,
thy will, not mine, be done.

Contents

Foreword

Chronic Pain Anonymous (CPA) is a Twelve Step program started in Baltimore, Maryland, by Dale L. and Barry M. in 2004. The fellowship now hosts meetings around the world, helping those struggling with the spiritual and emotional debilitation from living with chronic pain and chronic illness.

In CPA, we share our experience, strength, and hope with each other so that we may help one another recover from the disabling effects of chronic pain and chronic illness. Our lives have been characterized by countless doctors, diets, and alternative therapies, and by desperately trying anything to return to the lives that we had before we became ill or injured. This can be overwhelming, and many pursue this into isolation, addiction, anger, fear, and depression.

CPA offers friendship, hope, sanity, and peace. By practicing the Twelve Steps and Twelve Traditions as individuals and in groups, we develop a set of principles for living, both inside and outside CPA. We are amazed at how our lives improve by learning from and supporting each other.
There are no dues or fees for membership. We invite you to explore our website, try a few meetings, and discover how CPA may enrich your life too.

Wishing you daily peace, joy, and comfort,
Chronic Pain Anonymous

Introduction

How This Book Came to Print

The members of CPA have dreamed of a daily reader since its early days. It was first noted in 2008, a mere four years into CPA's existence. But because we were a brand-new fellowship, other projects were prioritized. The dream did not die, but it did sit on the shelf for a while. It wasn't until 2018 when the Literature Committee decided it was time to start making this long-talked-about daily reader a reality. Or at least to begin the process, which meant collecting submissions from CPA members who wished to contribute. From 2018 through 2021, that's exactly what happened. Email and video groups formed to write entries on various prompts. Along with individual member submissions, the Literature Committee received more than 400 entries! Once collected, these passages were beautifully crafted into 366 vignettes. Through the combined efforts of professional editors, members of the Literature Committee, and the year-long fellowship feedback process of editing, this book came to print, while still keeping the varied voices of our members clear.

Ways to Use This Book

The customary use for daily meditation readers is to read one vignette per day, as labeled. For example, reading January 1 on January 1, and so on for the entire year. However, you do not need to start at the beginning. Feel free to start this journey on any day of the year. If you miss a day, you can skip it and read the present day, or you can continue reading them in order.

But going in order is not necessary. If a page does not appeal to you, that's fine. Just find another one, or use the index to find a topic that is on your mind. Please don't feel restricted by the dates. Any reading can be used on any day. You can simply open the book to a random page. Read and focus on your favorite reading every day for a week. Go ahead, read February 29 more than once every four years—it's okay. The ideas are endless. How creative can you be?

Everything needed to conduct a CPA meeting can be found in this book, including: CPA Preamble, Twelve Steps, Twelve Traditions, Twelve Concepts of Service, CPA Declarations, One Day At A Time (bookmark), One Night At A Time (bookmark), Suggested Meeting Format, and an in-depth index. Common meeting formats include selecting a reading coinciding with today's date and then inviting each member to share on a topic related to the reading. Another option is to select a topic from the index, read a few of the corresponding pages to introduce the selected topic, and then open the meeting for shares. More details about these approaches can be found in the Suggested Meeting Format found in Appendix H.

Please Remember While Reading

Though there have been edits and changes made to the original submissions, please keep in mind that each entry was, at the outset, written by an individual, and is ultimately the expression of that individual's personal opinion and not the opinion of the Chronic Pain Anonymous organization as a whole. Likewise, CPA is not allied with any sect, denomination, political group or party, organization, or institution; does not wish to engage in any controversy; and neither endorses nor opposes any causes.

Any references to a Higher Power by a specific name, gender, number, or pronoun are that of the writer's understanding. If you like, wherever you find it appropriate and helpful for your recovery, please substitute the words for a Higher Power with those which you are most comfortable with. You are free to adapt and alter any language that you find benefits your journey with this book.

Living with chronic pain and chronic illness is not an easy path in life, but we find hope with one another. This daily meditation book is an avenue to share our members' voices. The hope is that CPA members find peace, joy, and comfort within these pages. Even though we may feel lonely in our pain, we find that listening to one another's experience, strength, and hope eases our isolation. These readings help us to stay connected to other members at any time, even between meetings or outreach calls.

We recognize ourselves in one another, and we believe that if someone else has experienced hope, then maybe we can too. We know that we are more likely to find personal growth when we apply these recovery principles together. Because of the nature of living with chronic pain and chronic illness, we compassionately understand that there will be many ups and downs ahead. The Twelve Steps gift us a way of life that allows us to have our bad days and not condemn ourselves for our mistakes. We clean up our messes and move on to do better next time.

These pages remind us to be gentle with ourselves at all times. After all, we are doing a great job at living through challenging circumstances. We remember that our recovery cannot always be perfect and that over time we will see our progress. A seed can only grow when it is left to flourish in the soil—we don't do it any favors by digging it up to see if it has taken root. So goes our recovery. We tend to it by doing the work of the Twelve Steps and not judging ourselves too harshly. We remember that years are built by taking life *One Day At A Time.*

January

In Chronic Pain Anonymous, it is suggested that we don't share specifics about our pain or illnesses. As I have gotten to know members one-on-one, of course those details come up. But in a meeting, we have the protection of anonymity, which provides a welcoming, nurturing ground for compassion and understanding.

When I was a newcomer, I was afraid I didn't really belong. Pain wasn't my primary issue. Fatigue and other symptoms were making my life unmanageable. I was vague with my shares—because I wanted to belong, not because I understood that we were supposed to share in a general way. It took a while for me to hear other people sharing about symptoms other than pain, but by then, it didn't matter. I was relating to people's shares: to their fear, isolation, anger, envy, and depression. I wasn't alone anymore.

I can go to a meeting and get as much from the share of a person who's been in CPA for a decade, or only for a couple of weeks. This is possible because our sacred space is honored—starting with the Serenity Prayer and closing with the same. There isn't anywhere else I can go to get those moments to share my thoughts and feelings without interruption. And there is nowhere else where I get to listen to others thinking and feeling similarly about their bodies.

Meetings are what I treasure most about CPA. It's here that I feel seen, heard, and understood. I know I belong—with pain or with symptoms, with this chronic illness or that type of chronic pain—it simply doesn't matter. We are all in this together.

In this moment, I will experience the peace, joy, and comfort recovery offers me, if only for a moment.

Chronic pain and chronic illness force me to return to Step One often. It is a kind of "home base" I tag, again and again, before moving on with some serenity.

Because I've always been a good "manager," I suffer from the illusion that if good, prudent management is good, hypervigilant care is better, and—by seemingly sound logic—obsessive management is best. Unconsciously, I equate "best" with *complete* management of outcomes. I am unwittingly suffering from an obsession to control and direct my pain and illness. My obsessions play a role in my emotional and spiritual debilitation, which CPA has helped me recover from.

When the truth of my delusion of control became clear, in a deep, whole-body understanding, I turned to the Twelve Steps of CPA. I began to see that I had to let go of a lot of old ideas and my intense need to control, if I want to survive. In that moment of truth, I was humbled enough to ask for help. I became teachable. I was ready to try another relationship with life.

In this moment, I will step up to this simple but profound process of CPA Twelve Step recovery.

Lately, waking up in this body every day is a struggle. Coming into reality—thinking about all I "need" to do today—I realize the events of the day are not necessarily up to me; they are up to my Higher Power, whom I check in with hourly, for guidance.

Today does not look like I wanted it to. I'm tired. I don't like holidays. I wanted to shower, unpack boxes, and prepare to start my new year in an orderly way. Fortunately, God's time does not follow any calendar. At some point today, my body will fall into sync with my Higher Power's plan; I'll spend time with friends in CPA meetings and end the day having fallen through laughter into peaceful rest. I'm hopeful that tomorrow, my pain will be gone…and I'll be strong—relieved of the impending fears of the disappointment that occurs when that does not happen.

But now, I have a safety net in CPA that draws me out of obsession with what I cannot do and the improbability of a physical solution. I know it will be there today and tomorrow, no matter how rough the start of my day is.

Part of my daily ritual is reaching out to at least one other CPA member to start my day. I find that by the end of my day, I've interacted with several CPA members in several contexts. I go to bed at night feeling like my life matters—it's a feeling of fulfillment, usually sprinkled with some laughter.

In this moment, I will find hope. It is a phone call or text message away.

I thought I knew about powerlessness and surrender. Each surrender I made led to tremendous relief, and I became a better person, living a better life. When chronic pain and illness entered my life, I had to go much deeper and really explore the meaning of powerlessness and unmanageability as talked about in Step One.

What I had missed before, and didn't comprehend until CPA, was the extremely important indwelling awareness, not just of symptoms telling me what to do or not do with my body, but a compassion for the Me who was alone, isolated, and suffering behind the storms and chaos of chronic pain and illness.

Whenever I ignore this compassion for myself, I inevitably end up in an extreme emotional state in which I can harm myself, and sometimes others. In this state, I'm not likely to think about sitting down and meditating; I obsessively berate myself (all night long sometimes).

The difference for me now, in CPA, is that I am willing to describe my suffering to a room filled with fellow sufferers, and immediately I am filled with the camaraderie of others nodding their heads in comprehension and love.

This fills my heart in a way that such shared understanding never has before. It can bring tears of joy, which I'm not yet comfortable showing but for which I am so grateful as I continue to learn to be vulnerable.

In this moment, I will choose to treat myself with the compassion and care I would extend to a friend.

Let Go and Let God is a slogan that takes extreme courage. For me, this slogan is the foundational principle of Higher Power (HP) reliance found in the Twelve Steps. And when I carry this slogan into my Step work, again and again I rediscover the power of the Serenity Prayer.

> *God, grant me the serenity*
> *to accept the things I cannot change,*
> *the courage to change the things I can,*
> *and the wisdom to know the difference.*
> *Thy will, not mine, be done.*

My need to control and direct my pain and symptoms cause my life, behaviors, and relationships to quickly become unmanageable. *Can I accept my powerlessness over my chronic conditions? Can I seek the assistance and wisdom of something greater than my own mind and best efforts? Can I take the risk of really taking a look at my actions, feelings, thinking patterns, motives, and gifts in a nonjudgmental way? Can I set aside what I think I know and be brave enough to change and to be changed? Can I admit to myself and to others the exact nature of my human-ness?* All of this requires letting go of fear and placing trust in my HP. The Serenity Prayer makes all this possible for me.

It takes great courage to *stop*: stop fighting life, stop fighting my body and my mind, and stop fighting those who wish to help me. My bravest CPA change of attitude was coming to believe that, somehow, some way, I am in the hand of a loving Higher Power.

In this moment, I will be given the courage to turn my will and my life over and really mean, "Thy will, not mine, be done."

I arise in the early morning stillness. My body has become conditioned to these early hours. At this time of morning, I read, contemplate, gather my thoughts, and ask Higher Power (HP) to guide my day.

I hadn't been able to do much of anything else for the past several months. I'd been shaken by the new medical conditions that arrived and will stay for the rest of my life. I hadn't adapted well, and I hadn't really asked HP to help me endure—to live with the "cards I've been dealt." In yet another moment of despair, I finally asked HP to guide me.

My prayer was not formal, not religious…just a thought that became a prayer. *Is there help out there?* I was moved to enter "life with chronic medical conditions" into an online search engine, and up popped Chronic Pain Anonymous. The answer to my prayer.

I had been given this gift, this connection that I found in CPA to help me. Understanding, comfort, and support were shared with me. And as I began to share, I began to change, learn, grow, adapt, and accept my new conditions. I am so grateful to have found CPA as daily peace, joy, and comfort have replaced my despair and isolation.

In this moment, I will acknowledge that actually my Higher Power stepped in and gave me hope in finding CPA, in spite of my fear and depression.

I have accepted that I am physically and/or cognitively functional for only a very few hours a day—on a good day. But I find I still want to explain, even within CPA, how I can't do things because my brain and body can no longer be forced to function, that my body now will just override and quit. Acceptance and humility—Step One—are what I need to turn to, repeatedly, in order to set boundaries.

I feared being labeled as lazy, snobbish, or uncaring, but now I have a different understanding. I am *powerless*. This helps me be less critical with myself and others, both inside CPA and in my other relationships. When I honor my limitation boundaries, it doesn't mean I'm being mean or uncaring; it means I am powerless and am practicing self-acceptance, self-care, and self-love (the three *S*'s of CPA).

I still find it so difficult telling a fellow member who reaches out for help that I just can't talk right then. I used to sacrifice my well-being to another all the time, but thanks to Step One, I now see it's my stubborn denial of self-care that makes my life unmanageable.

I have learned that when I practice self-acceptance, self-care, and self-love, that is a CPA victory.

In this moment, I will celebrate my self-care boundaries. I am grateful for my new understanding of powerlessness and unmanageability.

What does "admitting powerlessness" mean to me?

Admitting I am powerless brings me to acceptance of the reality of my circumstances. Acceptance releases me from feeling that I do not do enough or am not enough.

Admitting powerlessness also means I accept reality, even when I find it unacceptable. My dreams of working until retirement and being financially independent are gone. I'm not able to live alone easily, and I've needed a cane to walk since young adulthood. I am unavailable as a healthy, physically equal, and capable partner and companion, and I can no longer dance, sail, scuba dive, or ride a bike outdoors. I always need a Plan B and can't be consistent in my commitments.

Thanks to CPA, I am learning to accept all the feelings that come up surrounding these limitations, broken dreams, and hard challenges. I am powerless over them. I can now feel them and then let them go, as opposed to staying stuck in grief and suffering. I've learned that I can grieve but not endlessly suffer emotionally.

There are lots of positives in letting go of being adversarial with my pain/illness and my losses. Surrendering actually creates a void that begs to be filled with positive emotions and spiritual nourishment, or simple love of myself and others.

In this moment, I will admit my powerlessness, release negative thoughts, and make way for more ingenious, creative ways to live my current reality to its fullest.

When I attended my first CPA meeting, something happened.

Chronic pain and illness had isolated me, and until that meeting, I was unaware of how shut off I'd become. I seldom left the house or saw people. My focus was on how *awful* I felt almost all the time. Isolation had become a comfort to me. But during that meeting and the fellowship after, I realized: my pain and symptoms were easier to deal with when others understood. I relaxed. I can't describe the sense of belonging and rightness I felt. I had come home.

I am someone who loves and *needs* her alone time. I keep my cupboards stocked, have as many books as my shelves can handle; I have Internet service and plenty of streaming apps. I recharge by being with myself. But any asset can be taken too far. I had no idea how much I needed to connect with people like myself. Now that I have friends in CPA, meetings, and service work, I balance alone time with human connection.

My CPA program is based in working and living the Steps, nurturing my relationship with my Higher Power, and finding and strengthening my CPA recovery. But I cannot minimize the value of belonging. Connection with others separates me from my pain and other symptoms so that I am myself first.

In this moment, I will remind myself that although I have chronic pain and illness, I no longer feel alone.

Starting my day over at any time is a lovely freedom I can enjoy. When my day isn't going according to my design, I can take a breath, relax, and release my tension and frustration. I stop and reconnect with my Loving Source. Joy begins to creep into my awareness when I stop trying to run the show. Sometimes, abandoning my plans is the healthiest thing I do with my day.

If the pain or illness I am experiencing is more than I expected, I can pause, acknowledge the present situation, and readjust my expectations and plans. This gives me the chance to take care of myself by making a choice to rest or cut back on my activities. When this happens, I also have the opportunity to change my perception to one of grace rather than judgment for *"taking the day off."*

If I'm depressed, fearful, angry, resentful—experiencing any challenging emotions or situations—I do not have to be stuck in them all day. I can allow myself to feel the feelings, and then I stop, take a breath, and clear my mind. I might be feeling difficult things, but I don't have to be miserable all day. I determine what I can do to make a change if that's possible and useful. I might make a gratitude list, grab some literature, look at the resources on the CPA website, or contact another CPA member to help me.

In this moment, I will pause, take a breath, and start my day over.

Before CPA, I would classify days as all good or all bad. I know now that's not true. I now consider a good day as one in which I wake up, surrender, and accept that not much will be accomplished except for self-care for the day, as I make amends to myself for all the years I pushed way too hard.

When I remember past days as all good, it sets up unrealistic expectations for the future. When I see them as all bad, I'm missing out on seeing all the things that can contribute to happiness. When I wake up with very low energy or more symptomatic than usual, can I keep an open mind? Sometimes a good nap, or some other unforeseen help or event, can turn things around.

My Sponsor has taught me: 1) If I can't go back to bed, I may as well use the time to do something pleasant—perhaps connect with fellow CPAs. 2) Today and this time are precious, even though they're imperfect. 3) I really *can't* control or predict how I will feel in the future, so it's not healthy to project and catastrophize. 4) Focus on the yeses—on what is possible. (When I can't sleep, I can journal, read program literature, connect with friends, etc.) It feels good to let go of expectations and remember that physical and emotional feelings are transitory. Labeling things as good or bad no longer serves my recovery or my practice of acceptance and surrender.

In this moment, I will accept that this "bad day" feeling is just for now, not forever.

I equate Step One with humility, and my humility was born of desperation. I could not cure my illness or stop the pain from coming, but I also couldn't go on living like I was. I was only looking at the world through mud-covered glasses: feeling hated by fate, hating myself, my life, and my body. I have come to learn that this is not humility. It's humiliation and self-hatred and total lack of faith. In CPA, humility means I accept and love myself exactly as I am and realize I am not capable of healing myself with my attempts to control situations. By trying to control my conditions and pain, I was only creating more unmanageability and despair.

The good news is, it took just a drop of true humility (self-acceptance) to get me to that first meeting that opened the door to Step One in my life. I knew I wanted to live like the people who shared in that meeting were living. I wanted to live with humor, with hope, with the acceptance that *this is who I am today.* No more muddy glasses!

Doing Step One with a Step buddy helped me become aware of the unmanageability in my life. I discovered the part I played by not asking for help when it was really needed or refusing help when it was offered. Allowing others to feel needed is a gift I can give them by allowing them to help me.

In this moment, I will humbly love myself exactly as I am.

I have an obsession to control and direct. And I have learned in CPA that I only have control over what I choose to do next. So I ask myself, *What is the next indicated action?* If I'm feeling poorly or I don't have any energy, I can rest. Often I get stuck in "keep doing" mode and don't pay attention to what I'm feeling and what I need. This slogan helps focus my attention so I can take loving care of myself.

When I am not feeling well and there are items I need to complete, but I am overwhelmed, I use this slogan: *What's the next indicated action? Take out the garbage. Okay, this I can manage.* I don't have to complete the entire list right now. Just one thing. Just one thing at a time. If I need willingness, I talk to my Higher Power (HP) and pray for guidance, strength, and clarity. I can reach out and ask for support when my to-do list becomes my HP.

When my energy is low, my cognition unfocused, and my emotions are intense, all I have to do is the next indicated action. I find there is always something I can do. I can listen to music or find something to feel grateful for. I can read something that will nourish my spirit, or I can pray for someone else who is suffering. I can just pause, relax, and breathe.

Doing the next indicated action brings sanity back into my life. It brings a feeling of relaxation, of serenity, and reminds me that I am not hopeless or helpless. Here, right where I am, there are choices.

In this moment, I will do the next indicated action as guided by my HP, not my to-do list.

I love the slogan *Progress, Not Perfection* because it is full of grace that I can apply to myself or to others.

I have been practicing the Chronic Pain Anonymous program for about eleven years. I work the Steps. I attend meetings, do service work, and Sponsor people. CPA is a very important part of my life, so I often expect that I have it down. I think that when I have bad days, when I am weak or in extra pain and it repeats day after day with no improvement, that I must know what to do. I am experienced in this program.

The truth is, no matter how long I have worked this program, there are still many times when I need it, but I do not think to work it. There are times when I let depression or the fear of never feeling better into my day and let them rule my attitude. At some point, I almost always remember, *Hey, wait a minute, I have some tools I can use to help me out here!* When I remember *Progress, Not Perfection*, I am accepting that I am human.

I can use this slogan to treat myself and others with kindness. We are all a work in progress. Working our program takes practice: making mistakes and learning from those mistakes. It helps to remember that while none of us will be perfect, all of us can progress.

In this moment, I will acknowledge that I am making imperfect progress, and that's perfect.

My first year in CPA, I learned that *Rest Is an Action,* and that was a simple but life-changing slogan. It had been difficult accepting that I could no longer do as much as I once did. Earning potential and the ability to keep up with my responsibilities in my home and with my family were things I had to let go of and let a "new normal" in.

Even after hearing this new definition of rest, it was still a challenge trying not to do too much. I was still confusing rest with laziness. Resting seemed like a waste of time. I was taught that my home, yard, job, car, etc. have to be in tip-top shape; if they're not, I have failed/am bad. Yet if I did not rest and kept doing what I felt needed to be done, I would frequently end up with a decline in my condition.

In CPA, I've begun to see and act on the fact that resting is doing something. This is a miraculous shift in my perception. Resting has moved, in my mind, from something lazy and irresponsible to something valuable and useful. It is the opposite of a waste of time. Resting keeps me feeling better and often results in less pain. It is taking care of myself, which makes my life more enjoyable. It's a very constructive use of my time.

In this moment, I will remember that resting restores my energy.
When I accept this and become comfortable with rest as part of my
life, I more easily pace myself and have less downtime.

I used to think it was human nature to see what troubled me in life and automatically discount what was going well. My reasoning was that by focusing on the things in my life that could or were already causing me harm, I would find solutions and ways to make those concerns and fears go away. I was afraid that if I forgot about my problems, it would be like turning my back on an enemy that would later attack me. I didn't realize just how badly that was *not* working until I developed an *"attitude of gratitude."*

Gratitude proved to be an antidote for depression, worry, and fear. Bringing gratitude into a troublesome situation felt like a balm or topical medicine for my hurt feelings and fractured thoughts. Being purposefully grateful lifted my mood enough that I could think differently, and often solutions were more forthcoming.

CPA taught me that gratitude is an amazing tool. I use it when I have to pass the time, waiting on someone or something, such as during an MRI when I must keep my eyes closed and my mind busy! I start with the letter A and go on down the alphabet. Sometimes when I am relaxing to begin meditation, I breathe in gratitude. Making a list, even in my head, helps me to feel the spiritual elixir of gratitude.

In reality, there is much more in a day that goes "right" than wrong. I have much more to be grateful for than to be bummed out about.

In this moment, I will relax into gratitude.

I've spent years dreading nighttime because I worry so much about sleep. I've grown so accustomed to waking up often to manage my condition that now I automatically wake up at least every two hours. Doctors have impressed upon me the need for restful sleep but have no solutions for the unpredictability of my condition.

In CPA, I heard a lot of people talking about difficulty with sleep. It was a relief to know I wasn't alone. I heard my story, took a personal inventory with my Sponsor, and was able to examine where the unmanageability lay. I started practicing a new way of thinking around being tired, the resulting emotions, and to learn to let my Higher Power into my obsession about my sleep hygiene.

First and foremost, on days when I've had very little sleep, I get support from other CPA members. They remind me that I may be feeling extra hopeless or overwhelmed because I'm tired and that these days are usually when I make myself crazy by trying to plan the rest of my life or do too much. Second, I check in with my body, a hundred times a day if I need to, to see if I'm tensing muscles and bracing against exhaustion. Fighting physical sensations drains the precious energy I do have. Third, my Sponsor reminds me often that my Higher Power gives me all the energy that is required of me that day—if I'm unable to do something, it wasn't required of me. I usually find that I'm stronger than I think I am, and if I need to cry, I can do so, knowing that feelings pass and sleep comes to me when it can.

In this moment, I will practice changing my attitude about sleep and relax into being tired.

I am so grateful for CPA. I've met such beautiful people and made lifelong friendships. I have learned to have more peace and love within myself, and I discovered that, *Wow, my Higher Power (HP) WAS with me!* all along, when I'd thought I was abandoned and alone.

I'm using the tools and looking forward to doing the Twelve Steps and Traditions. I've learned to cope and deal with whatever comes into my path. Before CPA, something would get in my way, and I wouldn't proceed forward; I would be stuck. Am I still struggling? Yes, of course. In physical pain? Yup…lots! Emotional pain? Yes, but so much better! I struggle less and have a support system now—people who truly "get it" and are there when I need them. And I am there to make sure they're doing okay too!

I've got more obstacles ahead of me, but there are fewer crisis-laden "what ifs"—the kind that used to leave me crying uncontrollably and then paying for it later with pain. I'm able to stop now and tell myself: "Those 'what ifs' only lead to more suffering." I just take a deep breath and keep moving forward.

I am living life with a peace of mind and actual control of my reactions, all because of finding CPA and realizing my HP has been with me all along. There is no shame that my eyes simply weren't letting me see in the ways I needed to see.

In this moment, I will honor that my eyes are wide open and my life has changed!

Just for Today is my go-to mantra when I realize my mind has slipped into another fear-of-the-future spin cycle.

I've been sick for many years and am now aging. Often, as I am going about my business, I think, *How will this get done once I am a little more ill?* My head begins to spin. This is part of my insanity. I admit I still suffer from the delusion that I can control my condition, my life.

Just for Today allows me to feel good about what I am able to take care of *now* and to *stop* trying to fortune-tell my future. I don't know exactly how I will deal with all the future holds. To accept what comes with graciousness will keep me firmly in the present. Today is all I am guaranteed.

What I *can* do for tomorrow is live well today. What I will need most in the future is to be better at the very skill I need most today. I practice letting go of anything except what is in front of me, focus all my God-directed energy upon it, and do my best. So today, I keep practicing living fully in the now.

To do this, I often follow *Just for Today* with *God, Direct My Thinking.* This sometimes means I take a small step or two on a problem, then let it go for a few days—whatever my health requires and my Higher Power suggests. Once I've done what I *can* do for today, I can, in good conscience, let go.

In this moment, I will remain fully present and let go of thoughts of tomorrow.

I appreciate the CPA acronym *STOP (Surrender, Time-out, Observe, Prioritize)*.

As with all obsessions, the mental and emotional deterioration I get when pain is relentless becomes a cloudy, paranoid wall between me and all other humans.

A singular exception for me is when my rescue pets give clear indication that I am not in my loving-kind mind. In fact, I get such clear feedback from their ultrasensitive selves that I have learned to turn back from extreme states. I need this feedback from tender-hearted loved ones. It helps me remember to put this slogan into action as my next step, pointing me toward recovery.

I've heard it said that hypocrisy is love without truth or that truth without love is brutality. Today, I am able to distance myself from brutal and cruel interactions—with myself and others. My animals—and my body—tell me the truth about how I am doing.

I need this truth, it helps me *STOP* and reboot. I lose any connection to my Higher Power until I do.

In this moment, I will STOP and connect with my Higher Power.

Before CPA, it would have been hard for me to believe how *Acting as If* would really work. I would have gotten all hung up on the dishonesty of it and how that is truly not me. I am honest!

There was a time when I did not want to pray because many of my religious prayers are of gratitude, and I was not in an attitude of gratitude. In fact, I was very angry at Higher Power (HP) for all the injustices of my life. Then I read a humorous short story. A Sponsee was telling her Sponsor that she didn't want to do something because she didn't feel it and thought that it would be hypocritical. The Sponsor responded, saying, "That's correct. Heaven forbid— we wouldn't want you to be hypocritical. You can be a glutton, you can be a thief, you can be smelly, you can be disheveled and slothful, you can be a liar, you can be angry and rude... But no, you should definitely not be a hypocrite."

That got me to say my prayers. And, here's the good news: *Acting as If* does work! I've even started to thank HP for when things go wrong and I'm in a lot of pain. I don't usually mean it, but it does help remind me that HP is in charge and knows what's best for me—better than I do.

I often just want to be comfortable, but comfort does not help me to reach my goals. Often, I have to endure discomfort to get to what I really want.

In this moment, I will Act as If in areas of my life where I am unwilling or afraid.

In doing my Step Four inventory, I identified the character defect of comparing myself to others and judging myself as lacking.

A slogan that helps is: *"Don't judge your insides by someone else's outsides."* There are times I've dressed nicely, put on a smile, and presented to the world as a "well" person. The truth was, on the inside I was running on fumes, feeling miserable and disconnected. I was a master at acting "well" thanks to my invisible illness.

In CPA, I've learned there are levels of intensity and frequency, of both pain and illness. My body doesn't stay the same from one day, or one week, to another. On a good day—one with decreased pain and fewer symptoms—it may look like I'm "not that ill." When I'm having a bad day, I tend not to share it with others so they don't know how much discomfort is present. My safe place is my meeting, where I can share my feelings and my struggles. At meetings, others share their inner worlds, so I know everyone goes through the same ups and downs that I do.

If I compare myself today with myself last week, I can get caught in a trap, trying to figure out why am I not as well or why am I better than last week. What did I do wrong, or right? Those lines of thinking merely strengthen my obsession. Comparing means living in the past or the future. Sanity, for me, is found in the present moment, and in the program of CPA.

In this moment, I will release judgments about myself and others.

Every morning, I remind myself that I am, ultimately, powerless over my condition. As the gears in my head start slowly turning, the stark and simple truth of that powerlessness, once more recalled, drops me into the beginnings of acceptance for the coming day.

This means that I'm not fighting or resisting things as they are. Yes, I can try all kinds of medical treatments, alternative therapies, psychologies, and religions to improve my quality of life, but I'm not going to get out of the human condition in which both joy and suffering exist. My delusional disappointment is that somehow, I was not assigned the role of God. *I'm not God, I can't control everything the way I so badly think I ought to be able to. No.*

Instead, I pray and meditate, be in fellowship with others who understand, and be about the business of growing emotionally and spiritually. I act when I have been directed by an intuitive thought or a serendipitous meeting or event. I reflect conversations with one who knows me and my defects well. I am not leading but following. *And* I am acting. Powerlessness means I give up insisting, directing, and demanding, not that I give up living or trying.

In this moment, I will take the actions I am guided and inspired to take.

Surrendering to the fact that I've got this thing called chronic pain and illness, I now understand that if I want any kind of serenity, I have to move to accepting it. I may not like the situation, and I don't have to like it—I just have to accept it in order to pivot in a more positive direction.

Acceptance of things as they are right now does not exclude the possibility that I may be directed to try new treatments. But acceptance is essential for an open mind that is willing and teachable. I don't have the energy to waste on internal rants about how unfair this or that is. I don't believe that energy helps me or anyone else, and frankly, it's been my experience that it's really the kind of energy that harms me and those closest to me.

Some days, I find myself beginning to fire up over something— some wrong or slight or just the whole damned difficulty of it all— and I have to pull myself up and laugh a little. I am not royalty. The world does not defer to me. Instead of saying, "Oh, this can't be"—which is delusional indeed, since *it is happening*—I try to remember to say, "Oh, I'd not have preferred this. But it is as it is."

Today, I don't feel like bothering to be a royal pain to myself and others by resisting the current flow of things. I feel like taking it as easily as I can, doing all I can, and being okay with today as it is.

In this moment, I will live life on life's terms, not entitled expectations.

Loss and grief never seem to get easier for me. The cycle time has gotten shorter, but the pain of loss is always intense. Sometimes I get so angry when I have to face another adjustment to how I must live my life. And sadness at the loss of another part of my body or at more inability to function in the world is often under my anger.

I've learned that I have to take time and grieve. Sometimes, the functionality or mobility I think was lost comes back. For me, that's the insanity of living with multiple chronic conditions. Symptoms wax and wane. I get happy and nasty surprises.

I have a condition that produces a loud ringing in my ear. There are weeks and months that it is so loud I can't think clearly. It keeps me up at night. Meditation is impossible because all I can focus on is the roaring in my ear. And then one day, it is gone. There is no rhyme or reason. At one time, I searched for answers and chased doctors.

As I worked my CPA program on this specific condition with my Sponsor, I came to surrender it to my Higher Power and accept that this is *just for now*. In that process, I grieved the loss of peace and quiet and rejoiced when it left. As with all things in my program, I am never done. When it comes back, I will go through the process of surrender and turning over all my feelings again. I am grateful to have found a solution to living with my chronic, unpredictable condition.

In this moment, I will assure myself that recovery is a journey, not a destination. I'm grateful for the tools that help me each day.

I am powerless over my obsession with chronic pain and illness, the conditions and symptoms that arise without my fault or consent, and my relationship with the debilitating spiritual and emotional effects of both. My life is indeed unmanageable.

In early 2019, I found myself in constant pain unlike anything I had experienced prior. I was unable to get out of bed, make myself a meal, take a shower, wash my own hair, or handle the simplest tasks. I found myself unable to interact without reactive anger with my husband, the person I most love. I found myself unable to rise out of the pit of constant self-centeredness that turned all conversations back to me and my misery. I found myself unable to awake without wishing I hadn't, wondering how I was going to get through another day.

After three decades of active devotion in other programs, doing all the things one does to get to and remain in peace and joy, I had never felt such despair. I was baffled. I hated myself with a fervor I did not know was possible. This is how I crawled into Chronic Pain Anonymous. This is when my real emotional and spiritual healing began.

I wrote an entire notebook on my reactions to admitting powerlessness. The literature tells me I am powerless over the condition(s) and, most importantly, my *relationship* with myself, the world, and my living situation. This was a great relief because I knew it was *my reaction* to the situation that was causing my suffering and an unmanageable life.

In CPA, I am being shown other ways of responding that heal the spirit and emotions, soothe the weary body, and teach me that I am powerless, not helpless.

In this moment, I will help myself by working the Twelve Steps of CPA.

When I first came into CPA, any little body sensation surely meant catastrophe. I was obsessed! I calculated every action in regard to how it would affect my pain in the future, and I would agonize about every choice I made, assured I was to blame for any flare-up. My belief was that if I just managed my life well, I would be freed from suffering. CPA has taught me that it was this very "managing" of my pain and illness that was making my life unmanageable. *Who'da thought?!*

I love the slogan *Changed Attitudes Can Aid Recovery.* It reminds me that there is something greater than my mind that I can turn to when I forget that I am powerless. I can refocus my thinking by turning to that Power greater than my mind. I can write a gratitude list or turn over something to my God box. Most importantly, for me, is remembering that I did indeed make a decision to turn my will and my life over to the care of my loving Still Small Voice in Step Three.

Today, when my thinking turns to control and obsession, I pause, take a breath, and remember my program. *Oh right...here I go again, thinking I am responsible for my flare-ups. I am doing my best, and I am powerless over my chronic pain and illness. Still Small Voice, give me the next right thought or action.* When I do this, I surrender my obsession and trust that I will be guided toward a more peaceful, joyful, and comfortable life.

In this moment, I will remember that I suffer from obsession and turn to the Higher Powered solution of the Step Three.

I had a very difficult time with the concept of acceptance until recently. When I received my diagnosis, I was still working, exercising, traveling, socializing, and getting on with my life. I was "in control" and making sure everyone knew it. I had no relationship or reliance on God. Then, a traumatic event triggered a year-and-a-half-long flare. Everything was out of control! I thought, *I better grab on to something, or I'm not going to survive this.*

Acceptance and God are the most used tools in my CPA program today. When my pain is high, I go through my checklist of things I can do to reduce the pain—what is in my control. Once these things have been utilized, I say, "Acceptance is the answer." Often, this simple act relaxes me. It takes the pressure off and gives me permission to be okay with what is going on with my body.

When I'm fatigued and don't have the energy to get out of bed, I accept that I need to take care of myself and rest, and that's okay. When I'm depressed because I haven't had a "good" day in a long time, I remember that I've done my best. I accept the situation and pray for strength. When people look at me and say, "You look fine! Why can't you go to work, go to a party, stay up late, etc.?" I accept that I know my body and my capabilities. It's none of my business what others think or say about me. I pray that God will soften their hearts toward me. This not only changes how I feel about them, but it also changes how I feel about me.

In this moment, I will let go of what others think of me and keep doing the best I can.

When I came to CPA, the first thing that happened was that I found people who were able to accept their lives without living in constant resentment about their circumstances. This motivated me to attend meetings.

I began noticing that I was laughing with people who were quickly becoming my deeply compassionate friends. My despair began to lighten as I looked forward to attending meetings daily. This changing attitude, although not present at all times, allowed me to find some increased awareness of the aspects of my life, for which I am actually grateful.

I had been holding a lot of resentment. Chronic pain had stolen my career, my friendships, and my hobby of ballroom dance. Developing thoughts of gratitude, feeling friendship—and a bit of hope—allowed me to be more willing to explore how I was relating to my situation.

Today, after about a year and a half in CPA, my resentment has lifted. I can honestly say that I believe it is possible to create a life that I love, one day at a time, with the ongoing support of this fellowship. I am beginning to even find ways to be of service, both in this program and in the building in which I live. I am grateful I took a chance on CPA.

In this moment, I will express my gratitude by being of service to others. I will take a chance on CPA service.

I remember learning: "There is nothing more important than sleep." It's so fundamental that it can be easy to forget. As a person living with chronic illness and chronic pain, I need to expand this fundamental need to include *rest*. I need to do this because the sleep I do get is often disrupted and insufficiently restorative, and in part because my conditions need various *kinds* of rest every day. Sometimes I fight this need, thinking I can just tough it out. There are things I want to do, and I don't want to have to stop!

When a need isn't overtly obvious, I can interpret it as a psychological failing or character flaw—both of which carry a lot of social baggage. One thing that helps is getting validation (from myself, others, CPA literature, etc.) that my conditions are real, significant, and impactful—not a personal failing. I remind myself I didn't choose this, but I do have some choice in how I respond to it.

A Step One–related process that helps me do this is to make a list of all the conditions that have been officially diagnosed. It helps me see I am truly powerless over chronic pain and illness. And it bolsters my willingness to surrender when I want to keep fighting my reality.

To this end, I find it very helpful every time I'm in a meeting and I hear yet another person affirming, "Rest IS doing something."

In this moment, I will be creative in finding ways and the willingness to rest.

I have heard it said, "If you want to go fast, go alone. If you want to go far, go together." I'd learned to live alone with chronic illness, pain, and exhaustion for nearly four decades. Then, I discovered a new way of living in CPA.

I had never developed a relationship with a compassionate, supportive, and loving Higher Power. As I discovered the consequences of this, I found that I'd never truly been compassionate, supportive, or loving with myself, especially when it came to coping with my chronic conditions. I spoke viciously to myself. I persecuted myself for mistakes or falling short of expectations. And I shamed myself for my illnesses. CPA members helped me change the things I could but also shared how a relationship with a Higher Power had changed them. I had nothing to lose as I wasn't getting very far alone.

I didn't know where or how to begin. One of my Step buddies suggested I create a Higher Power "want ad." I listed all the attributes I wished "God" had and many that I wish I had. I then simply started talking to this Higher Power of my list. I felt silly and didn't expect much.

Before long, I began to realize my ad was answered! I was feeling lighter. I was treating myself more compassionately and not being such a pain to others. Character defects I had been battling for decades seemed to simply fade out in the light of this newly arrived loving-kindness presence.

Now, as I continue to travel far, I take my Higher Power and CPA village with me.

In this moment, I will re-enliven my commitment to the spiritual solution of CPA.

February

For Step Two, my Sponsor asked me to make a list of "tangible powers greater than myself." He said: "'God' is kind of an abstract thing. What are some things that you can interact with directly that can restore you to sanity?"

My list included:

- Meetings: I almost always feel more sane at the end of a meeting than I did at the beginning.
- Phone calls: Sometimes I get the perfect answer to my question. Sometimes I get to help someone else and not think about my own issues for a while.
- Literature: It's amazing how sometimes the section I choose to read has exactly what I need to hear.
- Working the Steps: When I do Step work, not only do I improve over time, but I also feel an immediate benefit. I'm in better shape spiritually and emotionally, and the rest of my day goes more smoothly.
- The Fellowship: Collectively, the CPA fellowship has more sanity to offer than my fearful thoughts. When I associate with the fellowship, I receive some of that sanity.
- Sponsorship: It often happens that when I'm talking to a Sponsee, my symptoms seem to recede. I can't tell whether my pain is less severe or I'm just less aware of it. And when a Sponsee asks a question, I give an answer, and think, *Wow, I can use that myself.*

For me, it's true: "God" sometimes feels abstract and far away. At those times, I can turn to one of these "tangible powers greater than myself."

In this moment, I will look for ways to connect to my Higher Power of my understanding, knowing that I can use meetings, outreach calls, literature, Sponsorship, Step work, or the fellowship when I am struggling.

When no cure for my pain or illness was forthcoming, I found myself in a long, desolate Dark Night of the Soul. Initially I felt abandoned by God, and then I became convinced there was no God. I could feel nothing. I was alone. I was sick, I hurt, and I was empty.

I saw faith in the eyes of the people at that first CPA meeting I attended. I was blown away by the down-to-earth spirituality and wisdom shared by people who obviously didn't feel well physically. Some were in bed wearing jammies, with stuffed animals and real live pets to keep them company. There might be tiredness around their eyes, and some hoarseness or drag in their voice, but they shared about life today, as it is, and it was not too bad! I can say without a doubt I came away from my computer screen over an hour later, and for the first time in over a decade—I felt my Soul again!

As I work the CPA program, I have come to embrace the fact that "control is an illusion." When I make a plan and decide what is going to happen, even if I have to force it, I sell myself short. The Power Greater than myself, who I am coming to understand again, has a plan for me that is out of this world! Somewhere along the way in my short journey thus far in CPA, I realized that all those years that I did not believe there was God or Higher Power, God always believed in me. God always loved me just as I am. I may not have had faith in God, but God has faith in me.

In this moment, I will practice faith and release the illusion of control to my Higher Power.

I have come to see that the Steps and fellowship of CPA are necessary for me to heal from the emotionally and spiritually debilitating effects of chronic illness and chronic pain. Collectively, people in the program have a more useful perspective than I do—they have something I want and have not been able to achieve on my own. Even if I have little or no specific faith at this time, I can choose to trust the group and the fact of its members' recovery.

I realize I am powerless in Step One, and I become willing to be open-minded about believing this spiritual process could work for me in Step Two. Now, I see that my next step is to *make a decision* to give myself over to this method of spiritual living in Step Three. I don't need to be sure ahead of time it will work. I just need to decide I'm willing to try it.

This is an action program, and no genuine and lasting change will come unless I let myself trust a Higher Power of my own understanding. How right it is that I'm asked only to trust my understanding, and perhaps experiment a little with surrender to the greater mysteries I don't comprehend but have sensed in my life? I now know that I no longer have to struggle to manage things on my own.

I grasp that just a little of my fundamental problem is a lack of power. I seek that deep and elemental force that undergirds and animates all. In this way, I can breathe deeply and relax. I can begin.

In this moment, I will open myself up, even just a little, to a Higher Power that can handle today's struggles.

I am a miracle. I am not what I was before I worked the Steps. Now, I have the opportunity to pass on the miracle, which I truly believe saved my life and demonstrated that there were great and small things for me to do still, regardless of the condition of my body.

Our book *Recipe for Recovery* reminds me the only way to really hold on to this experience is to pass it on to others. I can only do this when I'm ready. The transformation I experienced is a promise, not a hope. The recipe works when I follow it. When there is discomfort in my life, I turn back to the recipe or speak to another CPA member who has had success and ask for help to see what I am missing. I am not at fault, and mistakes are human. In fact, they are inevitable. But the recipe—the Steps and the program—is never far away, and I turn to it to guide me again.

If I have done well, it's expressed in my shares. Then one day, it just happens. I receive a phone call or a message from someone reaching out to ask if I would journey through the Steps with them. The first time, I was concerned. Did I really know enough to take on the responsibility of being a Sponsor? Would I screw it up and make things worse? My Sponsor reassured me that I am not doing this alone, but with my Higher Power, and that even the person who reached out to me was the work of that Power in my life, directing things. I need not fear.

In this moment, I will rely on the Step work I've done and carry the message of hope it's given me.

My journey with Chronic Pain Anonymous helps me face my fears.

My first fear was of going to an online meeting. I'd attended face-to-face meetings with a group of people I knew, while at an inpatient, thirty-day pain program. I attended my first online meeting "alone," from my home, with a fear of being judged, of not belonging, of being the "odd man out." I was welcomed and immediately felt at home.

Then I went to a hybrid meeting. I took a chance again and attended alone. It did not go well. As I was sharing, a man yelled, "Get over yourself." Ouch! I allowed that to hurt my feelings and occupy my thoughts for days. I asked people what I'd done wrong, whether crosstalk was allowed, how I should have handled that man's mean words and actions toward me. I attended once more to pay attention to the sharing guidelines and that man's behavior. The guidelines included no crosstalk; the man proved to just…be someone who needed recovery.

I faced a fear by attending again. I realized that I have to surrender; I am not in control. I expected *everyone* to treat me with kindness and respect. My self-pity was unwarranted—what the man had said was about him and had nothing to do with me.

Today, I go out of my way to welcome new people at meetings in hopes they will keep coming back. I thank that man for teaching me how *not* to treat a person who is new to CPA. I am filled with joy at every meeting I log on to, seeing the names and faces of others who are growing in the fellowship.

In this moment, I will continue to face my fears by planning to attend a CPA meeting.

Something I didn't know when I started in CPA was: I'll never work my program perfectly. Yes, I have an excellent set of recovery tools and use them regularly. I can make an attitude change. I can find gratitude in a difficult situation. I can reach out to my Higher Power and receive guidance when I am struggling. However, believing I can apply my tools every time I need them turns out to be part of my insanity—and makes my life unmanageable.

New conditions show up, symptoms come and go, pain waxes and wanes in intensity and frequency. I do my best to work my program through the good and bad times. One day, I reach out to a friend when I'm lost and confused, and the next day, I think I have to figure things out all by myself. Then I remember: *Oh yes, I can call someone!*

"Perfect" is an unattainable goal. My need for perfection is sometimes about wanting approval from others and often leads to blame and shame. This does not contribute to self-care, self-compassion, or well-being. I'm a human being with a range of emotions, old habits, and a body and brain that are not always reliable in ways I expect. It takes time to develop new habits, to shift attitudes, to let go of old belief systems. This is a process of progress, not perfection.

Progress is growth or development toward betterment. Surrendering expectations of perfection for myself is progress—my development toward betterment. The slogan *Progress, Not Perfection* helps me make sane and skillful choices for my well-being.

In this moment, I will celebrate progress and transform the belief that it doesn't count if it's not perfect—it's progress!. I can be content with "good enough." I am enough.

Acceptance is not something I did once and it was done. This is a tool I need to use often in my recovery journey as my body changes and more loss of functions occurs.

Denial is often my starting place. When I lost the senses of taste and smell, I ignored it. My thinking was: *This is temporary, it doesn't mean anything.* It took about a year for me to realize, *This ain't going away.* Moving past denial, I went to the Internet for answers and eventually spent money and time seeking a medical fix. *My body is broken, and the doctors will know what to do,* I thought.

Living with a chronic health problem means there are often no solutions. I had to learn to live with diminished and often absent ability to taste food. Chocolate had always been a treat, especially when I was feeling poorly. Now, most of the time, all I have left is a memory of this delicious experience. I had to accept that this was my new reality, disappointing as it was.

Here is why acceptance is crucial: without it, I would be spending all my energy mourning this loss and looking for the cure that does not exist. I do not have to like this new version of my body, but I *do* have to accept that this is how it is and no longer obsess about it.

In this moment, I will shift my focus to what is still intact and focus my attention on gratitude for the senses that remain.

For years, I had to take a type of medication that was risky for me but necessary. I was careful and took it as prescribed. I've recently had to discontinue this medication because it began to hurt more than help. The process of discerning this was very difficult. I had become the proverbial frog in the heated pan—the one where the heat can be turned up in such fine increments that the frog never realizes it's in trouble.

Without a CPA Sponsor, Tenth Steps, journal entries, and a great deal of Higher Power's grace, I would never have "jumped" out of that pan. I felt very scared. I had no idea how I would function without this medication. From previous experience, I realized I was at the edge of my comfort zone, which often led to good things I could not yet see.

Doing without this medication has meant accepting many more limitations. However, I began to experience new freedoms— essential ones. A mental clarity I'd lost somewhere along the way returned. My program became more meaningful, my conscious contact with my Higher Power deepened, and my fellowship relationships dramatically improved. I was much more grounded.

Does this mean I will never use this type of medication again? I don't know. Chronic illness teaches me that adaptations are constantly required. But now I can relax. I have found that staying open and accountable on an ongoing basis with a trusted, experienced person in CPA, like a Sponsor, is key when addressing my medication concerns.

In this moment, I will notice if I'm outside my comfort zone and commit to reaching out to my Sponsor or fellow traveler in CPA.

Before chronic pain and illness, I was a workaholic. I spent ten years struggling, constantly berating myself for not doing more. I went through cycles of forcing myself to get a new job, work for a while, and then end up in the hospital, followed by months of inactivity and depression. My chronic pain and illness dominated my life and made it impossible for me to work full time.

Service in CPA gave me wisdom and helped me grow. It brought me out of this cycle. I was not seeking work when I came to CPA, but my Higher Power (HP) had other plans! At the time, CPA happened to need someone in my field of study, and I felt that small, still voice (aka HP) telling me this position was perfect.

While doing service, I have felt myself blossom and thrive in ways I didn't think were possible with chronic pain and illness. The people I collaborate with completely understand my situation and limits because they are members of CPA as well. When something doesn't go as planned, everyone is understanding and supportive of the situation. I don't have to worry about flares impacting my service work because I know I have support and help when needed.

This gave me the confidence to slowly experiment with how much I can work. Using the pacing technique, I've now established a schedule that honors my limits, the needs of service, and other jobs I perform in life. It brings me such joy to see CPA flourish. I was able to help make that happen, and I did it in a healthy, positive way.

In this moment, I will feel grateful to CPA and my Higher Power for the many life lessons service has brought me.

I thought I was in CPA because I have a chronic health condition. As I listened to others share about their recovery and read the literature, I understood that my illness and pain are not the problem. It is my relationship to them that interferes with my serenity and happiness.

Some can drink a few glasses of wine and are not alcoholics, or they go to the casino and play the slots but don't have a gambling problem. I know people who have more serious medical problems than I do, but they don't need the recovery program of CPA. They don't obsess over their health. I do. That is why I need to be in CPA.

It is my obsession—my constant searching for ways to make my health problems go away that consumes my thoughts and makes me unhappy. It is my never-ending battles with a body that doesn't work the way I want it to that give me so much grief. It is my belief that if only I could get the right answers, I could finally live my life.

As I worked the first few Steps in CPA, I began to surrender my desire to be fixed and my belief that I am broken. This doesn't mean I've stopped taking care of my well-being. It means that my entire life is not focused on myself and my body. I'm not fixated on what triggers my symptoms, what I need to be comfortable, complaining to others, how sick I am, etc.

Someone told me that if I tell the same story more than three times about my health, then I am obsessing. This made me realize: others might be quite tired of hearing that story.

In this moment, I will be aware of my obsessions and ask for Higher Power's help if needed.

I have a bimonthly procedure that is incredibly painful and incredibly helpful, and I dread it every two weeks. My head is placed in a vise, and the mechanism is so loud that I am required to wear earplugs or earbuds. The first time, I wore the earplugs I was offered. Never having used them before, I got an instant earache that had to be medically treated. This only added insult to injury. What was I to do? The procedure hurts too much but yields such benefits.

CPA taught me that whatever procedure I am presented with, I can ask Higher Power (HP), *"How creative can I get in my self-care?"* regarding said procedure. How can I make an appointment a time of play? How can I make something that is naturally uncomfortable more pleasant? HP never lets me down.

The next time my head was in the vise, I wore my own earbuds and listened to British stand-up comedy. Now, I laugh and laugh and laugh out loud during the procedure. I discovered that my laughter actually reduced my pain level, and I come out of these experiences feeling lighthearted and giggling. I look forward to this "Comedy Club" appointment, and so do the technicians. They tell me they love when I come because they love to laugh at me laughing. My Higher Deeper Self's creativity changed my own attitude *and* brightened another's day.

In this moment, I will look for more ways to be lighthearted and laugh.

Chronic pain and chronic illness forced me to rest for the first time in my life. I was a superwoman, denying myself any form of self-acceptance or self-care, let alone self-love. Now I had no choice but to lie in bed and "rest"; I was bed-bound, barely able to make it to the restroom on my own. As I entered into my awful new reality, I had to force myself to rest. Force rest? The results of this forcing of course only increased my fatigue and anxiety in my already exhausted body and my depressed and terrified mind.

Then I found CPA and heard about resting *in the care of a loving Higher Power (HP)*. Wow! What a concept. It wasn't up to *me* to rest. It didn't have to be a chore. I could simply allow for rest, trusting HP to care not only for me but for everything in my life.

Today, when I take the action of rest, I do just that. I allow for rest. I relax and soften my body and mind; I breathe deeply and imagine myself wrapped in love and warmth and support. I have many different images for the concept of loving care, and they all support me by truly relaxing not just my body but my mind, emotions, and spirit as well.

Resting in loving care does not always equal a reduction of symptoms and fatigue, but it *always* creates a more peaceful, joyful, and comfortable feeling in the depths of my being. To me, this is CPA recovery in action.

In this moment, I will look for ways to allow for rest.

I find I require various ways to shift my attitude to help me discover God's will for me.

When the need for a yes or no regarding a request for my time and energy arises, I find that *sometimes* the only way to know if it's possible is to try it. Like a pair of jeans I try on and discover aren't a fit. I can return them without apology or lengthy explanation. This option lends a lighter attitude.

A daily gratitude practice has been a hugely helpful method to change my attitude. I used to make gratitude lists when desperate; they rarely made me feel better. In CPA, I've learned that gratitude takes cultivation. Daily noting of what's right shifts my focus from seeing mostly what's wrong. Over time, my outlook becomes more balanced: lighter and hopeful. I no longer expect to feel better on demand or hold that maddening requirement that I snap out of it and feel better right now by listing my gratitude. Instead, I understand it as an ongoing process—*a practice.*

I suppose the granddaddy of all attitude shifts for me comes in pausing to admit each day that I have chronic pain and illness. I don't have to like it, but I do have to accept it if I hope to live well. Morning reflection on the plain facts of my life wakes me out of that slip back into expectations more suited to my former, non-compromised state of health. Then, with fresh acceptance, I ask God for the courage I'll need for my current life—its joys and pleasures, its fears and sorrows. I repeat throughout the day: *God, may I go with the flow, be in the now, do the next indicated thing.*

In this moment, I will take action to adjust my attitude if necessary.

I think I am humble…until I ask for help due to my physical, mental, or even spiritual needs and see how well I'm able to handle either a lack of response from the individual I've asked, or if it's clear that what I think I need is not going to be someone else's priority. I do believe other people have their own lives to live. Accepting that though they may sincerely wish to help me, when I ask, they may not be able to, can be hard for me. Can I trust my Higher Power (HP), that the timing of anything—including what I think I need getting taken care of—is out of my hands?

In CPA, I'm learning to ask for help and to let go of the outcome. I learned this from listening to others who make efforts to practice this behavior. I no longer have to hold myself or others hostage to my expectations. I am learning to relax and trust, and to truly let go of outcomes. When I am able to practice a little bit of trust in my HP, I discover peace of mind and freedom from the stress that my old thinking causes me. There is always more room for growth in this department.

Someone shared with me the example of herding kittens: put several kittens in a room and try to get them to do what you want them to do. It isn't possible. I can ask for help in whatever area of my life I want and then let go of how that need is met. This is working for me, so far, and is a continual work in progress.

In this moment, I will let go and trust that Higher Power will help me get my needs met.

When I came to CPA, I'd looked in many other places for support: government and disability organizations, nonprofits, churches. I wanted help because it seemed so scary and impossible to handle on my own.

In CPA, I learned that I could ask, but I could not force people to see or hear my needs. I didn't cause my condition, and I would change it if I could. Before CPA, that thought—*I would change it if I could*—was a mission statement for me. I was glad to have some purpose, even if it was only to convince others I was worthy of services. Over and over, people said *no* to my requests for help. I felt like a victim, someone no one cared about, someone people thought wasn't in that much pain or wasn't that sick. In CPA, I found people who seemed more calm and accepting of the unacceptable.

CPA also taught me about the great power of prayer and meditation. I had been relying almost solely on myself; there seemed to be a lot I needed to do to make people understand my needs. But daily prayer and meditation helped me realize my Higher Power was far greater than myself, other people, and organizations. The more I prayed and meditated, the more I shed my victim role and could face life on life's terms.

My fears dissipated, little by little. Today, I don't feel like a victim. Yes, it might be nice to be freed of chronic pain and chronic illness, but I am okay and whole in spirit, even as I live with it. CPA helped me see myself as a full person as I move forward with my life, a day at a time.

In this moment, I will turn my fears over in my prayer and meditation practice.

In the past, I felt short bursts of potential hope because of a promised result from a new doctor, treatment, or medication—but I never had real hope. The rabbit trails I went down ultimately ended in failed results and feelings of disappointment.

Then one day, while desperately searching for yet another possible solution, I found CPA. I believe my Higher Power led me to this program. At my first meeting, a small seed of hope was planted. Although CPA was not what I expected, I felt as though my eyes and my heart had been opened. CPA offered a new and different way to live despite having chronic pain and chronic illness.

I heard shares, not about curing disease, but instead, heartfelt solutions to our associated emotional and spiritual pain. I knew I'd found "my people." As I began to experience real hope, I found that my body responded. I was experiencing life in a new way, with a new attitude. I felt lighter and more connected to the world.

Life is more joyful because of this changed perspective. Even when I am in bed all day, I can live my life as if the glass is half full. I do what I am able to and have hope for my future. With a new freedom from the obsession surrounding my pain and illness, I can truly experience life again.

In this moment, I will be grateful for CPA as a source of hope to which I will forever be connected.

With chronic pain and/or chronic illness, it's natural to feel envious and to compare ourselves to others who do not have this challenge. I often compare myself to my pre–chronic pain self and rue the things I'm no longer able to do.

I think comparing is part of the grieving process we experience when we try to come to terms with our situation and the changes it involves. This tendency is perhaps heightened by the advent of social media. We are surrounded by images of people whose bodies clearly have not let them down. Prior to chronic pain, I was a fairly active person. I had a full-time job, I was active in my community, and I am a father and husband (a son and a brother). I can still do quite a lot, but I get upset when it's a challenge to do things with which I'm familiar while living in an unfamiliar body. The temptation to compare myself to others often arises. I sometimes succumb to it, which aggravates my sense of frustration and misery.

I have started asking my Higher Power for help in managing this inclination. I notice when it arises, in an impartial, nonjudgmental way. It's actually quite amusing how my predisposition to comparing can manifest itself. There is a prominent politician in my country who is two weeks younger than me. When I see him on TV or read about him, I often think, *This guy is my age and managing the country's finances. I sometimes barely manage to make it through the day!* I am slowly learning to notice when I compare and to reach for a little self-compassion.

In this moment, I will accept myself for who I am and know that I do not need to be defined by what I do.

Hope is a word that eluded me for several years. I kept hoping that, doctor after doctor, treatment after treatment, surgery after surgery, would relieve me of my chronic pain. My constant focus was on my pain. What can I do to relieve it? How bad is it going to be today? What if I can't sleep tonight because of my pain? How am I going to get any chores done today? How am I going to participate in my relationship with my husband? I lived in moments strung together by fear. I felt like things were never going to get better.

I started coming to CPA and was shocked to find others who understood how I think, feel, and experience life.

I almost didn't come back after my first meeting because I got embarrassed during my share. I focused so much on what I felt about my own circumstances that I missed the hope that was there. During fellowship time after the meeting, someone gave me their number. I spent the next week talking one-on-one to another member who is my same age and struggles with my same pain. It was a Godsend. I kept coming back. I now go to meetings every day and hear the hope in being able to accept myself as I am—to accept my limitations not as negative parts of me, being kind to myself, knowing it's okay to be where I am. I want to learn so much about how to find self-love, self-acceptance…and honestly, just to find myself again. I lost myself since chronic pain started, but now I have hope I will come to find that I like myself again. Maybe even love myself.

In this moment, I will focus on ways to feel hopeful.

When the onset of chronic illness stopped me dead in my tracks, I found great relief in pacing to try to manage my energy envelope. It was such a useful tool until it became my obsession: *Okay, I have X number of hours out of bed for the day. Do I spend some of that energy on a shower or not, because showering really takes up a lot of energy, and it's only 8:00 a.m.? Okay, let me account for all the energy needed just to clothe and feed myself. Darn it, thinking about my energy just wasted energy. Argh!* Pacing became my master, not my servant. I fell under the delusion that if only I paced well, I could defeat reality.

When I arrived at CPA and read, *"The meaning of these Steps is based in faith, humility, and the ability to turn over the problems of our life to a greater power, without trying to control and direct the outcomes,"* I realized I was trying to control and direct my daily life—via pacing. If I wanted to apply the CPA program in all my affairs, I had to begin by giving my energy to my Higher Power.

As I practice Letting Go and Letting God, I find that Higher Power is much more powerful than a metaphor. When I pause and ask for the next thought or action, I find unknown reservoirs of strength, stamina, and courage, and creativity that I never knew I had. I no longer overanalyze my energy with extreme pacing. This "new normal" is peaceful, joyful, and comfortable because my actions or inactions are no longer up to me or my belief that life is limited by pacing "correctly."

In this moment, I will ask my Higher Power for guidance on the best way to manage my energy.

I was living a life of happiness and activity: golf, travel, books, crocheting, and being socially active filled my life. Then, it changed. For two years, I was bedridden, feeling hopeless, angry, and depressed. It felt like my life was over. Over the next five years, I tried all types of pain medications, every type of therapy, surfed the Internet relentlessly, with minimal relief.

I came to a point where I had to accept that there was nothing that could be done to eliminate the pain, that I had to learn to manage it. I felt defeated and alone. What was I to do? Fortunately, in my search, I ran across CPA. I found members who embraced me with love, compassion, and encouragement. They spoke my language. They understood me; I felt like I was home.

Acceptance of my situation and a deepening relationship with my God are giving me hope. I am redefining my life with activities that bring me joy and purpose. Online coloring, music, movies, visits with CPA members and family, walking when able, nature, seeing babies and puppies—all fill my cup. I genuinely feel more like who I was created to be.

In this moment, I will notice that I am a blessed person, exactly as I am today.

When approaching Step Nine, I was convinced the most important amends would be to my children. I had some fear that if I admitted my wrongs, somehow my amends would not work to repair the relationships. I wrote letters to my two children, in detail, about my wrongs and how sorry I was. My Sponsor reminded me that I needed to make amends to myself first. The concept of forgiveness and self-forgiveness was a lightbulb moment for me.

As I started to learn how to forgive myself, my children also opened their hearts, and a new foundation for our relationship was built. Both my children were very forgiving. I changed my behaviors to be kind and gentle to myself. Self-forgiveness gave me a new way to look at myself and, in turn, others. That allowed me to give kindness and compassion to others and to make amends. Some of my amends were a simple apology; that's all that was needed. Other amends required some changes in my behavior; these are still being changed, with time.

Working the Steps helps with my ongoing amends. As I learn to be kinder to myself, with the help of my Higher Power, I'm being guided to a more peaceful life with the people I love most. Praying for guidance from my Higher Power allowed for all of this to happen. My amazing Sponsor also helped guide me to make peace with myself and continues to support and give me strength to carry out my amends.

In this moment, I will focus on being kind and gentle toward myself.

All my life, I've had conflict with my body. From early childhood, I was engaged in a ruthless campaign of self-improvement. I was never good enough, could never do enough. Driven by self-will, I never succeeded in changing myself. Instead, after periods of frenetic activity, I collapsed into exhaustion and depression. Looking back, this was the only chance my body got to rest. But for me, rest was a four-letter word; once I regained some energy, the relentless cycle would start over again.

A huge impediment to my healing was my refusal to rest. I kept trying to force my body to perform the way it used to, the way it was no longer able to. I was unable to treat myself with compassion.

Through CPA, I am beginning to attend differently to my pain. I realize that all my exercise and management strategies over the years have actually been a form of bargaining. I've been saying, "I'll do all these things, I'll be really, really good, and the pain will go away." The pain isn't going away.

I no longer push myself when my body tells me it's time to stop. I am learning that my body is fine as it is. I am not separate from it, and when I treat it cruelly, I am treating myself cruelly. My developing relationship with my Higher Power is the foundation of this new relationship with my body. Through prayer and meditation, I am discovering how to be gentle with myself. (*Easy Does It.*) My body is not a thing to be improved; it is a gift to be appreciated. By resting in the loving approval of my Higher Power, I have found, at last, that change is possible.

In this moment, I will treat my body with loving-kindness.

I have been through many medical procedures since joining CPA, and I'm currently trying to decide about surgery. In the past, I've had a lot of anxiety around surgeries. I remember being seventeen, going into my first surgery; my mom, who was sober at the time, helped me connect with my Higher Power. We held hands and said a prayer together. I was scared about the anesthesia, so she had the anesthesiologist talk to me and help me build trust with him before I went in.

Fast-forward a couple decades to me joining CPA. I was getting a common procedure done, but my old fear was bubbling up. I was worried about how this could exacerbate symptoms and about how long it would take to get back to baseline. I scheduled the procedure for after my favorite Third Step prayer meeting, where I got to turn over the experience. This was just like holding my mom's hands and praying. I remembered that, ultimately, Higher Power (HP) is my surgeon. That thought is extremely comforting.

The procedure went smoothly. I came home to some delicious takeout—a treat for getting through the experience. I cleared my schedule for a week so I didn't feel pressure to accomplish anything while I recovered. This gave me the time and space to go slow.

Now, I am debating this new and major surgery; I am reaching out for help. I am asking my CPA friends for help and understanding. I am turning over my fear, every day. I'm an adult now, so when I choose a surgeon, I can meet with them, ask questions, and build trust with them before surgery.

In this moment, I will remember that I am never alone. I have CPA, I have guidance, and I have HP.

I have learned that I am powerless, but I am not helpless. I have no power over whether it rains. I have to surrender to the reality of rain. But I am not helpless. I can choose to take an umbrella when I go out, or wear a raincoat, or just not go out when it's raining.

The same holds true for my body. I am powerless over the thoughts that arise, over my digestive system, over my lungs, over my bones. I have to surrender to the reality of what happens with my body. But I am not helpless. There are things I can do to help myself. I can choose what and when to eat. I can choose to put heat on a part of my body that hurts. I can choose to recognize thoughts that don't serve me well and shift my attitude.

In CPA, I learned that the outcome of taking these actions is still not in my hands. I am still surrendering when I eat healthy foods. I am making choices as guided by my Higher Power, then turning the outcomes over to that power. I am making the best choices I can; I am powerless over the results.

There are always ways I can help myself. The key is in the Serenity Prayer: knowing the difference between what I can and can't change. I can't change my body. I can ask for the wisdom to know the difference and the courage to take actions that will help me cope with the realities over which I am powerless.

In this moment, I will ask for the courage to change what I can and the wisdom to know the difference.

Changed attitudes and actions can aid recovery. Yes, and…

Before CPA, I was drowning in the misery of all the changes my chronic pain and illness had brought to my life. On my own, I couldn't change my intense focus on every sensation, every negative thought, every debilitating feeling. It took something greater than me to effect a changed attitude.

Seeing smiling faces and hearing laughter in CPA meetings opened me to the new idea that I could be happy and disabled at the same time. The Twelve Steps taught me to surrender my stories, which led to the spiritual awakening promised in Step Twelve. For me, this awakening came in the form of Higher Power (HP), literally, changing my mind—giving me the choice and courage to choose to reframe my thinking and to release my need to label life as good or bad.

The freedom this awakening has given me is immeasurable. Some days, I need to honor my feelings of self-pity and sadness, letting that energy flow through me and exit. Other days, it is helpful to head such thoughts off at the pass. When I ask HP to give me the wisdom to choose which action is required, I honor the totality of my attitude—neither dismissing nor drowning in any story.

In this moment, I will choose to view life as an experiment, not a pass/fail test.

I really appreciate that CPA asks us not to investigate or discuss each other's treatments. In my other support group (of people living with the same disease), many conversations can quickly devolve into who is suffering more or who is administering what treatment better, etc. Part of my experience in trying to recover from my obsession of controlling my chronic conditions is getting into what I call "the conversation." This is when almost every interaction seems to turn into some mini health update, usually followed up by unsolicited armchair advice.

Medication talk can get even harder when you've had chronic illness long enough to learn that healthcare providers don't always know everything. I'm on medicines that, on their own, will eventually kill me if my disease doesn't first, but in order to live with my disease, I have to use them. I don't come to CPA to hear another person's opinion on this; I've had that conversation with myself and my care providers many times already.

It has been hard to relinquish control, to let each day be its own and not hate myself for the hard ones—which creates a whole other layer of suffering. I continue to work on surrendering and letting go. The added shame surrounding my use of medications is a big part of what I am working the Steps around.

What I have experienced in CPA is that there is an interest in my life that is more than medication compliance or updates on health outcomes.

In this moment, I will surrender, trusting in my current healthcare plan and knowing that as I work the Steps, good choices, both medically and spiritually, are indeed possible.

I could buy the notion in Step Two that I needed to be *"restored to sanity."* I was demoralized, depressed, and afraid because on some level, I knew my own resources were no longer up to the task of coping. But I had lots of baggage when it came to God and a deep irrational fear that I could only trust myself. I could, however, see that many in the fellowship of CPA had found a way out. They had what I wanted, but I could not seem to obtain it myself.

It was explained to me that I was not going to understand this power initially; rather, I would have real and vital experiences that would reveal it. In the meantime, I could simply trust the evidence of those in recovery who talked of no longer relying on their own power alone to cope with the destructive forces of chronic pain and chronic illness.

"It's something like falling in love. You have to experience it to know it. It's like that," my Sponsor would say. He suggested I just get started. I could address my petitions for help, "To Whom It May Concern." He said that if things didn't work out, the program would "refund my misery."

I thank God for such forthright, kind, and sensible people like my Sponsor and others. Finding my Higher Power became the great experiment of my life. And it's made all the difference.

In this moment, I will trust that experimenting with my beliefs in a power greater than myself is enough for me to experience spiritual growth.

I was open to a Power greater than myself in Step Two, although the word "God" in Step Three made me wonder if I was in the right place. My belief in a Higher Power/God developed gradually as I devoted myself to working the Steps with my Sponsor's help.

I'd tried my best to address my progressive chronic pain and chronic illness with innumerable attempts to cure or control my physical state. It was only after coming to Chronic Pain Anonymous that I began to see the insanity of my responses to my pain and physical limitations. In CPA meetings, I learned that if I put the God of my understanding first, and then my program, everything else would fall into place. I discovered my priorities had been reversed: I had put my career and other people ahead of my relationship with God. This was indeed detrimental to all my relationships, as well as my recovery, sanity, and health.

I am grateful for the opportunity to apply the Twelve Steps to other aspects of my life where I need help. The Steps work under any and all conditions. My faith and reliance upon my Higher Power grows as I listen, share, read, and participate in CPA meetings. While I usually prefer hearing the sanity and serenity that old-timers have gained, hearing newcomers share about the insanity also helps me realize I am in the right place. I certainly have more trust in God than I could have imagined before CPA. Listening gives me the most precious gift: hope.

In this moment, I will trust that I am in the right place and open my heart to listen to the hope that others share.

Until I came to CPA, I didn't think anyone would understand me and the choices I need to make to get through the day. The first time I shared in a CPA meeting, I often didn't get out of bed and dressed until late afternoon; instead of seeing looks of disapproval, I saw head nods. There was no judgment, merely shared understanding. When I talked to my Sponsor about the grief I felt because of the professional dreams I've had to give up, she looked at me with compassion and told me about how she dealt with this in her life.

We help each other in CPA by reminding each other we have permission to be idle, to rest, to not be productive every hour of every day. We give to each other by listening and not trying to fix or solve our problems. I can give to others even when I am prone in my bed, eyes closed, being warm and caring toward someone who needs a loving witness as they share their struggles that day. I can pass along the support and acceptance I received from others.

No one in CPA is an expert. We are always learning together on our recovery path. I'm grateful for everyone who said something at a meeting that positively altered how I responded to a situation later that day. I'm grateful to all the people who answered the phone when I was feeling poorly and showed compassion as I wept or ranted. I'm grateful for my Sponsor. And I am grateful for my home meeting and the love and support of the CPA fellowship.

In this moment, I will know I am of value even when I cannot get out of bed. I can still be loving and supportive within my body's limits.

March

Decades of chronic illness kept me working my first Twelve Step program: to change my attitude, to respond creatively, to grow closer to my God, but I felt very alone despite the many ways I tried to break my sense of alienation. One day, I found myself sitting in the parking lot alone after a meeting in that fellowship, weeping. Through my tears came this prayer: "God, I need some kind of support for PAIN, for this…ILLNESS."

I thought of purchasing another self-help book in hopes it would keep me going. The book I happened upon footnoted that it was used by Chronic Pain Anonymous. In a hot minute, I was on the CPA site, reading sample stories. One really hit me. I thought about how I'd like to talk to *that* guy.

So I found a meeting that night, and the host was *that* guy. Afterward, he spoke with me, late into the evening. It felt like a miracle to me—one that's been hard to beat. I like to recall it because over and over in my life, hasn't it been the case that the thing I needed arrived, eventually?

Often, my basic needs feel threatened by some difficult occurrence, and I must soldier on. Either things sort themselves or they don't, and I find I can, with God's help, accept them. It's been that way thus far; I can't speak to the future. I do know that when I note and affirm the many miracles, small and large, given me, I am reminded, again: *Don't quit.*

In this moment, I will remember that I am not alone.

Instincts can be tricky. It's not always easy to tell when it is my own will pushing through and when it is my Higher Power (HP) trying to communicate. In my experience, HP's will comes from a place of calm and peace, while mine typically stems from worry and panic. Noticing this difference is one way I've learned to identify whose will I am practicing: mine or HP's.

Working Step Three with my Sponsor, I connected with and came to appreciate my HP, but I can sometimes still feel distanced. During these times, I remind myself that I am trying my best and to *Let Go and Let God.* Letting go gives me a break. Instead of wasting my energy, stressing and obsessing over situations, and potentially making them worse, I can turn any situation over to my HP.

I keep items around my house to remind me to "let go" and trust in HP: a Serenity Prayer keychain that jingles when walking my service dog; my glass "God box," decorated with fairy lights; and jewelry pieces with the Serenity Prayer or recovery quotes. There are even some activities I've learned to help me turn things over: I can write about the issue and put it in my God box; revisit Step Three and my answers to the questions asked when working that Step; talk to my Sponsor; or meditate and imagine a peaceful garden I have created in my mind.

In this moment, I will remember that trusting my Higher Power brought something into my life that I was longing for. It brought me peace, and I will always be grateful for it.

"Thy will, not mine, be done." In CPA, we add this line to the Serenity Prayer. It reminds me that my serenity is based on accepting reality rather than on asserting my will upon reality.

This morning, when I woke up, I thought it would be a normal day. That was my will. The moment I stepped out of bed, I knew the day was not going to go as planned. My body did not feel stable, my head was spinning, and a fogginess had set into my mind.

Before CPA, I'd ignore the messages from my body—I'd disagree with reality. I'd pretend I was okay. I've learned the hard way that fighting with reality, fighting with the will of my Higher Power for this day, does not lead to serenity. I might check off the items on my list, but I make myself miserable as a result.

Today, the first thing I do is recognize God's will for my day. I accept what is true and surrender to reality. Serenity comes from aligning with what is happening in the moment rather than imposing what I think should be happening. With this shift, I can sort out what adjustments I need to make to adapt to this circumstance.

This day has been given over to my Higher Power. I don't know what the whole day will look like. I can always start my day over again. Living in this way brings me serenity.

In this moment, I will surrender my will and my preferences, and ask my Higher Power what to do next.

Sanity means: to have soundness of mind and judgment, be rational, behave in a reasonable way, be realistic, make good sense, make healthy and clear-headed choices.

When I first came to CPA, I didn't believe I would ever have sanity again. But this program works—sanity can be restored.

Insanity will never be totally gone; that's why I need to attend meetings, talk to my Sponsor, and work my program every day. I now know that when I've lost sanity, I can find my way back.

For me, sanity looks like this:

- When I am tired, I go to bed. (Good judgment.) Rest when tired. Even if it is noon.
- When I find a medication change causes problems, I call the doctor. (Reasonable action.) I don't try to figure it out myself.
- Before I go to a new restaurant, I look up the menu online and select what I can eat. If I need to make special requests, I can arrive with them already planned out. (This is a healthy choice.) If I'm going to someone's home, I may call and ask what they are serving and make a request for myself. If that's not realistic, I eat before I leave the house so I'm not hungry.
- When I travel, I start packing weeks in advance. I may arrive a day before an event or stay a day longer. I pace myself, arriving and returning home. I keep my schedule light, before and after the trip.

Sanity can just be good, common sense. I didn't seem to be able to do this before CPA. I often made choices that led to pain and suffering.

In this moment, I will remember that through my Step work and turning myself over to my Higher Power, I've learned a new way of living.

I am very new to CPA. I love the idea of the Twelve Steps, and know I have much to gain from them, all while being a little reluctant to jump in.

Just knowing I have a connection to this group is so helpful—that I can reach out to a meeting online or go to one in person. It's such a relief! I no longer feel alone in my pain. I am in physical pain almost all the time, but since coming to CPA, I find I am no longer fighting against my pain. I am learning to accept it and have faith that I can live a joyous life regardless of my pain. On days when I'm having a lot of pain, I have to take it easy and slow. CPA is teaching me how to slow down.

One coping mechanism I've developed is helping others. I find it interesting that when I help others, I avoid my own pain and suffering. It's as if getting outside of my head and focusing on someone else releases my grip on my pain. I am grateful to have CPA, where I can share the path of recovery.

In this moment, I will see where I might be useful to someone else.

One of the things that has really helped me in Chronic Pain Anonymous is developing a new perspective on resting. Back in my healthier days, resting was something I viewed as wasting time. If I was resting, I was not doing anything.

That's changed. Where I used to only be focused on what I could get done, now I am also focused on taking care of myself. It was a surprisingly difficult switch to make.

All my life, everything was about what I could accomplish. At work, it was taking care of my responsibilities, meeting deadlines. At home, it was cleaning the house, buying groceries, and cooking. Everything was about getting it done, crossing it off my to-do list.

When chronic pain/illness came into my life, I soon discovered this no longer served me. If I pushed to get everything done, I ended up in more pain and illness, which meant I could get even less done. At first, I struggled with guilt. There was a constant inner battle: I knew my body needed rest, but I also thought I *had* to get everything done. I was frustrated and in insanity—not facing reality.

When I finally accepted rest as a good thing, not an interference, it brought peace. I now realize that rest is not doing nothing—it is accomplishing something. It is giving my body what it needs so that I can live a life that is peaceful as well as productive.

In this moment, I will accept the benefits of rest in my life without guilt. It is part of balancing my life while living with chronic pain and chronic illness.

Before CPA, I had no issue with asking for emotional support because I had no emotions that needed exploration. I was just a normal guy. *What emotions?*

It wasn't until depression and anxiety drove me into Twelve Step rooms that I was desperate enough to ask others for emotional help. I discovered that expressing my fears and resentments, my confusion, and my faint hopes to those that understood was of enormous benefit, especially when combined with taking the suggested actions.

But I am still unable to request a specific favor of a physical nature. Something as ordinary as asking for a ride feels impossible. When I was able-bodied, I'd ask for that kind of help readily because I could and would easily reciprocate. Once I was too ill and disabled to return favors, I stopped asking.

I have some ideas about asking this—about being a "loser," a "freeloader," someone who made his own mess and now expects others to clean it up. I am not recovered in this matter; there is lack of humility, fear of rejection, and a deep belief that a man paddles his own canoe.

The abject honesty I find in the program has been as important as any specific guidance I've ever been offered. As for asking for help: I am trusting the process. For me, in CPA, the hardest things, requiring the most genuine changes, have shifted when I've had no choice but to grow through them. Humility gets me to move out of the way, giving my Higher Power the space needed to enter. My experience is that this works.

In this moment, I will ask for help when I need it, even if I cannot reciprocate.

When I was first introduced to the Twelve Steps, my perception of a Higher Power was attached to a specific theology. But there came a time when the concept of my Higher Power within that spiritual practice stopped serving me. It became a hindrance to who I was becoming.

As I worked the Steps in CPA and practiced them in my daily life, it became clear that I needed to go back to Step Two and find a new understanding of a Higher Power.

There was some relief in this decision, but it was a "spiritual bottom" of sorts. When I left that spiritual community, I disappointed my family; I lost friendships. It was difficult to do what was needed for my own growth and recovery when it meant disappointing others.

My authentic self emerged as a result of working the Steps in CPA. I cannot be authentic if I'm pretending to believe in something that isn't true for me anymore. Step Two helped me to see that I owe it to myself to recognize that I have a Higher Power that loves and supports me in every way. It is key to my recovery.

In this moment, I will give myself permission, and the space and time I need, to "come to believe" in my own Higher Power.

Acceptance is a daily practice for me. Living with chronic illness has meant learning how to wake up each day without knowing what the day will bring. I simply cannot predict how my illness will take shape today. How was I ever going to be able to find a place of acceptance if I never knew what I was going to have to accept on any given day?

I was battling my illness, and I was terrified of surrendering. It wasn't until I found CPA that I was able to do the deep work I needed to in order to excavate the emotional resistance I was experiencing about accepting my illness.

The first and most powerful result I received from my Step work in CPA was allowing myself to accept my illness—*Just for Today.* When I first heard that was an option, it was like a weight was lifted. I was convinced that if I accepted my illness, I was giving up. But it clicked into place when I cut things into smaller chunks. In fact, I usually chop up my day into morning, afternoon, and evening. So I'm really accepting my physical condition for just a few hours at a time. It's amazing how much I can handle in bite-sized chunks.

I needed CPA to help me see that accepting this day, just as it is—*One Day At A Time*—was the only way I was going to find inner harmony and a sense of peace.

In this moment, I will only face the next manageable chunk of time. I don't need to overwhelm myself with taking on too much of my day.

The stark, difficult realities of my symptoms are very real: when I hurt, I hurt. When I've not slept for a very long time, it seems I don't have access to basic brain functions that lead to well-being. I do not deny illness.

That said, much of my freedom from the emotionally and spiritually debilitating effects of chronic illness and pain comes from becoming aware of the ways that I respond to my symptoms. With growing awareness, as I continue in this program, I see that what I am *thinking* about my condition(s) causes a great deal of my distress.

I work to be aware of what I am thinking when I'm feeling rotten about life. I take the action of asking Higher Power for the grace to accept my life just as it is, right now, then for the courage to change what may need changing. More and more, I'm aware that what needs changing is my attitude toward my life as it is.

I reflect on what thoughts would reveal a healthier and even a more accurate view of things. I find my stressed thought patterns are often quite distorted. I'm becoming aware that when I take action by choosing—again and again—to continue, with help from my Higher Power, the practice of adjusting my attitude, so much stress and disease are often removed.

I am learning that this one seemingly small application of *Awareness, Acceptance, Action* can be large in its reward. For me, it's been one of the great gifts of CPA.

In this moment, I will pause and notice my thoughts. If they're mired in negativity, I will take action on behalf of my well-being by simply asking my Higher Power to help adjust my attitude.

When I first came to CPA, I wasn't able to set healthy boundaries. I continued to say, "Yes," when "No" was more accurate. Even today, I appreciate those in the fellowship who help me see when I am over extending.

Boundaries can be an act of kindness. They're my way of ensuring I don't spew my feelings all over another person because I couldn't say, "No," in time. They're a service, a tool—a form of love. To me, setting a boundary isn't about strength, it's about loving another person enough to say, "No," in a timely way.

My experience is that life doesn't always allow time for boundaries, but in most cases, I can find room to provide a little relief by simply saying, "No." "No" is a complete sentence, but I've found saying something like, "I don't think I can help with or do that today, I'm sorry," works well for me.

CPA has helped me tremendously in this area. Trusting all things will work out, all will get done in time, my Higher Power (HP) will never abandon me and always guide me to the next right step. When my connection to my HP has static on my end, I can reach out to the fellowship with an open mind. Faith is key. Faith that the other person will understand (sometimes it takes time), faith that what needs to get done will get done, faith that I can handle any repercussions with my HP leading the way.

Seeing boundaries as an act of love has helped me tremendously. I implode and explode less, experience more peace and serenity, and feel the program working in my life.

In this moment, I will trust my HP to guide me about when to "go"
and "do," and when to "stop" and "rest."

When I first came to CPA, I was in a state of total panic and fear. I felt desperate, unable to think clearly, and trapped, like a wild animal in my own body. I was obsessed with my symptoms and constantly distracted by the pain. All I could think of were worst-case scenarios. It took intense effort to listen to the shares and really tune in, but as I did, my mind and nervous system started calming down, and my breathing began to regulate.

Little by little, seeds of wisdom from CPA members penetrated into my soul as I began applying them to my life. Simple things like *One Day At A Time* helped me to stay in the day, in the moment, and let go of possible future outcomes, realizing God is with me right now. Our Serenity Prayer is an all-time favorite. Many times, I resisted the pain, fought with the pain, and sought doctor after doctor to fix it, but the Serenity Prayer says to "accept the things I cannot change." As I've practiced surrendering control, I find the pain can actually lessen while becoming more manageable.

CPA gives me permission to be gentle with myself and others. When I remember this, I have peace in my body and in the world. My attitude is improving. I accept that people don't have to understand my condition or fix it in any way, especially since many cannot understand unless they walk a mile in my shoes. I'm grateful for fellow CPA members who not only understand the despair of living with chronic pain, but their constant love and genuine compassion actually have the power to heal.

In this moment, I will be gentle with myself and others and use the
Serenity Prayer to guide me to the next indicated action.

As a CPA member, I've discovered that when a new diagnosis appears, even as I explore options, I need to work my program of turning outcomes over to a Higher Power (HP).

Recently, I developed a new condition and found myself weighing how best to work my program. I didn't want to obsess, yet I did want to find answers: identify the appropriate healthcare professionals to see and assess the treatments that might be offered. Acute illness or a new diagnosis, unlike a chronic condition, needs prompt attention and a focus on possibilities for getting well. Could I do all the necessary research and still work my program so I didn't make myself miserable trying to control everything and becoming overwhelmed with fear? I met with my Sponsor to think through a plan.

It was time to turn myself and the process ahead over to my Higher Power, pray for the best outcome, and not tell my HP what that was supposed to look like. I prayed for my HP's guidance as I did my Internet searches, went to doctor's appointments, and weighed all the options. I went to meetings and reasoned the situation out with a trusted friend. Was this new diagnosis interfering with my family life? Was I complaining a lot about the symptoms? What feelings needed to be addressed, such as fear, grief, and anger? I worked my Steps again to get perspective.

Recovery is a journey, not a destination. A new diagnosis highlights the journey once again. Even though I work my recovery program daily, I'm starting from Step One when a new diagnosis shows up.

In this moment, I will work the Steps no matter where I need to start. I will be compassionate with myself if I need to go back to Step One.

I often wonder about why I persist—what is it that drives me on. There is a part of me that, as a kid, if someone said something couldn't be done, I would always step up to the plate to do it. It was almost like I had no choice in the matter; a part of me just took over.

Perseverance has served me well in my journey through chronic pain and chronic illness, but when I don't put my Higher Power at the forefront of every decision, this very skill can cause me to enter into many battles I didn't need to get into. CPA has taught me to slow down and not waste precious energy. I try and turn over, to the best of my abilities, any situation that is causing me problems and conserve my energy to use it wisely and smartly.

Working the CPA program, listening, praying, and reaching out to others, I can look back and see when perseverance has served me and when it's worked against me. I am listening now for guidance on when and how to use my skills to help myself and others. I am so grateful God has given me this asset because there've been so many times I wanted to simply give up. Today, I feel that perseverance isn't *me*; I truly believe it's my Higher Power taking over.

I believe my Higher Power has given me exactly what is needed to deal with my chronic pain and chronic illness. I try to remember to come up for breath and enjoy the process instead of just fighting my way through. In CPA, I am learning a new way to work with perseverance.

In this moment, I will turn to my Higher Power and ask for assistance if I'm struggling to slow down.

For me, faith and humility are necessary for me to even begin to turn over the problems of my life to a greater power, which in my case is: a power greater that I cannot see in material form with my physical eyes. That takes a lot of faith and trying not to control, direct, or influence outcomes takes humility.

Each member of CPA is free to find their own meaning of a Higher Power. Our literature is made up of the collective consciousness of our recovering, practicing group members, and we are all human. Together, we do what none of us could ever do alone. That is but one example of a Higher Power.

It's easy for me to hear that faith and humility are required to turn my problems over and to work the Steps in my daily life. I accept that I "require" these spiritual principles to work these Steps to keep me out of the life of "no soul," where I lived for far too long due to the negative emotional and spiritual effects of chronic pain and chronic illness. But my process in working the Steps in CPA has been much gentler and deeper than following simple "requirements." It comes back to "meaning." When my soul was empty and my body sick and in pain, and I felt emotionally bankrupt, I was desperate for meaning. Having faith, having humility, helped me to take that first step, but then, I found more faith, humility, willingness, and meaning in the Steps, in the literature, and in the fellowship of CPA.

In this moment, I will find meaning by actively using the CPA Steps and tools.

As I continue to go to CPA meetings, talk with CPA members one-on-one, and have heart-to-hearts with my Sponsor as we read and discuss literature, I have come to embrace the fact that *Control Is An Illusion*. My outcomes—when I make the plan and decide what is going to happen—sell me short. The Power Greater, who I am coming to understand, has outcomes for me that are out of this world!

Somewhere along the way in my short journey thus far in CPA, I realized that all those years that I did not believe there was God or Higher Power, God always believed in me. God always loved me just as I am. I may not have had faith in God, but God has always had faith in me.

Knowing this, I now have not only willingness and ability but also enthusiasm for turning my problems—and everything else in my life—over to a Greater Power of my own understanding... without trying to control, direct, or *influence* the outcome. This is how I practice Step Three.

In this moment, I will practice Step Three and turn my concerns over to the care of my Higher Power.

I very much appreciate the kindness and compassion I have found in CPA meetings. I had no idea it was missing from my life since I became chronically ill. I have truly found "my tribe" here.

In those early years of illness when I was bedridden and housebound, I never thought I would smile again. Later, my symptoms began "cycling," and I had no idea how to be grateful for that. I had lost so much to despair. I now have online CPA friends who are inspirational, caring, and often, so much fun!

Recently, I realized I had missed something my friend had mentioned to me. I apologized for being so wrapped up that I missed it. She wrote me back, telling me I never need to apologize to her for what I share when it is honest. She asked me to always just be who I am, said that she goes for the spirit of what I say to her, and asked me to please not censor myself. I never want to disrespect anyone, so I try to be careful, but I've always valued emotional honesty and giving others "wiggle room" with what they share with me over being cordial, correct, and careful. With "my tribe," I can totally be who I am. I know they give me the benefit of the doubt if something comes out wrong or not quite the way I wanted it to—it's quite amazing. I could not be more grateful for the fellowship of CPA.

In this moment, I will be authentic in my relationships and give others the grace to truly be themselves.

In Step Seven, I see, once again, my own powerlessness—my ongoing need for help.

In my original Twelve Step group's earliest literature, Step Seven was simply a prayer. I still find, personally, that I need to give human, vocal utterance to my request—as supplication, as *asking*.

My own, personal, most oft-spoken Seventh Step prayer goes something like this:

God, take this fear I carry—which seems to be at the root of most of my character defects—and remove it. Give me the strength to bring something good out of the many ills of my self-will. Help me see that You—God, Eternal Presence, Abiding Love, Ultimate Mystery—are the source of the grace needed to drop all that stands in the way of my becoming as loving as possible. Remind me that in remaining under Your guidance, I may rest.

In this moment, I will use prayer to humbly ask to become as loving as I can be to myself and others.

I still have lots of difficulty surrendering when I feel that I *need* something, right in that moment. I know this is something that I need to work on.

I find the acronym *STOP (Surrender, Time-out, Observe, Prioritize)* to be incredibly helpful. I've been learning in CPA that when I find my mind or body in that rabbit hole of urgency, I must stop and take a time-out—nothing useful, helpful, or productive will come out of me trying to force a solution.

I'm also working on being more of an observer. Trying to separate all the emotion from an event or decision and prioritizing often can help me know what is the next indicated action—when I am ready—after the "time-out."

Another thing I've learned is that there almost isn't anything that can't wait twenty-four hours, especially in regard to decisions or things I'm not sure whether I should say. I try to take a day and sleep on all decisions and responses of magnitude.

Recently, I had an incredibly challenging day and did not wait even a few hours before sending off a questionable text. The results weren't terrible, and I think the relationship will still survive, but it's a reminder that I can always say something later, but I can't take back what I've already said.

In this moment, I will remember that I can take my time and pause to reach for CPA tools before taking action.

When I started my CPA journey, I had already been in another Twelve Step program, so I thought I had Step One down. I had been in chronic pain for almost ten years and had a diagnosis that I understood, and I thought, *Well, obviously I can accept my powerlessness and unmanageability. I've been dealing with this for too long to believe I have power over it.*

I recently had to change doctors, and at our first visit, my new doctor said she didn't believe my diagnosis was correct and we would need to start over with diagnostic testing. Then I saw the true extent of my obsession. Day and night, all I could think about were my symptoms and how I could speed up this diagnostic process. I began to believe that if only I thought hard enough about my pain or read enough about the human body, I could figure this thing out on my own.

After a few weeks of this, I became trapped in my own brain, and it hit me: *I am powerless over this entire process. I cannot force the right diagnosis or treatment to appear, and even if I could, it would not change my reality in any way. All I can do is continue to show up for the appointments, take care of my body, and give the results up to my Higher Power.*

Some days it's easier than others, but when I can truly admit my powerlessness and unmanageability and turn my will over to my Higher Power, I start to see how much more there is to life than my body and my symptoms.

In this moment, I will apply the first three Steps to anything that is disrupting my serenity.

It took me years to understand that resting when I'm feeling poorly does not mean I'm an idler and irresponsible.

Giving myself permission to rest, without guilt or shame, was one of the amends I made to myself when I worked Step Nine. It was such a novel concept. How dare I go to bed in the middle of the day and watch TV? Even though I was ill and could barely function, I thought I had to push and make myself do something to prove I was not a slacker.

I began to think of it as taking a sick child to bed. As a mother, I would never send my child to school or out to play when she was ill. Why would I do anything different for myself? In CPA, I've learned how to be a kind, loving parent toward myself.

I learned that when I rested, I actually got more accomplished. When I did get up and work on a task, my mind was clear and my energy was strong because my body and mind were well rested.

What has helped me is to see resting as "putting gas in the tank." For way too long, I made my body operate on fumes, which only made me feel worse. I made errors and tasks took longer. I wore myself down and aggravated my symptoms. I was not respecting my own body. I was forcing solutions instead of *Letting Go And Letting God.*

Moving into faith helped—trusting that all would get done in Higher Power's timing, not mine. Today, when my body was screaming at me, instead of emptying the dishwasher or finishing the laundry, I went to bed and watched a movie. It was a lovely, compassionate gift to myself.

In this moment, I will rest if I need to.

Acceptance has been vital in my recovery and in living a really good life despite having chronic illness and chronic pain. This does not mean I give up and things are just going to be bad. Acceptance is recognizing that things are the way they are and being able to experience peace.

I recognize that my life has changed and I can do less than I used to, but that is okay. I continue to do what I can to improve my condition. Acceptance is easing my frustration, despair, and resistance toward calmness, optimism, and hope. Acceptance has given me courage to make changes that have improved my life, and opportunities have come that would not have been here if it were not for pain, illness, and acceptance.

When I truly accepted the place of chronic pain and chronic illness in my life, I grieved. I went through depression, fear, and anxiety, but eventually I came through them. These challenging feelings come back, but the longer I practice living in acceptance, the less they affect me. Acceptance brings me peace and the opportunity to continue to live a fulfilling life instead of living a life of bitterness and despair.

In this moment, I will grieve if I need to and accept myself exactly as I am.

When I first started working a Twelve Step program, I had no belief in a Higher Power. If there was one, I thought He or She had abandoned me. My life had fallen apart. My partner left me. I was too sick to work or take care of my children. I had no money. I was scared, sad, hopeless, and wasn't sure if it was worth it to keep on living. I had hit bottom. How could I be restored to sanity?

My Sponsor guided me through Step Two. He kindly listened as I wrestled with old beliefs of a punishing God. He described his perception of a caring, loving Higher Power and said, "This is a personal and direct relationship."

He asked me to begin by merely staying open to considering the possibility that I could be restored to sanity. He asked whether I would be willing to explore the idea of a Power besides my own will and determination. My Sponsor had a strong relationship with his Higher Power and said I could "borrow" his belief. By going slowly, I approached Step Two in baby steps. I needed to trust that someone else believed in a Higher Power and that it could happen for me.

Over time, I came to believe, through my own experiences, that Step Two works. In retrospect, I can see there was a Higher Power working in my life all along, but I didn't recognize it. I was so sure that I was too broken to be restored to sanity and that no Power existed that could help me. I'm so grateful I was wrong.

In this moment, I will allow for the possibility of a Higher Power working in my life, and I know I can "borrow" a friend's belief in such a power if I am struggling.

Some days, especially mornings, my symptoms can be so intense that it's difficult for me to concentrate, let alone accomplish much. I often feel distressed during these times.

One morning recently, I was weak and tired. Life felt dark, and the work that needed to be done seemed endless—work I did not have the strength to do. I did not feel I even had the strength to trust God.

I decided to offer to God what I had: my "nothingness" and my "inability to do." Then, I just needed to trust that God, in His mercy, would meet me right where I was. This brought me peace. I was able to let go of feeling guilty for not getting much accomplished. I accepted that I need not try to be something more than I was able to be right then. This brought not only relief but sanity—the truth that I am indeed met and loved by my Higher Power, exactly as I am.

In this moment, I will not expect too much of myself and will turn to my Higher Power to meet me exactly where I am.

I woke up under a heavy blanket of dark thoughts today. I am trying to learn how to surrender in these moments (which feels counterintuitive)—spiritually, emotionally, mentally, and yes, even physically—whether or not my body heals. I'm learning what that means.

When I remember to not fight and to take time to stop, pause, and connect with my Higher Power, I can actually feel a hint of meaning and purpose in the uncertainty and fear of being chronically ill. In the quiet space in my heart, underneath the turbulent thoughts, I've always known there was a powerful opportunity here for spiritual growth. I knew this but didn't "want" this reality I'm living to be true, so I spent all day, every day, scrambling desperately to find a solution.

But today, it feels slightly different. I am more in my heart and relaxing into my reality. Observing the fear allows me to open to it and receive the moments as they come, instead of reaching so hard for some kind of hope that my life will be different. I don't want to run away from this reality anymore. It's too painful to live like that. I want to learn how, in the heat of these moments, to pray to find peace and ease and total acceptance.

In this moment, I will surrender so that I can actually see/feel/know the beauty that is with me inside, all the time.

A lot of my amends have turned out to be "living amends." There are a few that I have kept on paper as amends I will make if my Higher Power brings me into contact with that person again—because reaching out to some of the people I owe amends to after not seeing them for at least a decade could cause more harm than good. However, I make a living amends by changing my behavior, and I stay willing to make those amends, should the time come.

My rule of thumb with amends is to put myself in the other person's shoes for a moment and imagine that someone had done this to me. Would I want to hear their amends, or would I want them to leave me alone? Sometimes this can help me clarify whether or not I'm making amends because I feel it's right or because I'm trying to clear my conscience, regardless of how it affects someone else. As long as I turn it over and stay willing, my Higher Power has always shown me what to do next.

In this moment, I will focus on improving my behavior to work on my "living amends" until a situation arises to foster other Step Nine amends.

I practice Step Ten during the day sometimes, and mostly every night, along with my gratitude journal. If I am able, I write down the things that disturb me during the day as they pop up, and then at night it's a little easier to recall the events of the day. For example, someone did or didn't do something that I had an expectation about…I write it down and then look at it in the evening.

Since working the Fourth and Fifth Step, I have become aware that my greatest defect of character is being hard on myself. That's why it's essential for me to focus on what I have done well each day.

My inventory is very simple, of necessity. Brain fog and pain issues tend to cloud my thinking in the evening. I write at least three things I did well—sometimes more. And I also write anything I feel I could have done better. For me, it is as important to practice my daily inventory as it is to practice the Eleventh Step.

In this moment, I will practice Step Ten and think of at least three things I did well.

It's hard to remember to allow God into all areas of my life, big and small; hence, I require spiritual *practices* like Step Eleven.

Mine currently include every morning praying that I be given "knowledge of God's will and the power to carry it out" in all areas I'm focused on. I read selections from spiritual writings that seem right for the concerns of the coming day. Daily meditations have become essential to increase my ability to detach from distorted thoughts that add stress to my already stressed body.

All day, I ask God to direct my thinking—most often and specifically that my mind be moved off of worrying about that which I can't control. Often, I'm directed to take very small actions, letting the larger problems be managed or resolved *One Day At A Time* or accepted slowly. I ask for courage or strength to do difficult things—such as making a phone call I dread. I pray for discernment in perplexing issues and then listen for direction. If I feel guided to act yet feel unsure, I ask myself, *Is this direction increasing peace and clarity or increasing my disease and darkness?*

I've also begun a practice of day-long gratitude. Throughout the day, I am on the lookout for items for a gratitude list. Late afternoon, I jot down all those I can recall. Not only does this lift my mood when I'm at my most fatigued, but it gives my mind something positive to focus on. Once I have my list, I review it, looking for a special blessing embedded there—just one thing that nourished me spiritually. This allows me to enter my evening feeling *blessed.*

In this moment, I will ask my Higher Power for courage, discernment, acceptance, gratitude, or any other emotional strength needed to nourish me spiritually.

Letting go and admitting I was powerless was foreign to me. But I was so miserable when I arrived at CPA that I was willing to try anything and to be teachable, even though being powerless seemed ridiculous to me. How could letting go be the path to serenity and happiness? It was the complete opposite of how I had lived my life—I was a great manager. It was hard to believe. However, my Sponsor suggested I try it out. She said I could always go back to the old way of living.

Well, I never did go back. As I worked Step One, I found that for the first time in years, I felt relief, I had hope, and I was no longer lost and alone. It is a Step I return to daily, and now it guides how I live in all areas of my life.

Admitting I was powerless seemed like the worst way to live, but so far, no longer living in the delusion that I have control over people, places, and my illness has been the best way to live.

In this moment, I will admit I am powerless and become willing to be teachable.

When I began working the Steps in CPA, I realized in Step Two that my concept of a power greater than myself needed to grow. The Twelve Steps give me the freedom to explore my relationship with this Higher Power within the CPA program. It's a freedom I treasure.

Sometimes my Higher Power has been the program itself, and sometimes it's the fellowship.

The Traditions help me feel safe in CPA. We have a primary purpose. We have unity within our fellowship. There is no teacher or guru making sure that I'm doing things perfectly. I'm safe here. I believe in the power of these Steps; I became willing to believe that following these Steps might work for me. That is all that is required of me to work this program.

Today, I would say that my Higher Power is the power of the unity that binds us together. I'm seeking a spiritual solution to emotional and physical problems and am willing to do the work. If I show up to meetings or work with my Sponsor on a specific Step, I'm doing the work. Living with chronic illness and pain is not an easy way of life, but it becomes a manageable life with the help of CPA and my own concept of a Higher Power. CPA members inspire me to keep growing. They help me stay willing to believe that there is a spiritual solution.

I worked Step Two with hope, an open mind, and an open heart. As a result, I came to know my Higher Power, myself, and others in ways that changed my life forever.

In this moment, I will recognize how a Power greater than myself, through the Traditions, provides a safe space for me inside the fellowship of CPA.

I've struggled with how to practice Step Three. I'd admitted that some of my coping mechanisms were making my life unmanageable. So I collected a new set: I would attend tons of meetings, dissociate on the Internet or with TV, set feelings aside to do service, make endless lists, basically just *move* until I wore myself out.

These activities kept me from self-destructing. I'm grateful I found them! But when my health issues arose, it became clear they were not sustainable. I couldn't physically show up in the way that I had. Bombarding my discomfort with solutions that weren't working left me exhausted, symptomatic, and depressed. Feeling betrayed by circumstance, I became more sick, ashamed, and lonely, and I didn't know how to ask for help. I'd thought I could wield powerlessness in a way that would leave me invulnerable to pain and uncertainty.

Today, after a brief time in CPA, my Third Step toolbox includes economy of motion and energy: meditation, writing, gratitude lists to Higher Power, angry letters to Higher Power, and connecting with program friends (whom I've never met in person). I reach out to my doctors instead of the Internet when it's time to turn over a medical issue. And when these things don't "fix" me right away, I put my hand on my heart and let myself cry. I trust that feelings pass.

Today, there's more space for me to examine how my fear motivates me. I turn toward it with compassion: visualizing the fear behind the impulse to "do" as the voice of a worried family member who truly loves me. I am so grateful to have found CPA.

In this moment, I will look in my Step Three toolbox for methods to help me practice letting go.

April

Through working my Steps, especially Step Four, I discovered that I often felt obliged to be obedient—afraid to rock the boat and stand up for myself—when working with my healthcare providers. At times, the medical settings were intimidating, and I didn't want to upset the people I relied on for care by coming across as "difficult."

With support from my Sponsor, I began to make amends to myself by practicing self-care. The ways I took care of myself when it came to changes in my treatment plan included going slowly, asking questions, doing my own research, and speaking to other patients. I realized I could even say, "No," to my medical providers, if necessary.

As a result of working my program, I believe I make better choices regarding my healthcare, most of the time. And yet, just last week I had a bad reaction to a new medication; I had to surrender and cancel my plans. Unlike in the past, that didn't freak me out or get me angry.

This experience was a reminder that the unexpected is a part of this journey; it's guaranteed as a part of living with chronic health conditions. I can do the footwork, but I am always powerless over the outcome.

In this moment, I will make a choice that honors my integrity and self-care. I will let my Higher Power handle the outcome.

Before CPA, my pain frequently came between me and my loved ones. Disguised as self-justified anger or depression, pain hijacked my emotions. The loving part of my soul was clouded by fear and frustration. I was too angry and ashamed to ask for help. I turned away when helping hands were extended.

Early in my recovery, I was taught that the Twelve Steps can help me to "get right with God, with myself, and with others." This was a process; I did not believe in God then, and I did not trust anyone. I had relied fully upon my own abilities and believed I was the only person qualified to run the show. This changed when I found my Sponsor and started through the Steps. I slowly became willing to share my insecurities; her impartiality and acceptance led to trust. My Sponsor was the person who put my hand into the hand of a Higher Power.

My relationships are more loving, trusting, and fulfilling now that I'm working the CPA program. Meetings are an opportunity to share with others who understand and empathize. I've learned I can be honest about my condition and ask for help, without shame. My spouse is extraordinarily grateful for the newfound serenity and acceptance he sees in me now that I am "living with chronic pain, rather than suffering from chronic pain." I can see that there are innumerable good people in the world who want to help—it benefits them as much as it helps me. When I don't ask for or accept help from someone else, it deprives both of us of a hand-of-God moment.

In this moment, I will remember that admitting when I could use some help is a beautiful way to exemplify the principle that "I can't, God can."

I still hadn't stopped "whirling" when I did my first CPA Fourth Step. I was still trying to do everything, be everything, and control everything. That might sound like I needed more time with the first three Steps, but those Steps just ask us to believe and make a decision. So I attacked my Fourth Step with the same vigor as I was attacking life. I came out the other side a bit different.

As I worked on Step Four, I discovered things not only about my behaviors and my faith but about others' behaviors too. When it came to others, mostly I learned compassion. I realized they were trying to help me—a person going through something *they'd* never experienced and don't understand. Or maybe they had a somewhat similar experience and offered unsolicited solutions or advice (usually things I'd already tried and that didn't work for me). But in all cases, I realized they were loving me in the best way they knew how.

It took another Fourth Step to find some compassion for myself. Today, I am working this Step around why I feel shame when people treat me graciously. I want to be free of that shame and feel that I am deserving.

For me, practicing a Fourth Step is the beginning of the road to freedom. I do them frequently and get so many amazing realizations about myself and how I view the world. What a great gift this Step is: a way to free myself of the weights pulling me down.

In this moment, I will remind myself that if I have difficult feelings about a person or situation, working Step Four can provide clarity, compassion, and freedom.

There are bad days when I can't function at all. And days when I am walking happily along, and suddenly I run into a brick wall that was not there a second ago. I know these days will come, so I have movies saved to watch. When I feel wiped out and weak, I need movies that are light, that have no violence or tension. I treat myself with compassion and gentleness on those days. I cancel my tasks and crawl into bed. I do this with gratitude that I have all I need to rest and be kind to myself.

This attitude was not possible before CPA. There was a time when I got angry and frustrated, when I lashed out at family, when life seemed terribly unfair and cruel. I would fight reality, and that only made me more miserable. I have discovered over time that bad days do not last forever. They do pass. And there is nothing I can do to make them pass faster. With the acceptance of reality comes serenity.

I'm no longer scared or angry on days when my ability to participate in the world is curtailed. This is the rhythm of my life. I can attune to reality and have harmony, or I can fight it and have dissonance and suffering. It is my choice.

Through working the Twelve Steps, the love and comfort of my CPA friends, and trust in the love of my Higher Power, I've found a new way to be in the world that brings me joy and makes my life meaningful.

In this moment, I will remember that bad days do not mean this is a bad life. I have CPA, so I have choices.

In Chronic Pain Anonymous, we employ the principle of anonymity—putting humility and compassion into practice.

If, in a meeting, I say that I used to be a rocket scientist and giving that up makes *my* life particularly difficult, I am expressing myself, asking to be heard, hoping to be understood, and perhaps being of service to those who could profit from identifying with me. But am I sharing or comparing? Have I not, innocently—with no malice whatsoever—suggested something that is untrue and possibly off-putting, even hurtful?

Is it equitable to imply that I feel an especially keen sense of loss at the inability to engage in my previous vocation because, in my case, it was so "special"? Did I consider that others' losses are as significant as mine? Am I, unconsciously, trying to bolster my self-esteem by making sure everyone knows my former five-star status, real or perceived? Is this helpful for others or for me?

I could say: "I used to get a lot of meaning out of life by setting challenging goals, then achieving them." Or, "I am still grieving over career loss." I may want to talk about it more specifically outside of a meeting, perhaps with someone who identifies and has found help in the Steps, adjusting and letting go of what used to be.

In CPA, I focus on my similarities with anyone with chronic health conditions. In these similarities, I find compassion and healing. We are people of all backgrounds and stages of life, stages of illness. I want to avoid setting myself apart or above when I speak in meetings and instead focus on the spiritual solution we find in the Twelve Steps. When I put anonymity into practice, fellowship is about *us,* not *me.*

In this moment, I will remember everyone's experience is valid.

Many of us in CPA with sleep problems learn that though we may know a lot about good sleep hygiene, often it just isn't enough. My Sponsor taught me that sleep is just another thing in my life to accept that I do not control . For example, there are days and weeks when I wake up at night and know I am *not* going to be able to fall back to sleep, so I've stop trying to force myself to do so. I quickly get out of bed and do something productive, like write in my journal.

I cannot control when I will be able to sleep through the night, but I can control how I respond. It's often the case that when I'm up in the middle of the night, I have a lot on my mind, so I journal to help process it all. This is a beneficial use of my time, and I feel better spending it this way.

Part of accepting my sleep situation is knowing I probably won't be my best self the next day. For this reason, I almost never schedule early morning appointments. When people ask me, "What time can you be available in the morning?" I often respond that it depends on my sleep and I can't really know. Not having morning commitments helps me relax and not worry about what will happen if I cannot sleep. I strive for acceptance that this is exactly the way it is meant to be and I cannot change it.

One day, I may have greater insight or more tools to help with my sleep. Just for today, this is my best solution, and I'm finding it increases my serenity and deepens self-compassion.

In this moment, I will listen to and respect my limits.

After spending years trying every treatment under the sun to manage my pain, and none of them working, I was left hopeless, with no will left to live. I surrounded myself with others who, like me at the time, were angry, disappointed, and dissatisfied with life. It was the only place I felt minimally understood. We spent our days complaining, commiserating, and basically embodying the cliché "misery loves company." I engaged in self-destructive behaviors, doing anything I could to lessen my pain and avoid dealing with the reality of my life. With every choice I made, my life became more unmanageable.

After spending years living in misery, I was sick and tired of just surviving. I wanted to live. I was so lonely and thought no one would ever understand my physical or emotional pain. But I was wrong. I am truly grateful to CPA—to have a fellowship of people experiencing similar issues! I feel connected and very lucky to get to learn from others' experiences.

The people I surround myself with have a significant influence on my mental and physical well-being. We learn from connecting to others. When I see acceptance around me, it helps me to accept my own situation. When I see others focusing on gratitude for what they have and what they can do—the yeses and not the nos—it helps me do the same. I've even regained hope for my future.

In this moment, I will choose to not just survive, but to live.

The slogan *Just for Today* is a workhorse in my program. Often, I apply it this way: *Just for the next hour* or *Just for the next minute*. I remind myself the pain I'm in is not forever. So many of my health issues have changed over the years: some going away, some lessening in severity, some getting worse. Nothing stays the same. All I need to deal with is this moment, and that I can do.

This slogan applies when I'm happy as well as when I'm miserable. I want the happy moments to stay, but they don't, any more than the unhappy ones. Using this slogan's perspective, I can be resilient and get through any experience that feels overwhelming, impossible, or unbearable. And I can enjoy the good times, with no expectations that they'll last.

More often than not, I realize I'm okay in this moment. It may be hard; I may not want it in my life, but I am okay. I ask, *What might I use for support?* That's when other tools in my program show up, such as praying to my Higher Power, saying the Serenity Prayer, or calling a program friend.

This is not always as easy as it sounds. There are times I want to fight against this moment—it should not look like this, it's not fair, I want it gone. I'm angry that I have to feel this awful or have this treatment. In these moments I can return to the slogan *Just for Today*, remembering that as dreadful as it is, it will end, and this gives me hope when I am suffering. The situation will change. It has happened many times, and it will again.

In this moment, I will focus on what I can control.

Chronic pain and illness—and accompanying medications—often affect my ability to engage in sexual activities. But I now know that we can adapt. It doesn't need to be an all-or-nothing thing. By listening to others in CPA share their trials and tribulations around this topic, I have learned to acknowledge my basic human nature.

But am I not also free to choose to let sex go entirely, if that is my wish? Might it not be valid to work a program of acceptance, rather than of change? And I have let it go entirely, at times of great duress or simple aloneness and then, still later, asked, *Isn't there a way to experience my basic need for touch?*

There are those of us who have no partner, or who may have gone years without loving touch. I recall when I was single, I'd save my money and indulge in a good, deep-tissue massage when I could. I'd garner hugs wherever I could find them. I got a dog and pampered it with physical affection, including nap-time spooning! I bought a weighted blanket and a body pillow—those didn't do much for me, but experimenting is part of the path to finding what does work.

I found that even amid my chronic pain, I can find activities that are physically pleasurable, if only for that moment. By practicing willingness and open-mindedness, I learned that I can still find joy.

In this moment, I will allow for physical affection.

I have discovered different degrees of rest.

Rest can be doing any kind of activity, even active endeavors, that lead to overall restfulness over time. Whether it is an artistic endeavor, playing gently with my dog, or washing the dishes slowly, methodically, it can be restful. Sitting at the window and noting which birds come through my yard works sometimes, as do the times I can take a slow walk.

Rest can mean taking a breath and tuning in to the moment, saying a little prayer, and releasing the desire to be in charge of everything. A quick, heartfelt Step One, Two, or Three is a source of enormous rest.

Rest can mean going slower and doing half of what I'd planned (or a fourth or a tenth…).

Rest can mean choosing to just listen and let others talk at a meeting.

Rest can mean doing my morning and afternoon meditation. Rest can mean lying down and listening to music or a book on tape.

What I term "Emergency Medical Treatment Rest (EMT Rest)" means total rest: I brush my teeth, drink some water, eat a little something, and then go to bed—no phone, email, text, or mail, no chores. I do as close to nothing as possible, not even think. I may listen to music or something I am not really paying attention to. I may hopefully, nap. EMT Rest means the world turns without me this day.

CPA has helped me understand that resting is doing something. It's listening to my body, slowing down, rebuilding strength. Despite my personal dislike of it at times, because I need so much of it, I accept it. I rest in knowing it is the next indicated action.

In this moment, I will honor my need for rest.

Someone who lives with chronic pain and illness once told me, "It's hard to be on the physical plane and the spiritual plane at the same time." At the time, I was still trying to make it to in-person meetings, but when I would go, I would be in so much pain that I couldn't hear any of the message. It's hard to let my spirit go to a spiritual plane when physical pain firmly tethers me to my body.

It took some time, but I finally gave myself permission to attend virtual and phone meetings. I could stay home and lie down in my most comfortable position during the meeting, making it more likely that my spirit would absorb the readings and the shares.

Sometimes when I meditate, I have moments when I become completely unaware of my pain. I go back and forth, back and forth, switching from the physical plane, where I feel all my body's discomforts, to the spiritual plane where I am unaware of my pain. I also experience these moments of relief, of oscillating between the physical and spiritual planes, while I am being of service to others.

My friend's admonition is a reminder to be kind—to not beat myself up if I don't spend the entire day feeling spiritual because my body is almost constantly pulling me back to the physical plane. Furthermore, I can celebrate the moments when I'm able to be on both planes at the same time.

In this moment, I will support my spiritual journey by honoring my physical needs.

How do I keep moving forward through times when pain, exhaustion, and overwhelming emotions are so relentless? Five minutes with this pain can seem like too much. Five minutes in a doctor's waiting room can be excruciating. But trusting my Higher Power's sense of timing helps me to be patient and let the process unfold

The tools I have learned in CPA help me navigate my medical care, while the program helps me learn how to competently apply them. Sometimes the answer about a surgery or procedure is "not yet." One of my favorite prayers is, "God, bless it or block it. Please let your will for me be clear and show me a red flag or obstacle if I am not meant to continue." I have more acceptance of not getting the answer I desired. I used to plow headfirst through life, without as much consideration as I devote now.

Today, I have spiritual resources. I remember that the outcome could be beyond my wildest dreams. I have overcome seemingly insurmountable challenges with help from my Higher Power and CPA. The inspiring messages I hear in CPA meetings encourage me—if my friends can do it, so can I! And if I have trouble envisioning even the possibility of a solution or a miracle, I know I can ask one of them to share their experience, strength, and hope with me.

One of my greatest miracles was finding CPA, and I am truly grateful. Five minutes with CPA is much better than five minutes without it.

In this moment, I will remember I am not alone and have a whole community of resources.

Sometimes I'm so far from acceptance that I can't see it at all from where I am. It's nowhere on the horizon. Not even a silhouette in the skyline. I don't know—maybe it's somewhere on the other side of the world?

It is during these times that I lean on the CPA program the hardest. I lean on my Sponsor. I lean on the friends I have made, and I lean into meetings and the literature. I know that I will get through the current situation.

I won't always be in acceptance, and I won't always be out of it. I'm just grateful to know what to do, either way: accept what is before me, and if I can't, lean into the program even more. For me, acceptance is cyclical. It waxes and wanes. Each time I'm in acceptance, it seems deeper, truer, and the times I'm out of it have lessened. That's *Progress, Not Perfection* in action.

In this moment, I will acknowledge being on the path of acceptance, wherever I am on this journey.

Humor is a go-to tool for me, especially after surgery.

At my post-op appointments, I continue to call the chief resident assigned to my case "The Devil." He gets it. I'm joking. Humor helps, and I enjoy these post-op encounters, even when I am there to deal with serious complications. It is not their fault my body is resisting the treatment. With the Serenity Prayer and a dose of good humor, we are making progress toward finding solutions I had never imagined possible. Though the recovery is taking longer than expected, all I have to do is ask, and unexpected solutions show up. But in the meantime, adding a bit of levity to an otherwise heavy situation helps me to cope.

But humor doesn't just help me to deal with uncomfortable topics. I also use it to improve my mood. After a particular meeting, a group of people regularly stay for fellowship and just tell jokes for twenty minutes or longer. Every time I attend, I leave feeling better emotionally, spiritually, and on lucky days, physically as well.

In this moment, I will allow for humor in my life.

On a very high-symptom day, I was in fellowship time after a meeting, and we were all brain-foggy, trying to remember the definition of recovery in CPA. One member recalled part of it: that we have the ability to live joyfully. My reaction, and I even said it out loud, was: "There is no joy in chronic illness!" A difficult day can really cloud my perception.

Joy is a much different feeling from happiness. Joy is bone-deep; it locks in and has lasting effects. There can be plenty of joy in living with chronic pain and illness. It is all around me if I'm willing to take the time to look for it. And that's the key: *Taking The Time.* Often when I'm bogged down with daily tasks and doctors' appointments, or my symptoms are flaring and my pain is high, it's a challenge to stop that frenetic energy. But when I pause and *Take The Time,* I can recognize that joy is floating just below the surface, and I can release down into it, if I so choose.

I'm reminded of the joy in my life every day. It lives in the love I have for my fellow CPA pals. It lives in the love I have for my husband and son. It lives in the love I receive when our kitten wants to cuddle. It's in the memories I have of the ways I used to savor my old life. And it's in the fellowship time after a meeting where I can be me—whether I am in my joy or I'm seeking it.

In this moment, I will take time for joy.

Recently, I realized that I did not know what surrender means or how it worked in my life. I thought of surrender as something that happened in battle: I give up, you win, I lose. I read the dictionary definition of "surrender." Still lost, I committed to trying an action I did not fully understand—like when I began to practice prayer a couple decades ago. I didn't believe in prayer then, but I do now! That practice led me to believe in a power greater than myself. My strategy, to learn what surrender meant, was to get outside, throw my worries to the sky, and say, or shout, the word "surrender" two or three times.

I recently did this during a particularly hard trip to the grocery store. A friend drove, and I finished shopping first. Exhausted, I could not find an available chair. I pushed my over-heavy buggy to the automatic doors. Standing outside, I threw my arms to the sky and shouted, "Surrender!"—twice.

I must have looked crazy. I went back inside, as there was still no sign of my friend. Aimed toward the flower department, I found a bench turned backward against the wall. I was able to sit and wait for my friend more comfortably. It worked. I surrendered.

As we walked out, I glanced at the place where I'd stood and shouted, and I thanked my Higher Power for making space available for me to rest. No one knew what I had done but me. Now you do too. I'm continuing this practice: open a door and shout, "Surrender!" whenever I can. Through this performative exercise, I'm learning to embody surrender.

In this moment, I will remember that surrender is a practice.

I received some stunningly good news. It could be said that "there was dancing in the streets," yet I responded with trepidation rather than joy. After taking my inventory, I realized my guarded stance against joy, hope, and relief had protected me from crushing disappointment most of my life. This unskillful reaction had especially protected me in regard to my chronic conditions. My need to brace for the next cycle of pain, the next random symptom, or the next diagnosis was my attempt to feel safer and less vulnerable. Ironically, this inability to feel joy at this welcome news made me feel sad and out of sorts—the opposite of safe!

My CPA Sponsor suggested I greet all emotions as welcomed guests, with as much self-compassion as I could muster. I heard myself say, "This is a moment of genuine suffering and concern. I'm sure I am not the only person responding this way. What kindness can I offer myself in this moment?" I asked my Higher Power to allow these ambiguous emotional energies to flow through me, without resistance on my part because I know "that which I resist, persists."

After a few deep breaths, I was able to gently detach from my feelings of differentness and isolation and the belief that there was something wrong with me because of this unexpected reaction to good news. I told myself, "You are awesome. I love you, and feelings don't define you." I gently patted my chest saying, "It's alright, it is all right." Self-acceptance, self-care, self-love, and self-compassion are perhaps the greatest gifts CPA has given me.

In this moment, I will show myself compassion.

When I came into CPA, I was feeling beaten down by my body and the people in my life. They pushed me to do more than I was able— emotionally, physically, and financially. I took on commitments that further limited my time and energy that might've been used for self-care. I was only adding to the mess.

I first came to a Saturday night meeting, then another, a week later. That second week, I felt a tad more courageous. I'd taken on one of the suggested challenges: letting go of at least one of my outside commitments. I kept coming back, each week for a month, reporting each time about that feeling to my group—courage.

I realized I could go to as many meetings as I wanted and keep cultivating that seedling inside of me. I was able to remove an abusive ex-spouse from my life, after struggling for over a year to do so. I set limits on how much time and energy I would invest in my family and started moving toward a safer and healthier home environment.

Thus, with the help of other CPA members, my Sponsor, and Step study group, I was able to surrender. That took courage.

Today, I sit, surrounded by boxes I'll slowly unpack in my new apartment, trusting in my Higher Power that I'll have courage to continue to face life's ongoing challenges. I'm learning to stand up for myself and the serenity I need to progress. I no longer make decisions under duress or based on fear. I'm embracing this challenged body with the love and attention it needs.

In this moment, I will remember it takes courage to participate in my recovery.

Anonymity is the spiritual foundation of our recovery because it puts my personal agenda second to the common good.

In a meeting, if I say, "I used to be an Olympic swimmer, so giving that up makes my life especially difficult," it's like saying, "I have a more difficult time than you." Plus, it encourages and promotes our differences rather than similarities.

When I want to share on this topic, it's useful for me to examine my motives. Am I unconsciously trying to grasp at self-esteem by making sure everyone knows of my former status? Have I considered that others' losses are just as significant? For instance: there are those who fell ill or were injured so young they never had a chance at a career. For all I know, that might hurt more than having lost one.

Certainly, my process of letting go of my former identity/roles/activities needs to be shared in meetings, even, at times, with some specificity. But it can remain inclusive, not exclusive. Rather than saying, "As a former member of the NYC Ballet, it's different for me, having to settle for short walks," I can say, "As a former member of the NYC Ballet, I miss dancing keenly." Or simply, "I miss dancing, it was my life." The latter statements do not make the claim that I am any different. We all have activities we miss and past lives we grieve. In the end, I am free to share as I like. Meetings have breathing room—I can be direct and still be inclusive, not exclusive.

For me, the spiritual practice of anonymity is worth thinking about because I need a fellowship that is about *us*, not *me*.

In this moment, I will focus on the similarities I have with others.

Decades prior to my chronic pain and chronic illness, I hated my body; my chronic conditions only exacerbated my self-loathing. I could never walk past a mirror without something harsh to say about what I saw: ugly, haggard, too thin, too old, too sick, too weak, too frail, etc. I employed every positive affirmation any self-help guru had to offer in an effort to alter my poor self-image. I took pride in loving those close to me unconditionally, yet I could not extend that same love to myself.

In one of my first CPA meetings, I heard "self-acceptance, self-care, and self-love." (I added a fourth "S": "screwed.") I didn't know what any of these really meant, let alone how to apply them. How could I love this body that continually let me down and, frankly, went out of its way to torture me? How could I accept being bed-bound? How could I practice self-care when I couldn't even shower?

My Sponsor assured me that willingness to work the Twelve Steps of CPA was all I needed. As I came to really accept my powerlessness to control and direct my illness, symptoms, and pain, I found the tone of my self-talk began to shift. After my Fifth Step, my black-and-white thinking moved into kinder, more compassionate, "gray" tones. And I knew the spiritual awakening promised in Step Twelve had occurred when, for the first time in my life, I had *nothing* to say when I looked in the mirror. The Twelve Steps of CPA and my Higher Power had done for me what decades of my best efforts could not: enabled me to outright love my body exactly as it is, in any given moment.

In this moment, I will practice self-acceptance, self-care, and self-love by speaking kindly to and about myself.

My partner and I have gotten playfully creative in attempts to avoid the inevitable amplification of my humanness when I am in pain. They know that when my door is shut, that means, "Enter at your own risk!" Their tentative, gentle knocking comes with this playful knowledge of said "risk." We have found this inside joke not only lightens both our moods but also diffuses my painful situation. This way, future amends are rarely needed.

"Thank you for your patience with me" has been another helpful tool and helps me avoid constantly saying, "I'm sorry." Not only does it indicate to those around me that I am not myself, but it is a beautiful reminder to treat myself with compassion and patience. When I am at my worst, the pain makes me feel unsafe and angry or tries to tell me lies about my self-worth. But humility tells me I can still love myself exactly as I am and ask my Higher Power to help me not wreak havoc with those around me.

CPA has led me to real self-acceptance, genuine self-care, and authentic self-love—safe in the awareness that although my pain can bring out my most unskillful human aspects, I can still be loving and lovable.

In this moment, I will accept my whole self, skillful and unskillful characteristics alike.

As a person with chronic pain and illness, I have learned that much of my anger is simply my body expressing pain and fatigue—no defect to uncover or complex analysis needed. What I need is rest and self-care.

When experiencing "legitimate" anger, I've come to understand that most of it is rooted in fear—fear I won't get, or will lose, something I think I need. An insurance company refuses a claim. I get hot. Isn't it because I'm afraid I'm not going to get what I need? Someone says something unkind about me. I start scaring the dog with my ranting once I hear of it. Isn't this fear that others will not think highly of me?

What about all the *extra* frustrations and difficulties that come with chronic illness? Don't I have a right to my anger about *that*? Absolutely! But if I get stuck there, I find that returning to Steps One, Two, and Three, and sometimes Four, helps to process it.

Anger can jump up quickly, so the first thing I do is employ the suggestion: when unbalanced, practice "restraint of pen and tongue." In this way, I don't damage others. I observe the anger passing through my body and bite my lip. If I do lash out, I make amends as soon as I cool down. If it is rest I need, I take it. If there's a genuine issue, I take an inventory, looking especially for fears. Finding these, I take them to God. Focusing not on the person, entity, or situation that has prompted the upset, I pray for my fears to be removed.

In this moment, I will remember that anger and fear are normal human emotions.

Doing the next indicated thing often refers to the process of narrowing my focus down to what needs attention right now—it is a way to move forward when feeling overwhelmed.

Sometimes, just picking up the simple tasks of life, one after another as they present themselves, is a very profound practice. What's indicated is governed by the next obvious need. However, I think of this process, too, as an indication from a Higher Power.

Sometimes my actual needs are not obvious or are a consequence of choices I've made. In such moments, I turn to a specific meditation practice that suggests I ask my Higher Power for direction; pause during my day when agitated or doubtful; ask again for the next indicated action; relax, take it easy, and trust the answers will come, as long as I separate myself from dishonesty, self-will, and self-pity.

It's not always easy to see those character defects in play. I find it helpful to ask, *Is this a Godly thought? Would a loving parent suggest this? Could it lead to greater clarity, peace, or connection with my fellows?*

The ability to sense God's will for me increases with my willingness to listen to *any* answer that comes, including ones I dislike. I need to listen, reflect, and possibly discuss, and then act and let go. Whatever the outcome, the experience helps me develop this sense.

In this moment, I will use my actions as a way to connect with my Higher Power.

For me, facing fear and managing worry are a large part of my CPA recovery. I relax in knowing I am doing all I can, with God's daily direction. Currently, I am having repeated panic bouts about finances; I have some hard, scary decisions to make and imperfect data. Such is life. I am not special in facing this challenge. But no one can expect to be free of fear—so I ask for the courage and the grace to walk on, with purpose.

I meditate, talk to my CPA people, go to meetings, and address what can be, using small chunks of time and energy. Sometimes I will *not* face my fear directly or right away but will find a distraction: a walk, a movie. This gives me a break and allows for a shift in perspective. I also take care to not get overtired because fatigue is to my fear like a struck match to a pile of gasoline rags. At such times, I don't need more counsel or another plan: *I need a nap.* Rested, I will be able to think clearly and listen for God's direction. I am continually learning that what works for me is surrendering, with humility, to a personal Higher Power. Though I sometimes doubt, my faith is renewed when I realize that through the most difficult times of my life, I somehow had the strength I needed to face my fears and difficulties and to recover.

In this moment, I will remember I am not alone when facing my fears.

Working Step One in CPA, I was surprised by my shame around admitting I was ill. I had never really admitted, even to myself, the true state of my mind and body.

Admitting illness, in my mind, was cementing it in my consciousness. I thought it was my responsibility to transcend it. I was in a no-win loop. If I am intrinsically defective, this is all my fault. Then I had the huge realization that shame is a subtle form of control, a means to grasp power. Somehow it seemed better to feel at fault than to feel powerless. But taking Step One, fully, demands I relinquish the shame and guilt around experiencing illness and pain.

Fortunately, the rest of the Steps in CPA address and result in the release of shame and guilt and have given me a way out. Though I lived the Twelve Steps daily for decades prior, I never was able to shake the shame before CPA. Now, when I feel shame arise, I meet it with compassion and kindness, knowing that part of me feels terrified and powerless, and that shame is the only survival tool it knows.

Thanks to Step work, Sponsorship, the literature, and the fellowship of CPA, I now have an expanded concept of a Higher Power—Love. I am certain I'm safe, loved, and cared for in a way that includes a joyful invitation, patience, compassion, tenderness, and tactile comfort.

I am more grateful to CPA than I could ever convey.

In this moment, I will greet shame with compassion and kindness.

I spent a number of months working on my Step Four inventory. It was largely an emotional inventory—which was quite radical for me because, prior to CPA, I falsely categorized my pain as 95 percent physical. My Sponsor lovingly guided me through the process of "finding and facing my pain." I read about, did written exercises on, and used guided imagery to examine my feelings of powerlessness, fear and anxiety, isolation, anger and rage, ambiguity and blame, jealousy, grief, and exhaustion. This multifaceted approach resulted in a number of "ah-ha!" moments.

I had a few of these moments surrounding blame, in particular: *"I should have known I would react poorly to the anesthesia!" "This person on the phone is a useless idiot and my health insurance provider is out to get me!"* and *"My boss is putting pressure on me to perform the way I used to, but I'm too scared to tell him about my increasing pain."* I discovered that frequently, my response to an ambiguous situation is to blame! Surgical outcomes are uncertain, financial coverage by insurance is not guaranteed, and the ability to continue working with chronic pain and illness is questionable. I feel comfortable when things make logical sense, and uncertain and insecure (fear-based) when things are ambiguous. I was trapped in a cycle of anger and blame. These are harmful emotions, yet this cause-and-effect behavior continued until I became aware of it. These days, I admit powerlessness, accept my uneasiness, and then take action,

In this moment, I will be grateful for this awareness and acceptance I am coming to through my Step work.

The *Three As* is a frequently used tool in my recovery program. The first "A," *Awareness*, is something I still work on. There are ways in which I live in denial and am not aware of my own behaviors and attitudes. When I first heard someone in a CPA meeting say they used their illness to get out of doing something they didn't want to do, I recognized I did the same thing on occasion. Until that moment, I was not aware of this. My first reaction was disgust with myself. I felt ashamed that I'd used my pain and illness as an excuse and was dishonest with myself and others.

The next part of the formula is *Acceptance*. Now that I was aware of what I'd done, I spoke to my Sponsor and worked Steps Four through Nine. In this process, I came to accept that I was not always truthful. My illness had become a way to avoid going places and doing things that did not appeal to me.

The last stage is *Action*. In this case, the action was to make amends. I am making living amends by no longer using my illness as an excuse.

The *Three As* provide specific steps, applicable to any situation or challenge. I have gradually altered the way I interact with others and how I respond to my pain and symptoms. As a result, I live with more serenity and peace.

In this moment, I will be honest with myself and act accordingly.

Acceptance is not a judgment. When I accept something, I am not saying it is "okay" or "good" or even "God's will." Acceptance is simply acknowledging the situation, good or bad, happy or sad, easy or challenging.

In CPA, I am leaving behind an unrealistic obsession about how I want things to be and seeing reality as it is. I may feel it is good or bad, happy or sad, fun or challenging. My emotions about my reality can help me, in my meditation and prayer, to understand the next best step to take.

There is an ease with which I can move forward as I shed the frustration of my unrealistic ideals and begin to tackle life as it really is. The fight and struggle are relieved. I believe that if I'm fighting and struggling, I am working too hard and proverbially trying to force a square peg through a round hole. I can stop such things when I simply accept the situation.

Acceptance is a strength for me, the same as surrender. It strengthens me because I stop wasting energy on what I cannot control and begin dealing with what is right in front of me.

I don't often start at acceptance, but through meditation, prayer, daily Step work and discussion of my frustrations and fears with others in CPA who understand and help me see reality, I get there. My close friends in CPA are a huge aide in my coming to acceptance. They are lovingly honest and help me see what I cannot see on my own.

In this moment, I will simply see things as they are. If I need help, I will reach out to another member of CPA for support.

I hate having to take medications, and finding acceptance feels impossible. I struggle with each medication change. Every time, my self-esteem takes a hit. I even try to convince my doctors not to prescribe necessary, additional medications. Often, I try to appear stronger than I am, to persuade or even trick my doctors into cutting back on my medications.

When I was working my Fourth Step, this pattern showed up as a resentment toward medications, the doctors who prescribed them, and myself. In the past, I addressed these negative emotions by trying to control the situation: I would simply stop taking the medications. Then the downward spiral would start. My symptoms would increase, and I would feel shame for not being able to overcome the need for the medication or for having stopped it in the first place. Fighting the need for my medications never worked.

After I worked Steps 4 through 9 around this issue, my relationship with my doctors and medications became far more serene. I now view myself as a member of my medical team, fulfilling my role as the one who describes my symptoms and my efforts, and letting my doctors recommend treatment. I can discuss with my Sponsor any resulting emotional upheaval. I'm not alone anymore.

When I let go of the isolation and the illusion of control, acceptance becomes attainable.

In this moment, I will ask myself, "Is there an area where, today, I am trying to exercise the illusion of control?" If so, I will turn to my Sponsor and the Steps to analyze my role in the situation, and then receive and accept the help I need.

Before I began this process of recovery, my days always felt like they were building toward something. So when the chronic pain or chronic illness would inevitably flare, I felt these "bad" days were holding me back. Now I break the day into sections, moving through each one, as it arises.

Even though this has been a helpful tool, difficult-to-handle things still happen.

Recently, there was a day when my symptoms got worse and the pharmacy mismanaged my medication. Once again, the cyclical narrative of despair, loneliness, and being a burden arose. I picked up my *Recipe for Recovery* book, and through hearing my own story reflected back to me, I was reminded that recovery is day by day, moment by moment.

I find myself increasingly paying attention to the quality of moments in my life. My disease and pain do not allow me to miss any moment. They stretch out, and so my choice now is to try to make them meaningful and a part of my spiritual path.

For me, this is about making the path the goal. With that emphasis, I can start a day over, in any moment—even right before bed. I've found that the only true influence I have is on the next moment, not on the previous one. So I turn my mind, in the moment, to freshness, sanity, and authentic positivity...again and again.

In this moment, I will focus on the journey, not the destination.

May

One of the many weaknesses unveiled in my CPA program was this: I prided myself on not asking for help, and, as my needs increased, I would become even more heroic in my inability to ask for help. Through recovery, I can see things from the "other side," and it's clear that what I once thought was a "sane" and rational response is actually a symptom of my insanity.

As more and more people were pushed away by this behavior, the isolation I was left with became further proof that I should never ask for help or ever get in the habit of asking. The proverbial snake chasing its tail and devouring itself—that was me. I was even quoted once, saying that for me, asking for help is like pouring hot acid down my throat.

Recovery has shown me that asking for help is part of surrender, but it is also an opportunity to practice grace. This is all easier said than done, but the quality of my relationships has only increased the more I directly ask for help. I am beginning to realize that I may not be the only person in the universe who finds meaning and value in helping other beings.

This is, and will be, a constant struggle for me, but I am learning that recovery is lifelong; so too is learning to ask for help. I will struggle again, I will forget or refuse to ask for help and suffer again—it's a pattern that accompanies me. What is different now is that I meet each of these moments with recovery tools, and that makes a huge difference.

In this moment, I will risk asking directly for the help I need. I will trust that honesty with those I love increases the quality of my relationships.

In Step Five, I found great healing in making myself known to another. I chose this person carefully. I knew I needed someone who'd already worked this Step, someone with both the needed insight and the compassion to help me put things into perspective.

We thoughtfully began to discard that which no longer served a purpose and made life harder. I began to set down and leave behind my load of old ideas, fears, and resentments.

It was scary to let go of my old ideas, but I was able to trust the process, having seen what it has done for others in this program. They had something I wanted. By giving up my blame, resentments, and unreasonable fears, I opened myself for new energy, which, as a person bearing serious health conditions, I could use for more constructive endeavors.

I learned there is no shame in letting my humanness be seen; this is a fellowship where we confess our faults freely, recognizing it as not just normal but exemplary to understand our shortcomings. I was relieved to finish the process of taking a searching and fearless inventory, and I'm able to relax more now—no longer putting out extra energy to hide and reject my humanity.

I remember waking the day after taking this Step with a feeling I'd known once but could no longer name. I decided it must be that I was feeling *connected*—to my God, to my fellows, and to myself.

In this moment, I will practice accepting my humanness.

Every share I've heard in a CPA meeting has taught me something. Only four months into the program, I still identify as a newcomer, but I know I'm in the right place. I see what I want in others. They have learned to be happy and serene—I could not see this as being remotely possible before I came. There is "wiggle room" allowing us to be ourselves as we learn to walk this road of CPA recovery. But what I especially appreciate is the humor!

I realized recently that for years, I've been overly sensitive with able-bodied people. I was constantly angry, had hurt feelings, or felt my boundaries were being violated. Ergo, I was very overprotective of myself. My brother visited me recently and told me my "edge" is gone. He said that since I got sick, there's been an "edge" to me. He thought he needed to be careful with how he spoke to me and what he said, but he's feeling comfortable with me again. I thought about how a CPA friend told me never to apologize for sharing honestly. That is something I want: for others to be open with me and not feel they need to censor themselves. And according to my brother, I must be picking some of it up.

My desire for compassion and understanding are being met in this program and fellowship. So, for the most part, I've stopped seeking that from people who don't recognize that I need it and stopped getting hurt or angry when they don't meet my vague expectations.

I'm quite amazed that in CPA, I'm actually learning new things...when it looked for years like my life was going to be a series of forgetting things.

In this moment, I will examine the role I play in my relationships.

When I see a character defect crop up—such as self-pity, non-acceptance, or being a pain because I am in pain—it does not serve me or anyone else to beat myself up over my lapse. I am a human being, not a robot. When I notice that I am not living the solution, I remember that life, including my emotional and spiritual status, is an ongoing process, not a static state of being. I can't expect to move immediately into feeling better.

Instead, I can note that it is growth for me to notice I'm forgetting the solution. I know then to ask my Higher Power to gently remind me to give myself the same compassion I routinely show friends as we struggle with the very real difficulties of living, day in and day out, with chronic health problems.

Sometimes, I begin by asking for help accepting that I'm not in a state of acceptance or serenity *at all*. I might ask for help letting myself be sad over another loss, without slipping into paralyzing self-pity, or accept, for a while, feeling angry, without nursing that anger into a corrosive resentment my health can ill afford. Often, I need to acknowledge that my fear is still there—like the crow that comes to sit awhile, atop the tree outside my window—and then go on, with courage.

I'm endeavoring to remember that living in the solution in deep and meaningful ways grows out of facing difficult emotions and challenges. The blossom is rooted in darkness. Let me be that perennial that comes back, again and again, more lovely in its bloom because of its regular, necessary absence.

In this moment, I will accept my recovery as an ongoing process.

I don't know about you, but when I walk over the threshold of any medical room, I shrink instantly, from my tall, adult stature to that of a five-year-old, voiceless child. I do not wish to either blame them or shame myself any longer. CPA has provided me with new ways of seeing and communicating that allow me to act and eventually *feel* different.

What sticks to my flypaper mind, when I don't ask for help from my Higher Power, are the painful but countable times I have been belittled, misdiagnosed, shamed, and dismissed by those to whom I have turned to for help. However, there are also countless instances when they, and plenty of others behind the scenes, have cared for me in ways I will never fully realize, and without whom it is doubtful I would be alive. Remembering that changes me, and thus my experience.

Step One invites me to admit that not only I but all medical professionals are humans who are powerless to know what they never learned or to fix the unfixable—beings who want to help me and perhaps feel frustrated at their own powerlessness. Additionally, each human I encounter has battles they are fighting, about which I know nothing. Now, when I walk into a medical appointment, I ask each staff member and the doctor how they are doing and listen with an open heart. Instead of feeling beholden to an authority figure I both fear and depend on, this simple practice allows me to feel shoulder-to-shoulder with others.

In this moment, I will be kind to those I encounter.

I often find myself stuck between *should* and *want.* I wake up and I think I *should* start off my day with prayer, but I *want* to just lie here before eventually getting up and starting my day. In the afternoon, I think I *should* do my physical therapy exercises or take a short walk, but I *want* to zone out and keep watching TV. At night, I think I *should* meditate, but I *want* to go to sleep.

Then one day it occurred to me that what's in the center of *should* and *want* is *feel.* How would it *feel* if I began my day with prayer? Would I feel more connected to my Higher Power? How would it *feel* if I did my physical therapy or took a walk? Would my body feel stronger? Or does my body feel like resting today? How would it *feel* if I meditated before bed? Would I feel more at ease with a quieter mind? Would I feel proud of myself?

When I find myself struggling to get motivated to do something I *should,* or beating myself up for doing things that I *want,* I ask myself this: How would it *feel* to do that particular activity? How would my body *feel?* How would my spirit *feel?* How do I think I would *feel* about myself after I did it? When I remember to check in with myself in this way, I find that I am more motivated and much less likely to be *"shoulding all over myself."*

In this moment, I will do what feels right for my mind, body and spirit.

The other day I picked a fight with my husband. He was not doing anything wrong. I was in a lot of pain, feeling quite cranky and irritable, and I was lashing out at him. Thanks to my Higher Power, I remembered to *STOP (Surrender, Time-out, Observe, Prioritize)*.

First, I *surrendered*. Pain was all-consuming. I was miserable and powerless over how uncomfortable I was in the moment. I realized I needed to step away, to *take a time-out*, so I told my husband I was not going to continue the fight we were in and walked away. I *observed* what I needed and *prioritized* that: took something for the pain and went to bed.

When I felt better, a day later, I realized how much I had fallen into insanity. The issue I was fighting about was not real—it was just my unhappiness with my pain showing up as unhappiness with my husband. There really wasn't an issue between us. I dropped the matter and made my amends to him.

There are many times when my pain or symptoms are the catalyst to being unpleasant to others. When I am able to *STOP*, I get clarity and don't have to create any new wreckage.

I can use *STOP* whenever I find myself spinning out of control, having a challenging health day, struggling with a decision, or having a conflict in a relationship. At those times, if I keep pushing, I end up lost in confusion, overwhelmed by my pain and symptoms, and back in my obsession. I'll just barrel ahead, forcing solutions, rather than pausing to work my program. But if I *STOP—Surrender, Take a Time-out, Observe, and Prioritize*—I can find my way back to balance and sanity again.

In this moment, I will remember to STOP when facing a challenging situation.

I struggle with grief all the time. So much of the difficulty with my illnesses is the unpredictability and not knowing what to expect. I've been told not to act like a fortune-teller and think that I know how things will look in the future.

My resistance to my current situation or my expectations of the future makes me feel worse. When my Sponsor and I discussed Step One and "acceptance of the unacceptable," they told me about the concept of rolling grief. When I accept my life as it is, I am accepting that I will have a continuing relationship with grief. There will be so many ups and downs, and I will have emotional reactions to these circumstances.

Once I understand that grief is here to stay, I don't have to resist it. I look at it like the current of a stream. The current is moving downstream, and it's only hard on me when I try to walk against it, or when I'm clinging to a rock, trying to stay in the same place. The joy of the journey happens when I let go and allow the emotion to wash over me and actually carry me to my next destination.

When it feels overwhelming, I remember that I can pray to my Higher Power to remove my resistance, I can attend a meeting and share about my struggles, and I can reach out to someone to let them in. Then I will be able to realize that there is a possibility of many outcomes, and I'm not a fortune-teller. I can let go.

In this moment, I will remember that my grief becomes less all-consuming when I stop resisting it and share the load with someone else.

From a letter I wrote to myself, when I began to forgive myself on this journey with chronic pain and illness:

…I am not only forgiving you, but forgiving the society that has made us feel abnormal. It's been a difficult road. I've learned we enjoy being alone. Solitude allows for us to be creative in our own space, giving us room to pursue different levels of freedom. This includes practicing meditation in quiet places, reading, studying, thinking, writing, crocheting, sewing, and other crafty projects.

I forgive our past mistakes that led to negative emotions, thoughts, and behaviors. I see now that self-directed negativity makes us sicker. I'm working on changing the narrative and examining my standards and expectations. I'm giving the past less of our time and focus to allow for more creative freedom in the present moment. I forgive myself for getting stuck in the past. I am learning not to repeat past mistakes, and I'm excited about what's to come.

I forgive our body. I've been given more chances than most, and I want to spend the rest of our time doing what we enjoy. I am letting our body have the grace it deserves. I have been praying for more self-acceptance and to accept what I cannot change about our chronic illness. I resolve to live with more self-care and kindness.

In the process of forgiving myself, I'm finding more joy in the little things. I'm also taking care of my body, recognizing the ability to be creative from within, and feeling grateful for my new knowledge and understanding. All of this fills my soul with more room to be forgiving and at peace.

In this moment, I will honor forgiveness as a journey and respect wherever I am on the path.

Just Do The Next Indicated Action is an important tool and core practice in my recovery. While valuable at any time, it becomes increasingly useful the more overwhelmed I feel or when my mental faculties aren't working well.

For example, it is difficult for me to manage many different kinds of tasks. There is always more than I can do. But instead of being immobilized by anxiety and feeling overwhelmed, narrowing down my focus to what I can do *next* helps me to take action. Sometimes the next action is to take a break: to rest or sleep; to check out of the mental whirlwind and tune in to my deeper source of wisdom and discernment; to seek guidance. Or it may be to seek help from a recovery buddy who can stay on the phone with me while I get started on the next indicated thing (then check-in afterward, for accountability and to celebrate the achievement). Sometimes I'm only able to take a simple action, but not one relating to a critical task.

Sometimes I give myself permission to do *anything.* This provides freedom from the internal pressure to get the "most important" things done first. Inside this freedom, it's easier for me to check in and receive the guidance my Higher Power has to offer. There's less mental static and buying into the judgments about what I *must* do.

As I use this tool over time, my stress and my feelings of being overwhelmed decrease. I can remember that I've used it before, that it has helped me take action even while feeling overwhelmed, uncertain, and lacking clarity. I don't have to figure out, or be responsible for, the bigger picture. It is a form of *Letting Go And Letting God.*

In this moment, I will take everything one step at a time.

CPA has no opinion on individual members' sexual morality, preferences, or behaviors. But the values CPA points to as important to a life well-lived, like honesty, empathy, awareness, and some modicum of selflessness, may be important to consider when looking at my need for touch. Chronic pain or chronic illness expresses itself within my body and my mind and thus affects all aspects of my life. I am a physical, emotional, and spiritual creature, so it's no surprise that my physical maladies as well as my emotional and spiritual conditions are not separate from my sexuality.

I've learned that both my character defects and assets play out in the sexual arena. For example, if I have difficulty communicating with my partner outside of the bedroom, I typically find *that*, not my physical limitations, to be what is disabling my sex life. Maybe I've lost much of my self-esteem, and, almost unconsciously, I've withdrawn to avoid further disappointment. Perhaps I've stopped trying because it can feel too much like one more chore. Or maybe I have some old ideas about what sex ought to look or be like—that if I can no longer be the brilliantly skillful sexual partner I may have once imagined myself to be, then why participate?

And what about my partner's emotions surrounding our changed circumstances?

I've found that with sex, as with many fundamental program issues, it's better to take the time and find ways to sort things out. An investment of time looking at an issue pays regular dividends that don't require the initial effort, ever after. In the area of touch, I've found an overall program of emotional recovery can really help.

In this moment, I will remember I can use my program tools in all areas of my life.

Chronic pain and illness can turn our lives upside down. Many of us are no longer able to follow the path we dreamed for ourselves or do the work we prepared for and set out to do. Some of us believed that achievement equaled success in life. Loss of abilities, jobs, finances, potential, friends, and spouses all leave us not only grieving but wondering if there is a reason to go on living.

CPA can help us discover new and meaningful ways to live. When my illnesses severely progressed, I needed to depend on caregivers to help me get through the day, to rest for hours at a time. My brain became so foggy that it was hard to put together a sentence. Then I found CPA.

Quickly I discovered that finding a group of people who understand and are going through a similar journey provides a sense of belonging. Attending meetings provided a purpose for each day. As I listened to others share, I learned it was good to be compassionate to myself and even to love myself—creating more purpose and meaning in my life.

The Serenity Prayer provided a mantra and helped me face and grieve losses. I could not control my illnesses or how doctors and the many people who did not understand or believe how ill I was treated me. Letting go and letting love into my life became a mission. Daily, I can surrender to this Power of Love, ask for guidance, and seek to do its will. I realized this new purpose for life had more depth and seemed far more important than my old purpose of *doing* and *accomplishing*.

In this moment, I will remember I can still find purpose and meaning whilst living with chronic conditions.

When chronic pain and chronic illness irreparably altered my life, I lost all sense of direction, purpose, and identity. I struggled every morning with thoughts of dread: to have awakened, yet again, to another meaningless day. I was bedbound and hopeless. A friend intervened and taught me to crochet. It brought color, texture, and a sense of accomplishment right into bed with me. I began collecting all types of yarn; for my birthday, my husband installed shelves to hold it all.

In CPA, I've learned the value of self-acceptance, self-care, and self-love. Nonetheless, I believed that because I could no longer work to bring income into the house, I should not be spending money. I began hiding yarn purchases in the car until I could "safely" bring them into the house, without my husband's knowledge.

As time went on, my dishonesty ate away at my serenity. It made me feel worse and worse. I prayed for the courage to come clean and confessed what I had been doing. My husband's response shocked and amazed me. He told me that he viewed my crocheting, and all that included, as part of my "medical treatment" and that he had witnessed the benefits it had on my spirit. I knew it was meditative and gave me fulfillment and joy, but I didn't know he could see that too.

In this moment, I will consider the things that bring me small joys as necessary to my well-being. I am worth it!

How do I know the difference between my will and Higher Power's will? My will always comes with an urgent, pressuring, and panicky tirade of mental dialogue that propels me into exhausting action and exacerbated symptoms. When I listen to that voice and act, it almost always ends with the need for even more frantic action, or worse, the need to make amends.

My Higher, Deeper Self speaks in a quiet, brief voice that creates an "ah-ha" sensation that is comforting and often humorous.

The prayer *"Thy will, not mine, be done"* releases me from my obsession to control and direct everything and reminds me that when I listen to that "small, still voice," my life is always easier, lighter and, dare I say, more miraculous—in ways I could never have achieved myself.

I have come to believe that something greater than myself knows what is best for me, and my only job is to stay grounded in the present moment and ask and listen for Higher Powered guidance. This works for me every time; I know a new freedom and ease of living in the midst of chronic pain and chronic illness.

In this moment, I will get quiet and pay attention to the "small, still voice" inside.

On my best days, I know I will reach a point where, unless I isolate myself and dial down the stimuli dramatically, I'll collapse emotionally. If I'm with others, I'll lash out at them. It doesn't matter how resolved I am to be pleasant or how much I pray about it. At that point, I don't need another suggestion—I need a nap.

I live with my spouse, and I let her know when I'm approaching "tilt mode"—without burdening her with details, simply indicating it is that time now. It's time I isolate and rest, entirely. Later, we can be together, pleasantly, even when I may be but partially restored. We both know I won't be up for much conversation and certainly not for problem-solving discussions. When I am rested, we communicate well. That's what allows for the mutual understanding and accommodation necessary for a healthy relationship, even with sometimes crushing burdens.

Before CPA, I thought I *never* blamed others for my pain. In truth, I expected: *Since I am the sick one here, you ought to be working on your character defects so I won't have to be patient with them.* I've learned that it probably *is* my issue and that perhaps I am too tired to judge the situation at hand with any clarity.

I am thrilled to have the awareness and the opportunity to do my self-care, communicate with care, to be less of a pain and more of a lover and a friend.

In this moment, I will take time for myself if necessary and make amends for any poor behavior toward my loved ones as soon as I can.

Forgiveness is like sunlight, a gift from my Higher Power. I didn't do anything to deserve it, and I can't bend it to my will. I become still, and it arrives. When considering forgiveness, I think about the parts of the word, specifically the "giving" and the "for." It's about finding something worth "giving for." To me, that something is the freedom to live this day as I am, in this body, with this life. This isn't the life I thought I would have, but it has become precious.

In my experience, forgiveness is something that comes through the actions of prayer and meditation. From spending time with and paying attention to my Higher Power, I gain awareness. Awareness isn't always a comfortable place to be, and I am learning to be compassionate and gentle with myself when I have these uncomfortable feelings. I discovered the first person needing my forgiveness is myself.

I still struggle with the contribution I made to the worsening of my chronic pain. Engendered by my need to control, my frantic desperation and fear led to actions that exacerbated my injuries. But I am learning today, in the gentle and compassionate care of my Higher Power. This relieves me of the need to control. When I give myself over to that care, my desperation to be "cured" is lifted. While my physical pain remains, my mental and spiritual anguish are eased.

In this moment, I will acknowledge that forgiveness brings me acceptance, and acceptance gives me freedom. Through connection with my Higher Power, I find that I am exactly where I need to be.

In taking Step Five, I value being transparent—not feeling that I want or need to hide my faults. It's freeing to recognize and admit my shortcomings to another person and to my Higher Power, and to have the understanding and acceptance of both during this process. So it's important to choose my partner in Step Five carefully.

I shared my Fifth Step with my Sponsor. I found it so helpful to have someone else's perspective. There were some things that I was ashamed of, but when I shared them, I found they were natural and understandable results of things in my life. I was able to quit carrying guilt and give myself compassion as I experienced acceptance from my Sponsor and from God.

The process of talking through these things gave me the wisdom to know if it was time to drop some out of my life if they no longer served me. It was a healing Step. Taking it left me free of things that had been secret problems and with a greater sense of self-worth. I love that Step Five fits right where it belongs in the process of working all of the Twelve Steps.

In this moment, I will take action if there is something I need to share with a trusted individual.

When I think that progress is unending forward and upward movement in a linear way, this is unrealistic thinking. It's not how life or healing or the recovery process work—let alone pain or health or anything else in the changing world. I have to let go of the insanity of trying to make life as it is happening fit the way I think it should.

I now see progress as forward movement from wherever I am right now. My health may have taken a dive. My ability to remember I have tools and use them may be significantly impaired or shut down for a while. Onward does not always mean upward.

Sometimes, progress looks like survival mode. Survival is a foundation upon which thriving can happen. The more challenged I am, the more foundational my responses need to become. Harm reduction is a useful strategy during these times, also self-acceptance, self-compassion, and prioritizing self-care.

Progress, for me, is taking the risk of trying a different coping strategy, experimenting to discover how that might turn out. I can turn a "mistake" into information, an opportunity to learn new ways of responding. Progress is also forgiving myself when I'm caught up in playing out older strategies that come with unpleasant consequences for being an imperfect human being, responding imperfectly to an imperfect life.

Taking a risk rather than remaining immobilized in uncertainty and fear, with whatever scrap of willingness I have left, provides some glimmer of a possibility that this may be my best way forward.

In this moment, I will make progress by taking one, next indicated step, even when my discernment seems offline and I fear it may be the wrong thing to do.

My pain can coexist with my faith. I tried it the other way, and that was dark, scary, and depressing. When I let chronic pain and illness take over my life, I lost the ability to recognize faith or anything like it. I expected to be let down, over and over—especially when it came to being sick. I once had a very strong faith, but now found I had none at all.

Once I attended a CPA meeting where I could see and hear others who lived like I did, then talked to them in the fellowship after the meeting, I got some hope. Faith followed, eventually. I think, now, that I needed to connect with others…but I may never know exactly what changed for me by going to CPA. I know that life is good today and the despair is gone, the darkness is gone. I'm okay with not knowing "why"; it's not necessary. Today, I have faith that I will be continually guided in this program.

My understanding of Higher Power (HP) has expanded. It includes a much "grittier," down-to-earth version of HP. It's also a stronger version. Life can be "harsh" and "unfair." But I've come to view terms like "harsh" and "unfair" as based on my expectations. My world has become smaller in many ways, but my vision of life has expanded.

So, yes, my faith can coexist with my chronic pain and illness, but more than that, it exists *because of* my chronic pain and illness. Today, I don't worry that I don't "believe in God" because I've found that God definitely believes in me.

In this moment, I will allow my pain and illness to coexist with my faith in my Higher Power.

It took me a long time to come out of my shell in CPA. When I first started coming to meetings, I was quiet, reserved, and shut down. I felt like chronic pain and chronic illness had sucked all the life-force out of me. Then one day, I opened up and was vulnerable for the first time. I think I expected everyone to stop and take notice and give me special attention. Instead, the meeting went on as normal. I sat and stewed, feeling like I'd just exposed a very raw part of me.

Fellowship time began, and no one said anything about my big brave share. I wrote in the chat, the words, "I can't," meaning, "I can't do this vulnerability thing," and I left. The topic being discussed was dancing; apparently, other members thought I'd left because I was saying "I can't dance." Later, someone reminded me that we don't crosstalk in meetings, and that's why no one had addressed my share. I began to feel better.

While I still have vulnerable moments in meetings, I've learned to share the really raw stuff with my Sponsor and close friends, especially when I'm looking for any sort of feedback. I've let the fellowship get to know me—in my good moments, in my funny moments, and in my dark moments. It took time for me to learn to trust the fellowship and the program. Now I look back at my "I can't dance" outburst with laughter. I have the pleasure of watching newcomers come in and slowly share their experiences and their personalities in meetings.

In this moment, I will enjoy watching the process of newcomers working the program and setting down the heaviness they come in with, just as I did.

I have Sponsored others twice in CPA—once with a man, once a woman. One is best advised to find a Sponsee of the same gender, but that general rule is one I'll break for specific circumstances. Sponsorship is a significant responsibility; a person's spiritual life is being fostered. So when I Sponsor, I review the literature carefully.

I'm not a preacher or priest, and even if I were, my role as CPA Sponsor only includes sharing my experience, strength, and hope as I've discovered them, working the Twelve Steps. I am well-steeped in other Twelve Step programs; I naturally draw upon these, of course, but when Sponsoring in CPA, I focus on how our literature presents the Steps.

Getting my head into our books is a great way to see the difference between what my head says and what the literature says. I can find myself so wise, at times, that I may find myself selling *my* way of approaching a Higher Power, though I don't mean to be doing so, or I find myself using therapeutic techniques that have no business in Step work. CPA literature can ground me when Sponsoring.

Sponsorship has meant that I work the Steps, to some degree, again from start to finish. When a Sponsee responds, not so much to me but to a Higher Power they encounter in the Steps, I see and feel their spirit ignited, and mine gets reignited. I feel gratified and satisfied, the way I am, at times, when putting away, at day's end, a right tool, well used.

In this moment, I will remember the best way for me to maintain unity in Sponsorship relationships is to align my experience, strength, and hope with the CPA literature.

Since I've had my pain and illness, I've struggled with unrestful sleep. Even on days where I seemed to get enough, I would wake up exhausted. Doctors and specialists told me: sleep is important, especially in dealing with pain and illness. But the medications they provided only made me feel worse. I felt utterly defeated and had given up hope for a solution.

Another suggestion was to take naps during the day. As someone who only found meaning in productivity, the idea of a nap seemed wrong. I could not wrap my mind around the idea, so I completely dismissed it. My denial increased my suffering. My body was screaming, begging, and pleading with me to sleep.

I suffered for three years until I found CPA, where I learned that *Rest Is an Action.* People in meetings shared about their experiences with sleep and rest, and I saw that I was not alone in my experience with sleep or even my attitude toward it. This helped me realize: maybe I could be productive *and* take care of myself. I discovered that I actually become more productive when I rest and take naps.

CPA may not have solved my sleep problems, but it has helped to change my attitude. It's given me a gentler outlook and allowed me to change my toxic belief system. When I gave myself permission to rest, much of the suffering I was experiencing diminished.

Through CPA, I will do what is best for me and my health, listening to the voice of recovery rather than the voice of the emotional obsession of chronic pain and chronic illness.

In this moment, I will give myself permission to rest when I need it.

First of all, when I found CPA, I couldn't believe I'd found a fellowship that understood my pain, isolation, and fear. But secondly, and most importantly, I couldn't believe I'd found a place where I could laugh again.

I've noticed many health benefits from bringing laughter and humor into my life. It has helped my immune system and improved my overall mood, and it even helps relieve some of my pain. This kind of medicine is not only free but readily available. Therefore, I not only practice this medicine, but I share it with my CPA fellowship when I can.

We are all on this journey of recovery. We are all trying to get by and live another day. This life is not easy. So, I suggest: try humor. Practice laughing in the mirror or watching a funny video. Or even try telling a corny joke. The best that can happen is laughter—your own and others'.

I can't eliminate my pain or someone else's, but I can invite someone to smile, giggle, or laugh. I find that keeping a sense of humor is helpful not only to me but to everyone around me as well. My goal now is that every time I share a gratitude, I include a corny riddle or joke. Maybe everyone won't find it funny, but if two or three get a giggle or laugh from it, I think I've made the world a better place—a lighter, more enjoyable place, right in this moment.

> *Knock, knock*
> *Who's there?*
> *Cereal*
> *Cereal who?*
> *Cereal pleasure to meet you!*

In this moment, I will remember and apply Declaration Eight: "We will laugh and see the lighter side of situations."

I have had periods in my life when it seemed that every time I thought I was on solid ground, another tsunami came and washed me away. Sometimes it seems like I just can't catch a break.

This is where my program helps me. Yes, I go down. I feel defeated and I am angry. I have to fight to get up again. But the cycle time is shorter, and the intensity of the experience is less when I use the slogans, the Steps, the literature, meetings, and program friends.

Step One, I surrender to my reality, even though I don't like it. Step Two, there is a Power greater than me that is there for me, even though it sure doesn't look that way right now. Step Three, I turn myself over to the care of my Higher Power (HP).

Once I feel sane again, after the storm of feelings, I ask my HP, *What am I supposed to receive out of this experience? What am I supposed to learn?* I pray for guidance. I trust that there is something of value, which doesn't mean it isn't awful and I would rather not be doing this, but this practice gives me agency and hope. I am not a victim. I am resilient, and HP will show me the way forward.

When I don't know what way to go next, I have faith. That is how I have navigated these experiences. It looks pretty on paper, but it is not in real life. It is not graceful or easy, but with the program tools, I get stronger and my faith gets deeper.

In this moment, I will allow my feelings room to express themselves, then turn to the first three Steps to help me feel grounded once more.

"But, but, but...I want, I need, I must..." This is how I lived before CPA.

When I committed to turning my will, life, and my body over to the care of my Higher Power (HP) in Step Three, I had to constantly remind myself to relax, soften, breathe. I had to accept HP's will and timing as perfect, even when circumstances and appearances frightened me. I don't give up my hopes, dreams, and desires; I just surrender the form of the outcomes and timing of these things.

I knew I wanted to move to a place that felt like paradise...and it took seven years of waiting. Things had to happen in those seven years in order for my dream to come true. I knew that forcing my will in pursuit of my dream would only get in HP's way, create frustration in me, and exacerbate my symptoms. So, while I waited, I continued to put my best efforts toward research, footwork, and preparations. I treated it like a hobby instead of a job, and when HP pulled the trigger on the move, everything fell into place "as if by magic." This complex endeavor was the easiest thing I had ever done in my life. And it was, indeed, perfect!

Chronic pain and chronic illness do not have to rob me of my dreams, but living with their effects does demand reliance on something greater than my best efforts. When I surrender my wants, needs, and musts, I trade struggle and hardship for divine ease.

In this moment, I will practice Step Three and look for the path that HP has laid open for me.

"Rest" was once a condemnable action, a negative word used to describe "laziness." It has become a necessary tool I use in my day-to-day life. Chronic pain and illness forced me to realize that I am unable to move at the pace I once did. This felt unfair, especially given my young age, and I didn't accept it.

I did start resting at various times during the day, but not until I'd pushed past my limit and hit a wall. Bruised, tearful, unable to keep pushing, I would concede. I rested, but never without the shame of being in bed while the sun was still out. I'd look at myself through the eyes of a judgmental authority figure, the word "lazy" hissing in my ear. I'd look out the window at the bustling city, imagining that I was the only ambulatory person lying in bed.

Because of Chronic Pain Anonymous, what was once "laziness" is now something I do to restore myself, to return to a state from which I can greet the rest of my day with some peace and serenity rather than frustration and anger. Now, I know that I am not wrong, I am not bad, I am not lazy for retreating to a restful space to care for myself, even though it often means lying in my bed, the sun shining, the city charging forth around me.

In this moment, I will take time to rest even if a part of me still resists my need for it.

When I first became sick, I was the breadwinner of the family. As I began losing my ability to work, my fear of what would happen to us grew. I wasn't sure how our family could survive without my financial support.

One of the first things I realized was that my faith in my spouse's ability to handle financial matters was really low. Money was an area where my controlling nature wasn't easing. My fear was tearing me up inside and causing things to be strained in our home.

One of the practices an old Sponsor helped me with was inviting Higher Power (HP) into all my financial affairs. When creating a spending plan, I'd write a prayer on the top of each page. Some of my favorites were, "HP, guide my dollars," and "HP, help me remember that You are my employer." Prayers have now found their way into my passwords and comments on our financial spreadsheets.

The biggest change in my behavior has been talking about money with my spouse regularly. We hold hands and pray before we discuss money.

My general sense of doom is underscored when there is vagueness around money. I still write down every dollar I spend, and so does my spouse. We discuss how much money will be needed in the future and where we stand right now. By watching my spouse handle financial problems and discussing them with one another openly, I have grown my faith in him and his ability to hold our family together. He has done a great job. We've moved into a more accessible home because of his efforts.

In this moment, I will remember each day that I am guided and loved by my Higher Power and that HP has solutions I cannot even begin to dream of on my own.

It took me a while to learn that whether or not I slept, or how well I slept, was not the determining factor of my happiness. I have no control over whether I'm able to fall asleep, stay asleep, or go back to sleep after I've woken in the middle of the night. I'm powerless over my sleep. This is a new concept I've learned with the help of my program and friends in CPA.

I discovered that being angry at 2:00 a.m. only made things worse. Obsessively trying to figure out a solution makes me more tense and less able to sleep. Taking care of myself in the wee hours is the best way to deal with the nights when sleep eludes me. I listen to an audiobook and close my eyes. Although I may fall asleep, that's not my goal. I may go into another room, turn on the TV, or read a magazine. I have a friend in another country for whom it is daytime, so I call her. All this helps me get to morning. I've let go of solving the problem, and I accept the moment. This brings peace, even when it doesn't bring sleep.

I've also let go of the belief that if I don't get enough sleep, I can't function. It turns out, I can function. And if I notice that my thinking is compromised, I cancel my activities for that day. If I notice I'm irritable and snapping at others, I choose to be alone until I can regulate again. I love the days when I wake up after a night of refreshing sleep, and I no longer dread the days when that's not the case.

In this moment, I will stop judging my sleep and telling myself stories that hold me back from enjoying my day.

All my life, I've heard, "You're so hard on yourself!" I responded by being harder on myself—about being so hard on myself! Once my body required me to slow down, all of my fearful thoughts and resulting behaviors were magnified. I couldn't avoid them anymore. How was I supposed to generate that elusive thing called self-compassion?

Working Step One with my Sponsor led me to the realization that I hadn't felt safe in my body for a long time. It occurred to me that self-compassion might be instinctive, not something I could conjure in my mind. As someone who has always dissociated from situations in order to cope, I hadn't spent much time staying with discomfort.

I allowed myself to begin to feel my body, slowly building up a meditation practice that focused on sensations. I spent time relaxing my shoulders into the deepest part of my exhale, allowing my parasympathetic nervous system to take over for a few seconds. And then, I cried. A lot. I realized I had always pushed away feelings of sorrow, demonizing them as self-pity before I had a chance to gently investigate them. Witnessing these feelings of sorrow while in moments of release, I saw that my fear and anger were perfectly human experiences my Higher Power had afforded me. Shutting feelings down was effectively shutting out my Higher Power.

CPA has changed how I see myself and my life. It's given me the realization that I can *choose* what to do next—call my Sponsor or a program pal, write, yell into a pillow, or cry, and listen to other people who explore self-compassion as a practice.

In this moment, I will allow my emotions and sensations space for expression and release. I can ask my Higher Power for support as I do so.

Don't just lie there. Do something. My mind has always told me I have to do something to be worthy of love and acceptance. I must do more, must be better, stronger, or faster than I am. Then, chronic pain and chronic illness stopped me dead in my tracks. I could no longer distract myself from these unskillful beliefs with activities, and the emotional and spiritual debilitation that arose paralyzed me as my self-loathing continued to grow.

At one of my first CPA meetings, I heard, "Do half of what you think you can do," and "I am enough, I have enough, I know enough, I do enough." It took time for these concepts to become a working part of my mind. I had to practice. My mind tells me I *should* be doing this or that; CPA taught me, when this happens, to pause and ask Higher Power (HP) for the next right thought or action. Sometimes there is a gentle whisper, *"Go do the dishes,"* or *"Stay flat."*

When I listen to the "shoulds," my brain habitually turns toward and my life becomes unmanageable. When I listen to something greater than my mind—taking a shower when my HP tells me that that is the next indicated action, for instance—this is cause for celebration, not beratement. Doing HP's will instead of my mind's will allows me to live peacefully, joyfully, and comfortably, no matter what my body and mind are doing.

In this moment, I will quietly pause and ask my Higher Power to direct me to take the next indicated action, even when the action is "rest."

Around age twenty-seven, chronic illness arrived in my life. Right away, I had to accept that my illness does not have a cure or a clear timeline of life expectancy. I always have hope about things, but I had to lower my expectations. After a hopeful treatment with side effects nearing death, I changed my understanding of acceptance to include no control. It was clear that time was limited.

My spouse and I lived the next several years doing as much as we could to organize our life. We managed to accomplish many of our goals, and our efforts were fulfilling. We both had our professions. I loved working two miles from the Pacific Ocean. Our daily life was good. Then, the illness and pain progressed. I tried to hang on to the life I loved but could not do it anymore. Retirement disability became another opportunity to practice acceptance.

To my surprise, I have lived beyond doctors' expectations. (Another lesson in no control!) My husband got a once-in-a-lifetime job, so we moved. I think I will always grieve my sunny Southern California lifestyle, but believe it or not, my days are better now because I finally found my place—in a CPA meeting.

Sitting in my meeting, I realize how the practice of the Steps has turned around my thoughts. Most days are actually good now. It's still hard for me to hear yet another diagnosis. But I just return to Step One: realizing I am powerless, my life is unmanageable, and acceptance is all there is. I'm still living, so gratefully, and with much more acceptance, mindfulness, and understanding.

In this moment, I will be grateful for being alive, in exactly the life I have.

June

When having chronic conditions, as well as developing new medical issues routinely, acceptance is key.

I used to live by accepting a bad turn of some kind by trudging forward and staying positive until life got better, or I adjusted and had a "new normal" I could accept. Nothing wrong with that.

But at this stage of my life and my conditions, this process no longer works quite that neatly. I have had to admit that my so-called "new normal" is that I am now in constant change and am likely to always be as I age. So I no longer have the luxury of waiting until I have a new plateau I can fully accept—one to be "okay" about.

Now I accept that I will always be experiencing some new change in my life's conditions—denying some, grieving some— but ultimately accepting everything as it is and calling it "okay," while the process goes round and round.

When I start my day recalling the ultimate unmanageability of my life, I am reminded to continue accepting things, small and large, as I go through the day. I am not preoccupied with inner narratives, spun to convince I-don't-know-who that this or that isn't right/isn't okay. I now have the mental space that so my Higher Power can direct my thinking. I can now see what I do have, what I can do, and what meaning and texture is still here for me.

In this moment, I will remember that when I look through the "glasses" of recovery, I see the world differently.

I remember the first months and years after chronic pain/illness entered my life. I was devastated and depressed because of how much my life had changed, how much I'd lost. So many activities that had brought me joy, fulfillment, or self-worth were now impossible. I felt lost, but I struggled to keep up my pre-illness pace because I thought I should. This was my insanity. The whirlwind of confusion, feeling worthless, not knowing what to do, grief, and wondering why this happened to me was crazy-making.

CPA helped me see how my Higher Power could change all of this. It gave me directions on how to turn my life over to Him when the whirlwinds would inevitably come. With the help of members and the tools of the program, my insanity began to be dismantled.

I was able to address my sadness and grief, or any other issues, with the help of my Higher Power. I learned to turn things over to Him, to make new decisions and changes in my life that shifted much of what was making me insane. Those changes and decisions happened in Step Three; working Step Two made all that possible.

Step Two gave me hope, which supported me to do Step Three. This has resulted in a life that is fulfilling and good. It is not perfect. There are still problems and struggles, and sometimes sadness and grief, but Step Two brought me out of my insanity and despair and helped me to transition into what is, one day at a time, a satisfying, fruitful, and a better future.

In this moment, I will remember that turning to the Higher Power of my understanding can restore me to sanity.

Through working my Steps, especially Step Four, I discovered that I often felt obliged to be obedient—afraid to rock the boat and stand up for myself. This is especially true when working with my healthcare providers. At times, the medical settings were intimidating, and I didn't want to upset the people I relied on for care by coming across as "difficult."

With support from my Sponsor, I began to make amends to myself by practicing self-care. The ways I took care of myself when it came to changes in my treatment plan included going slowly, asking questions, doing my own research, and speaking to other patients. I realized I could even say, "No," to my medical providers, if necessary.

As a result of working my program, I believe I now make good choices regarding my healthcare most of the time. And yet, just last week I had a bad reaction to a new medication; I had to surrender and cancel my plans. Unlike in the past, that didn't freak me out or make me angry. My emotions and catastrophic thinking did not overtake me. I responded with acceptance and serenity.

This experience was a reminder that the unexpected is a part of life's journey; it's guaranteed as a part of living with chronic health conditions. I can do the footwork, but I am always powerless over the outcome. What I can do is relax into surrender.

In this moment, I will make choices that honor my integrity and self-care. I will relax and let Higher Power be in charge of all outcomes.

I revisit the Twelve Steps every few years and work through them with another. Because I'd done Step Four many times, my Sponsor suggested I focus my inventory on fear.

I decided to answer one question, again and again and again: *What am I afraid of?* I did this over many weeks. As I repeatedly answered the question, the more fears I discovered. Some were oldies but goodies, some were new.

It was liberating to have all my fears out in the open. All the demons that haunt me, that keep me stuck and unable to move, were exposed and therefore no longer so frightening. There was a clear map of all the ways I'm paralyzed by fear, and all I was going to give to my Higher Power (HP) in Steps Six and Seven.

After I spoke all the fears out loud in Step Five, I felt such relief. My Sponsor heard my list and defused many of my fears. He helped me see how they were not real; it was just my mind playing tricks on me. Some were the past, haunting me; some were negative projections into the future that were only my imagination, not truth.

One surprising result of this inventory was hearing HP's guidance clearly for the first time. This led to a major life change. I now have a real, interactive relationship with my HP. It is the miracle of the program. I didn't have any expectations when I started and wasn't looking to make big changes. Today, when a fear shows up and starts to loom large, I work all Twelve Steps on just that fear. This has become a powerful tool I use to work my program.

In this moment, I will shine a light on my fears by sharing them with another.

In Step Six, I became entirely ready to have a new relationship with my pain, my illness, and myself.

I am not defective. Steps Four and Five showed me that I am human and that I've developed skillful and unskillful responses to my pain and illness and to life itself. After decades of believing and behaving as though I had to be superhuman to be worthy of love and acceptance, I am now entirely ready to have God remove this delusion.

I recently had an extremely high-symptom and high-pain day that required medication. As a woman in long-term recovery, I am mindful of taking medication as prescribed, yet I had a human, mind-fog moment and took two pills instead of one. My pain was addressed; however, I felt "buzzed." I made a mistake. This served as a reminder that reliance on my Higher Power is needed in every action I take.

Instead of beating myself up, fighting the side effects of my error, and allowing my mind to launch me into *False Events Appearing Real (FEAR)*, I shared my error with another CPA member and "took the rest of the day off." Thanks to CPA, I have a new relationship with my pain, my illness, and myself. With humility, I understand that my responses are simply human, not defective, and my Higher Power is *always* there to lovingly support, guide, and comfort me regardless of my mistakes.

In Step Six, I became entirely ready to willingly accept my humanness and trust that when I seek guidance from my Deeper Self/Still, Small Voice, I will be lovingly directed toward my greatest good.

In this moment, I will forgive myself for making mistakes that I am guaranteed to make as a chronic human being.

I am a new member of CPA but have been dealing with chronic pain for twelve years. I was active all my life, and when that all changed, I reluctantly fought to accept that my Higher Power knows what I can handle. CPA has been a blessing, to say the least.

Early on, my bad days were filled with anger and self-pity, tantrums, and depression. Today, I accept my bad days for what they are, but my struggle is with wanting understanding from my spouse and other family members. You can't see my chronic pain on the outside. No one knows how much energy it takes to be somewhat normal or how I'm able to "hide" the pain to just have a taste of what life was. (Then it can take days to recover.) Coming from a family that values work and where no one has ever dealt with chronic pain, I find that they cannot relate. So on those bad days, I practice self-compassion to recover/heal, and I extend the same compassion to my loved ones. I remember that this is a challenging journey for them as well.

I try to do at least one kind act for someone, whether it be a text/call or email from bed, or just being an ear to listen. I'm fortunate that my kids have accepted "what Mom can do now," which is listen, be present, and be there when they get home from school.

I refuse to lose hope on bad days because I know I'm still here for a reason. It's up to me to recognize that reason, every single day.

In this moment, I will remember I am lovable not for what I do but for how I express love.

I think it's so amazing how we *all* can feel so alone and in such dark places at times. When I think no one can possibly understand what I feel, I attend a CPA meeting and someone shares the same feelings I am having. It's inspirational and comforting, and it allows me to "exhale."

I recently tried a new prescription and had a bad mental and physical reaction. It took me to a dark place—I felt very confused and disoriented. I couldn't participate in a family celebration; instead, my family had to take care of me. The guilt I felt was excruciating. I was angry at my Higher Power (HP), thinking: *How much more do you want me to go through?* The medication finally cleared my system and my mind. My family and support team held me up in prayer and provided for what I lacked. I am so fortunate.

My strength and hope come from my HP, which takes many forms. A beautiful picture can warm my heart. Often, a song will remind me of *One Day At A Time*, and the spring returns to my step. My CPA friends exemplify and inspire me to be raw and real. They lend me their strength, which allows me to exhale. And when I share my experiences and see others experiencing the same inspiration and comfort, I know I am in connection with my HP.

In this moment, I will pause, take a deep breath, exhale, and trust fall into CPA.

Two very important aspects of living with chronic illness and/or pain are surrender and acceptance. I find both are necessary to living in peace and serenity. And I'm not sure I've considered them separately. I've often used them interchangeably.

Do I need to surrender to be in acceptance? Do I accept in order to surrender?

I can see surrendering as an action I need to take frequently. In Step One, when I accepted I was powerless over pain/illness and that my life had become unmanageable, I surrendered and began to relax a bit. I gave up the frenzied search for a solution that would give me back my former health. This resulted in less stress.

In Step Two, I came to believe and accept that there was something greater than my best efforts. I surrendered control. In Step Three, I surrendered my pain/illness only by accepting that this was a chance for a more peaceful alternative for living. The combination of Steps One, Two, and Three led me to a place where I could begin to accept my life as it was and surrender my obsession to control.

As time has passed, it's become more natural, less of an effort, to surrender and accept the situations in my life. I remember my first months in CPA: the grieving and anger, the fear, panic, and confusion. Those things still appear from time to time. However, they are now the exception, not the rule. I am very grateful for this journey of surrender and acceptance and the peace it has brought to me.

In this moment, I will remind myself that peace and serenity are possible as I accept and surrender.

I have at times struggled with comparing myself to others in the fellowship. *They are sicker/not as sick as me. They are smarter than me. They live in a better place. Their recovery is better than mine. MY RECOVERY IS BETTER THAN THEIRS.* It was easy to see the distortion and insanity in my thinking, but I couldn't stop.

My Sponsor suggested that I actively begin to *look for the similarities rather than the differences.* Focusing keenly at meetings, I once more heard the shared dilemmas of living with serious, chronic health issues: loss of friends, medications, mobility problems, isolation, lack of needed help, pressing financial concerns, and more. Focusing on the similarities helped me identify with others and participate in this program. I was freed from the despair of comparing myself to others.

Then, one evening during a meeting, I had a personal epiphany: *Who am I to know how troubled a person is, whether it be over an issue I think trivial or catastrophic? Do I not have a few issues, which I know others would think of as small things, that cut me to the quick?* It really isn't so much about the particulars that trigger the destructive elements of emotional and spiritual debilitation; it's the obsessive, negative reaction to life that is my problem. Working my CPA program is how I find relief.

In this moment, I will let go of comparing myself to others by focusing on my CPA program.

The most difficult moment for me, when facing the healthcare system, is when I am told I'm going to need something seriously new or different—especially a surgery. Due to past experiences, a form of PTSD kicks in. My heart beats rapidly, my gut clenches, my knees weaken, and the ghosts of past hospital experiences begin to pass through me. When this happens, I understand: with PTSD, one does not so much expel these types of demons as learn to accept them, with care and awareness.

Instead of being thrown by these upheavals or blaming myself for not having gotten over them, I recognize them as simply symptoms of another ongoing condition I have. It's predictable, it's just another condition—an outsized fear I live through at times. I must treat these "symptoms" with self-care and God-care. This helps me not to run in desperate circles or try to force feelings to go away. I would be doing the same insane thing as trying to force any of my other conditions to cease existing.

The best medicine for me is knowing I can talk to other CPA members. I am never judged as a whiner or one who is invested in my ills and who doesn't really want to let go. Fellow members lend me their understanding for as long as it takes. They gently remind me of my Higher Power until I slow, and that little hole I seem to carry brims again with love.

In this moment, I will remember I cannot force my pain away, but I can reach out for comfort and support.

I have the tendency to discount gratitude as a tool for achieving serenity. It can sound so ordinary—everyone's always talking about a gratitude list. It sounds like a nice little task but not something that really accomplishes anything significant. I've been surprised to find my perceptions were not accurate.

Gratitude has become an important tool for me. When I'm caught up thinking about things I'm unhappy about, such as things I can no longer do because of my chronic pain/illness, it brings me down. When that happens, I've found that thinking about the things that *are* good shifts my spirit and outlook on life.

My illness resulted in me having to leave my job; that made me sad. But the extra time I have now gives me opportunities to spend time reading and praying, and many other things I love doing that I didn't have time for while working full time. Whenever feelings of sadness or negativity are weighing me down, I can always find things to be grateful for. I pay attention to those things and actually list them. When I do, I always feel better. When I'm in pain and writing is nearly impossible, I still make an effort, and the results are inevitably positive. My pain somehow shifts.

Now, I encourage my Sponsees to give gratitude a try, whether for the first time or as a new practice, and see how it shifts them. It is one more tool we have available to truly enhance our well-being, and we don't have to spend money to use it! We can just decide to do it.

In this moment, I will write down something I am grateful for and see if anything shifts in me.

One of the gifts CPA Step work has offered me is the renewal of my creativity. Chronic pain and illness had robbed me of my adventurous, creative spirit. I am mostly housebound and, more often than not, bedbound. My excitement for life had vanished, and it was just "me and these four walls." I was losing my mind to boredom, depression, and a general sense of uselessness. My Sponsor suggested I humbly request that my curiosity and courage be returned as part of my Step Seven work.

Higher Power (HP) sent me a surprising response via a rare trip to a thrift store. First, I found a beading kit for $2.99 and couldn't wait to get back into bed and begin investigating. Next, it was a bag of crochet needles and some yarn. And thanks to online tutorials, I am now an unstoppable crocheter. It provides immediate gratification as I see "art" develop by my own hands. Playing with color and textures literally brightens my day, and I find the repetitive hand motion to be downright mediative. Bed-crafting is one of my Step Eleven practices, as it reconnects me to the present moment and quiets my fearful mind.

These are all things I can do in bed, any bed! I even take my crochet supplies with me for hospital stays. I am grateful to discover that although I usually cannot get out into life, I can bring creativity and play into my bedroom.

In this moment, I will creatively honor my HP-given creativity in my most comfortable location.-

To me, surrender means letting go: letting go of results, letting go of outcomes, letting go of trying to "figure it out," For me, surrender is the complete opposite of control. It is acceptance of what is and of my humanness.

My debilitating obsession to control and direct my pain is part of what brought me to CPA. Sometimes I struggle with the surrender suggested in the First Step because I want to be able to make the healthiest, most proactive decisions regarding my healthcare. I find myself obsessing and second-guessing whether I made the "right" decision and ultimately blame myself for not being "good enough" or "smart enough." Obsessing over these things only causes me more anxiety and pain. My pain feeds off of my anxiety, and my anxiety feeds off of my pain. Surrender means gently making a decision, letting go of the results, and trusting that my loving Higher Power will take care of the details.

When I try to manage the details of my life, I end up struggling against, or outright fighting, that which I have no control over. And for me that is the definition of insanity. Sometimes surrender simply means asking for and accepting help to be restored to clarity. Asking my Higher Power to guide me toward the next indicated action is the best example of surrender I know.

In this moment, I will surrender what I am trying to control into the hands of my loving Higher Power.

Looking back at my history with chronic illness, I see just how early I was aware of "something not being right" with my health. I also see how early I started pushing myself to keep up, trying to be "normal." Even after receiving a difficult diagnosis, I continued to try and work. The debilitation got worse, but I continued a "push, then crash" cycle, behaving as if there was nothing wrong with me.

Before coming to CPA, I judged myself for all of this pushing and blamed myself for how sick I had become. I obsessed about whether or not I had made my health worse and got mad at myself for possibly doing lasting damage to my body.

But I am beginning to really believe the *Three C's* regarding my chronic illness: *"I didn't cause it, I can't control it, I can't cure it."*

CPA and the *Three C's* are helping me to forgive and have compassion for the *me* that pushed and crashed for so long. I know that I did the best I could with the information I had at the time. Living with chronic pain and illness is hard enough; why make it harder by holding myself responsible for causing it? Besides, I'm not that powerful.

With my Higher Power's guidance and the support of my brothers and sisters in CPA, I now try to make healthier decisions and then let go of the outcome, whatever actions I have taken. Along the way, I practice the *Three S's*: self-care, self-acceptance, self-love.

In this moment, I will release the belief that I caused my conditions, that I can control them, or that I am powerful enough to cure them.

How can I feel joy while in pain? It seemed mysterious at first. When I heard a CPA member crack some jokes shortly after a surgery or saw a friend meet a new diagnosis with a shrug and a smile, I was stunned.

Lightheartedness through difficult circumstances is modeled in CPA. I heard people share how grateful they were for a simple pleasure in their day. As I went to more meetings, joy began to feel attainable again.

When joy is shared, it is multiplied; sometimes this can be a welcome shockwave that blows aside my despair. I also know that sorrow shared is lessened. I set aside my pain and my negative emotions by sharing all of my emotions with people who understand. This letting go lets the joy flow in and then splash back out into my days.

I will share with you a joyful moment after a recent surgery. I sat outside in the sun and felt a delightfully warm breeze tickle my hair. My loved one saw me smile and smiled back, and then we both chuckled. My husband asked, "Why are you smiling?" I said, "The spring air feels so nice rippling through my leg hair!" Our chuckles turned to joyful peals of laughter that reverberated again when I told a CPA girlfriend about this unexpected delight from my postsurgical hygiene challenge. Being present, accepting each moment as it comes, helps me to be joyful, even when in pain.

In this moment, I will remember I can find joyful moments when I am in pain. I just have to seek joy out.

My ignorance of mortgages became apparent when my new spouse and I received a letter notifying me of the ending of my adjustable-rate mortgage. We feared the worst, as published rates were considerably higher than what we had been paying.

As a couple in long-term recovery, we had already decided to turn our marriage over to the care of a loving Higher Power (HP), but I just wasn't able to do the same with our finances. After all, I was the one responsible for the original mortgage decision. After seven stressful days, I told my partner that I was willing to take responsibility for my risky decision, that I was powerless over the past but had now made the decision to turn my marriage *and* mortgage over to HP. I surrendered into my powerlessness, came to believe HP could help, and made a Third Step decision. One week later, we received another letter informing us that, beyond all logic and reason, our new mortgage rate was ridiculously low, and our monthly premium was cut in half.

My HP is way more powerful than percentage rates, bank balances, and financial institutions. My job is to get on board by surrendering "all my affairs" into the care of my loving Higher Power. When I do, things always turn out better than I could ever have imagined. My faith gets replaced by trust that my HP indeed has my back when I let It.

In this moment, I will come to believe my finances are in the loving care of my HP as I practice CPA principles in all my affairs.

My greatest fears fester in the unknown. Becoming severely debilitated was a journey into that dark, terrifying space. I don't know what condition my body will be in each morning, if the next treatment or surgery will help or harm me, or how many years my body will be able to go on like this. I face unknowns every day.

When I first came to CPA, I wanted out of the unknown. I wanted answers; I was on a quest, seeking treatment and doctors with determination and desperation. Though I am married, with a wonderful son and great friends, everything they suggested annoyed me. I felt completely alone.

Working the CPA Steps with my Co-sponsors has given me the strength and courage to see what underlies my fear. My biggest fear is becoming more of a burden to my family or leaving my son without a mother too soon. Facing my own mortality isn't a walk in the park, but I'm doing it. I can walk hand in hand with my fear, making the most of each day I have with my family.

I used to believe that fear and faith can't live together, but now I believe that the essence of courage is the marriage of faith and fear. I have learned how to develop that necessary close connection with my Higher Power (HP) to help me in those times of excruciating fear. Prayer and meditation are where I find comfort, and often I get immediate guidance as to how to face my present fear and make a new choice. I can't prevent death or debilitation from happening. With my CPA friends and close contact with my HP, I can create the best "today" possible.

In this moment, I will live peacefully, joyfully, and comfortably with my fears.

In my recovery journey, I learned a lot about the importance of not revealing who and what was shared in the meetings and that we leave our professional titles at the door. It was drilled into me that we are simply members among members, and I learned about the importance of keeping our meetings safe for members to share intimately. As I grew in CPA, I realized there were even more types of anonymity supporting me.

One of the things I love about anonymity in CPA is that, when we share about our medical concerns, we share in a general fashion and leave the specifics to private conversations. I consider that to be very important because it reminds me again that I am just a member among members. If I don't know another's specific diagnoses, I can't compare their severity to mine. Before CPA, I constantly compared myself to others. *Compare = Despair* was a slogan I heard early on in CPA. Now I am on the lookout for my comparative thoughts and remind myself that my chronic conditions and pain are no greater or less than another's. We all belong because we all suffer from the emotional and spiritual debilitation of living with chronic conditions, not because we suffer from X, Y, or Z. Every one of us is simply a member among members.

In this moment, I will embrace anonymity as a spiritual principle that creates humility in recovery for me.

It's been very hard for me to have compassion toward my body since I had to stop working. So much of my identity was wrapped up in my work and the recognition that I received in my community for my contributions. I was really angry at my body for failing me.

In CPA, I am learning to have compassion for whatever is going on with me, whether it's physical or mental distress. Working the Steps is helping me to cleanse any remnants of self-loathing and self-doubt so I can love myself, no matter what.

Early on in CPA, I joined a non-CPA, self-compassion workshop. I attended for a few months; then I began to be overwhelmed with all I was doing. I was going to many meetings, doing lots of service, working the Steps, and starting a Co-sponsor meeting to work the Steps together as a group. I also had a lot of doctors' visits because for the first time in a long while, I was advocating for getting good healthcare for my pain and illnesses. One day, it occurred to me that the most self-compassionate thing I could do for myself was drop out of the self-compassion workshop. I stopped going to as many meetings, knowing that my Higher Power was guiding me to the best outcome possible.

With almost two years in CPA, I have learned so much about self-compassion and am taking much better care of myself. I have pain, but I am not *a pain*—as is often said in meetings. This now rings true for me.

In this moment, I will forgive myself for overdoing and remember that I am powerless over chronic pain and chronic illness.

I am having a moment of genuine suffering. I am angry. I am angry at my body, my doctors, my medications, and my god. Thoughts like *this isn't fair* and *why me* play in an unstoppable loop. That which I resist, persists. My body tenses and my anxiety increases.

I breathe deeply and remember: in CPA I have learned not to fear my anger but to honor it by allowing the anger energy to move through, and thereby out of, my being.

I also remember that others are experiencing the same kind of feeling. This brings me comfort—not that others are suffering but knowing that I am not alone. Anyone experiencing these circumstances would no doubt be angry as well. It's not just me.

The CPA principle of self-acceptance, self-care, and self-love encourages me to ask: "What do I need in this moment of suffering?" "How can I be kind to myself in this very moment?" and "What wisdom is my anger trying to impart?" I can greet my anger as a self-loving emotion. It is a signpost that a self-care boundary has been crossed, indicating that self-love is possible for me. My anger actually demonstrates that the obtuse concept of "self-love" is actually present in me. With self-compassion and my Higher Power's guidance, I find I can arrive at a place of serenity, peace, and true self-acceptance.

In this moment, I will choose to gently and compassionately acknowledge my anger.

My first glimmer of hope in CPA came when I read the *Recipe for Recovery* preface: "Many of us with chronic pain and chronic illness have cognitive and energy deficits, and reading can be challenging and overwhelming. We have written this book to present the Twelve Steps in a way that is manageable for anyone, whatever their condition." Oh, thank heavens—they get me!

When I went to my first online CPA meeting, I saw folks in bed saying they hadn't showered in seven days. *Again—they get me!* I heard people laughing about crying and crying about laughing. *Wow, they really get me!* And as I delved into the literature and heard that we suffer from the emotional and spiritual debilitation of living with chronic pain and chronic illness—*Glory be, I'm home!* I finally had hope because I was no longer alone. Others understood the suffering I was experiencing!

Before CPA, no one understood the impact my conditions were having on me; no matter how much they loved me and wanted to, they just couldn't get it. CPA gave me the priceless "identification" piece. Its absence had been a huge part of my isolation and depression and the mounting frustration of having to constantly explain or reassure others about my illnesses. CPA gets me. And I will be eternally grateful.

In this moment, I will celebrate having found Chronic Pain Anonymous.

There are days when I tell myself I should no longer be allowed to have "negative feelings," but I've learned that this is just another way of avoiding acceptance. When fully accepting the positive and negative aspects of myself, I can continue to grow and become my better self.

Working the Steps brought up many different emotions and forced me to lay everything out on the table: the good, the bad, and the ugly. I quickly realized I'd been unhappy with myself for a long time. I had lost my identity. What I thought made me a helpful friend, hands-on parent, and joyful partner, what made me "me," was gone.

I haven't always lived a conventionally healthful lifestyle. For many years, I told myself, "Tomorrow will be the day I change, tomorrow I will not be negative or hard on myself and others, tomorrow I'll work on choosing healthier habits." It was my decision not to be physically active and to avoid engaging in social activities. Then I was robbed of the choice to do so.

Now my whole life revolves around my pain and disability. It's exhausting. The uncertainty of when/if/how/why a flare comes keeps me from knowing when I'll be able to be present physically and/or mentally.

In Step One, I came to see that my unwillingness to fully accept the situation was holding me back. Experiencing true powerlessness allows me to surrender and pray for the willingness to change and become the best version of myself.

In this moment, I will lovingly honor all my feelings, whether they be the good, the bad, or the ugly.

I obsess about my level of suffering: Am I a warrior or am I a wimp? I like to think of myself as a warrior. Many days, I have to push through tasks when it would be easier to rest. Frequently, I feel overwhelmed with trying to be actively involved in the lives of my spouse and children.

But how can I know if I'm exaggerating how badly I feel? How can other folks with the same diagnosis or similar symptoms do tasks/activities that I can't? How can I do some tasks/activities that some other ill people can't? How can I know if my perceived "#7" pain/fatigue level is higher or lower than someone else's #7 pain/fatigue level? What if someone else uses stronger pain medication than I do? How can some folks still hold a job and others can't?

I am beginning to see this type of thinking and comparison as an obsession that doesn't get me anywhere. I need to listen to *my* body and trust what it tells me. If my body dictates that it needs to stop and rest, *I need* to pay attention. Allowing myself to trust my perception of symptom levels and choosing self-care accordingly gives me peace.

Comparing myself to others and obsessing about my perception brings anxiety, guilt, and shame. Getting caught up in that obsession clouds my thinking. It hinders me in making clear choices in moving ahead with the next steps to fully live and enjoy my *own* life.

In this moment, I will listen and take direction from my body, regardless of what others are doing.

My understanding of how to share my experience, strength, and hope dramatically changed for the better a few years ago.

Some of my recovery friends were at my house, chatting about this-and-that after our Step study meeting had ended. One of my friends was a relative newcomer, and she urgently asked us for some feedback about a situation that had come up in her life. She was planning to reunite with someone that she'd had a falling-out with and was not quite sure how to act at the approaching reunion. The woman to my right responded by asking for more information and details about the falling-out, which my friend gave. I felt emotional about my friend's plight, and I tried to use words to support my friend with positive energy and love, but not much else. Last to chime in was the wise and reflective woman sitting to my left. She started off by saying, "I was once in a similar situation. I don't know if this applies to your case, but the way I handled it was by…"

My friend's gentle experience, strength, and hope entered the conversation like sunlight through a window shade. Since then, I have kept in mind that my personal experiences are the most treasured assets I have to share with others. I also remember that this sharing is best kept for when the other party is actively seeking suggestions.

Unsolicited advice is something I find far less of in CPA than in the rest of my world, and I am grateful for that.

In this moment, I will remember my personal experiences are the most treasured assets I have to share with others.

For me, acceptance is seeing the reality of my life and not being at war with the circumstances. I don't get there right away. I need to go through anger, grief, forgiveness, guilt, sadness, and the humility of surrender before I become open to another way of living.

I can't have acceptance until I have awareness. I became aware of what it is I struggle with when I worked the first five Steps.

Accepting does not mean that I like reality all of the time. I don't have to like it. I felt sad and disappointed, and I needed to grieve. But surrendering liberated me from misery, and I could experience serenity even before acceptance.

By sharing my recovery journey with my Sponsor and fellow CPA members and turning to a Higher Power (HP) greater than ourselves, I can come to accept my circumstances in the moment, just as they are. I can then make choices based on self-care and kindness toward myself, as guided by my HP.

I can choose to rest because I see reality—I see that sitting at the computer for two hours is too much, and I accept it. I can make a choice to take care of myself: sitting for shorter periods, using the computer in bed, or not using the computer for a day. I surrender to reality, to my Higher Power's care, and I accept what is.

In this moment, I will creatively adapt my self-care needs.

The principle of anonymity brings about humility in me. I don't have to compare myself to anyone else. Members don't compare pain or symptoms, and no one gets a medal for dealing with the most amount of misery. I'm just part of the fellowship and am appreciated for showing up. In CPA, I am an equal, not better or worse than others.

Anonymity makes CPA a safe place. No one will reveal that I'm a member or anything I've shared in a meeting. This makes it possible for me to be honest about what I'm struggling with and how my program is helping me. Since I'm not worried about being judged, the harsh voice in my head has been able to quiet down, no longer criticizing myself for all that I can't do anymore. I feel safe knowing I will be heard and cared about just for being me.

I lost so much when I became ill, but in CPA, I am enough just as I am. Even on the days when I'm angry at the world and my body, I can speak of my experience, and no one tries to fix me or tell me what I'm feeling is wrong. They listen with kindness. I am returned to sanity simply by being heard and understood.

In CPA, anonymity assures our unity. No one gets judged by external criteria. It doesn't matter what we did for a living, where we live, how our body does or doesn't function. Our unity, focused on our recovery, is all that matters.

In this moment, I will be grateful for CPA's foundational spiritual principle of anonymity.

I find contact with other CPA members to be incredibly enriching, soothing, and inspiring. A phone call, a meeting in person, an online group, or just a text to someone to express whatever I need to express has been critical to my recovery in this program.

There are times I may not feel like going to a meeting or taking time to respond to someone, but I'm almost always rewarded when I do. Sometimes I'm able to help someone else just by being present and available—and that is a gift to me. Often, I say just what *I* needed to hear. Someone else's experience may help me in that moment, or it may become part of my toolbox, to use in the future. Being around others who are growing and learning about living a fulfilling life in spite of chronic pain/illness helps me cope, make decisions, and improve my attitude.

When a "healthy" person gives me advice or input, I'm much less likely to give it credence than the input that comes from my CPA friends, who have lived my challenges and heartaches. They understand the difficulties of travel, the struggles with self-value, and how seriously I have to think to make decisions about things that are simple to most people. (Should I try to bowl on the family outing? Should I just stay home?) They understand the guilt I sometimes feel because once again I committed to do something but then had to back out. The comfort I receive from my CPA friends knows no equal, with the exception of the unconditional love of my Higher Power.

In this moment, I will remind myself of the great gift of fellowship. I will relax into its comfort and inspiration.

The *Three As* have profoundly changed my relationship with my pain and powerlessness.

Awareness was a challenge for many years; I fought through pain and turned a blind eye to my well-being. Obsessed with trying to control my symptoms, I pushed myself to carry out tasks. My body had to reach its absolute limit before I became willing to look at myself. I saw that I was "doing things" as a way to cope with situations I did not want to face. My awareness today lovingly shapes how I now live with pain and illness.

Acceptance is the key to dealing with circumstances that are beyond my control. Surrender and admitting powerlessness form a peaceful trilogy with acceptance. To me, these words mean tranquility and trust. Acceptance has opened up new opportunities for me. I'm now more open to seeking help. I've found support through various organizations and individuals who only appeared after I made myself vulnerable by sharing the true nature of my condition.

Action has become a gift instead of a burden. Because I see and accept that my energy is limited, I budget it more sensibly. Sometimes I'm unable to participate the way I would like. Other times, I do push myself to participate. Regular contact with others in CPA, openness with my loved ones, and practicing the principles in my daily life are actions that support my health and spiritual growth.

In this moment, I will practice loving Awareness *of my capacities and limitations,* Accept *help where appropriate, and take gentle, respectful* Action *where possible.*

There are a couple of areas in which my humility has deepened through my experience in CPA. The first is "status." When I first began attending meetings, I noticed things such as financial status, educational status, social status, etc. The differences between myself and others was something that initially felt significant to me. As time went on, I found that these perceived differences faded. It did not matter what type of work someone did or how much money they made. Nothing that might separate us really matters at all. The "chronic" common bond we share makes everything else unimportant and brings us together for mutual support.

Another area of focus had to do with me comparing my pain/illness to others'. At first, I thought, *Why me? Why did I have to have these problems?* It felt unfair. *Did I do something that caused this? Was I being punished for something?* Constant dwelling on this only caused me more unhappiness and anxiety. Then came the opposite thoughts: *I am so fortunate compared to some people in the world. Others have much worse problems than I have, so why should I need any understanding or help?* Again, I was focusing on differences out of my control.

For me, the solution to all of this is humility. Humility means accepting where God has placed me in life. To humbly accept where I am is relaxing and allows me not to waste energy dwelling on things that are not important.

In this moment, I will consider humility as one of the keys to my serenity.

My daily spiritual practice includes morning and afternoon meditations, attending at least one meeting, and connecting with a fellow CPA member. I am mindful of my thoughts and emotions, and, if needed, I can start my day over several times. If I have an emotion that needs expression, I do my best to acknowledge it, feel it, and let it pass in its time without clinging to it. I am also mindful not to act out when emotions are intense.

This isn't always easy. Maintaining balance takes effort. I need to routinely adjust my thinking and attitude when I find myself holding on to or fighting challenging emotions. I am just beginning to make some real progress. I find simply naming my feelings out loud reduces their power and immediately shifts my attitude toward self-compassion. I've only recently discovered that when it comes to illness and pain, daily mental and spiritual mindfulness seem to ensure I have healthier relationships and more serenity.

Having daily practices in place makes improving my attitude more accessible. One new development for me is the way I am making my gratitude list. I now look for "What's right?" throughout the day. Actively looking for little mercies makes the entire day more pleasant. When I find myself in my old, typically unconscious default mode of "What's wrong?" I pause, take a breath, and start my day once more, on the lookout for blessings.

In this moment, I will remember that maintaining mental, emotional, and physical balance does take effort, but I am rewarded with greater serenity and joy.

July

As I am learning to replace my old thoughts, habits, and behaviors with ones that serve me better, I have found laughter is nourishing for my soul. When I feed my soul with a happy behavior, the pain fades into the background and does not have the tight grip it did a moment before.

I choose laughter every day. No matter how bad I feel. It is good medicine for my soul—which has suffered with my physical pain. Through actively laughing every day—by choosing this action—I can separate how my body feels from my inner self, and I am healing from the disabling effects of chronic pain and illness.

One way I am able to accomplish this is by being present and engaged with all that is around me. Only then am I able to find all the joys in the little things. Meditation, mindfulness techniques and the Steps help me to focus on the present instead of the past or future. CPA has helped me realize I have choices about how I think and what I focus on. My favorite tool in my toolbox for getting back my smile and some ease is laughter.

In this moment, I will choose joy. I will find at least one reason to laugh today, and when I do, I will allow myself the pleasure.

I came from a pretty chaotic childhood, and for the most part, my escape was hard work and a determined self-will. As life progressed, I could not shut off this go-go attitude and practice. It became addictive in its seductive illusion of control. Chronic illness and pain changed all that. Not all at once—it took years for me to hit a bottom of hopelessness. Then, as my CPA recovery started, I began to see my inability to rest, just rest.

If it weren't for my illness and pain, I would not have slowed down. Being present and coming to rest is, in fact, the heart of my recovery. I meditate a lot; that is my full-time work now—to train constantly to be at rest in the world. I also paint…in a slow process, where the breath connects with each stroke, and everything is examined in eternal time. I wouldn't have come to this type of rest in my daily life without sickness. I believe that my training in coming to rest and painting in eternal time may end up being of far greater significance to my loved ones than anything I've done before.

I believe that when our bodies are sick and in need of care, they are asking for rest, and for those of us who live with chronic illness and pain, we must train in being at rest, so we can live, so we can listen. It is training, and it's hard, but the payoff is both rewarding and tremendously unique.

In this moment, I will make time to rest. I will allow myself to be still and know that by just being, I am enough.

When I found out about CPA, I doubted that it was what I was looking for because I was primarily facing illness more than pain. Would these people understand me? Would I feel a sense of unity in CPA—the kind I'd known and relied upon in my other Twelve Step programs?

In phone meetings, I found myself stuck in comparing. Whenever I heard someone talk about driving or working, I thought, *They don't understand me, this isn't for me.* But I always got a nugget of truth I could identify with, so I kept coming back.

In video meetings, I found my connection. I saw others in bed, on disability, not able to work, and sharing about the struggles of trying to take a shower. I saw others in pain, illness, or both who were laughing and courageously facing their struggles. I shed my cloak of comparison and picked up that old tool: looking for common ground.

Today, I feel united with all my CPA friends: those who go to work every day and those who can barely get out of bed. Questioning my body, having emotional pain around accepting my normal for today, wondering how I'll get through the next twenty-four hours—these are the notions that bind me with others.

CPA is my place to lay it all on the line. My family will never truly comprehend the absolute joy of successfully showering, but my CPA family celebrates with me, each and every time! I found the unity and support I was seeking in CPA—because I stuck around and didn't quit before my miracle happened.

In this moment, I will listen in a CPA meeting for similarities, not differences, and keep coming back. I will trust there is something here for me.

Last week, our family went camping. We headed for a campground we'd never been to before and missed a turn, ending up on a dirt road. My husband knew of another campground farther along this road, so we decided to keep going and check it out. We traveled that dirt road for twelve miles, only to find the campground not to our liking; we turned around and bumped back over the road again. By the time we arrived at our original campground, my body had enough of being jostled around.

The next morning, my symptoms were up. The camper bed was not overly comfortable; I didn't feel rested. I felt raw and was emotional over trivial things. I wished I didn't have to deal with anyone. It was also our wedding anniversary.

My husband and kids went for a walk to the nearby lake. After they were gone, I tried to figure out how to salvage the situation. I remembered a CPA tool: *STOP (Surrender, Time-out, Observe, Prioritize)*. I was able to pull the CPA Toolbox brochure up on my phone and think about how I could use this slogan. I determined what would soothe my mind and body. I took pain pills, put on my sunglasses; did some slow breathing; observed the trees, the sound of the wind, and the warmth of the sun; repeated relaxing words; did some writing; and poked the campfire. Later, I was able to walk down to the lake and play a game with our daughter.

Using *STOP* can help bring clarity to out-of-control symptoms and feelings. I become aware of my needs and the next action I need to take.

In this moment, I will listen to my body. I will use the tools of CPA to give my mind, body, and spirit what they need.

My first couple of years in CPA were difficult. I was trying to understand the art of acceptance while at the same time attempting to find a "fix" for my condition. The two ideas were somewhat opposite. I couldn't accept my condition, especially when it flared, so I kept searching for a cure. I remember very difficult days when I called my Sponsor and asked how she coped. "*Just for Today,*" was her reply. "I can do anything just for today." She told me she added it to the end of her sentences, whether they be thoughts of worry or thoughts of achievement, to remind her that everything, regardless of how it is judged, is *Just for Today.*

I tried it. "I fixed myself breakfast, just for today." There was a freedom. I didn't have to worry anymore about all the days I couldn't make myself breakfast! I didn't have to worry about the days I was unable to manage my condition and found myself in the ER. "I am in the ER, just for today." Sometimes a trip to the ER lasted a week, but each day I was there was "just for today."

Over time, this phrase helped me learn to stay in the present moment. It helped my brain slow down and sometimes even cease its incessant desire to look to the future for the worst or to look to the past for all the *I should've dones.*

In this moment, I will remember to take life one day at a time, knowing that my daily condition is fluid and this too shall pass.

In Step Six, we're entirely ready to have God remove all these defects of character. That word *entirely* sometimes causes confusion. My own experience has made it clear that a quick temper, a tendency to distrust, and a stubborn insistence to control are not qualities that easily depart, despite my wish they'd go. I need help.

As I've accepted help and begun the Steps, I've had experiences that have shown me I can change for the better. In Steps One, Two, and Three, I began the process of releasing my debilitating ideas. Humbled by emotional pain, I became willing to let go of the grandiosity and the stubbornness that was keeping me from the road to freedom.

Listening at meetings to those who openly share the traits they've had to abandon in order to ease their self-inflicted suffering, reading stories of hope and recovery that tell of releasing emotional hindrances common to living with chronic conditions, I become more open to change. Steps Four and Five brought into focus my own, specific, often deeply set, maladaptive personality snares that can hold me back.

When I understand how these traits are causing me more pain than I'm willing to accept, I become willing to have them removed. I choose to believe that my Higher Power can lead me on toward this ideal.

The sure experience and proven effectiveness of the program's Step process gives me hope, inviting me to begin the lifelong journey of stepping ever further away from that shadowy twin of mine who has long dogged my footsteps. I listen when I'm told that I'm lovable just as I am. I am *willing*.

In this moment, I will realize I am loveable just as I am.

Step Seven is about humility. In this Step, I am deepening my understanding that I am not in charge, even over my defects of character.

At the end of our Serenity Prayer in CPA, we say, "Thy will, not mine, be done." That is the essence of Step Seven. I don't tell my Higher Power (HP) how to remove my defects, when, or in what order. As I do Step Seven, my mess is out of my hands.

What a relief! My energy is so limited. It's a waste of energy to always be trying to "fix" myself. With this Step, I am turning myself over to my HP and doing the next indicated action. With this shift in my attitude, there is greater ease and peace in my life.

But it isn't that I am sitting around doing nothing—I am actively working the tools of my program. Through these efforts, my HP removes my defects. Some of my actions are: talking to my Sponsor to help me reason things out when problems arise, doing my Step Ten inventory, journaling, and getting help from special workers, such as a therapist.

A specific action I've taken in this Step is to use a "God box." I write down all of my defects and put them in the box; I've also written them down, gone out to the desert, and done a ceremony to give them to my Higher Power. In all these actions, I am practicing humility: asking HP to do for me what I cannot do for myself.

In this moment, I will do the next right thing in my recovery. I will listen for Higher Power's guidance and trust in the process.

I came to CPA as a novice to Twelve Step programs. I had heard about the Twelve Steps before, but it felt a bit too "cultish" to me.

I saw CPA on a social media post and thought it was worth a shot. At that point, I'd been struggling with chronic pain for about six months due to complications arising from an elective procedure. My emotional pain was as bad, if not worse, than the physical pain; I felt I had nothing to lose and hopefully everything to gain.

I gingerly joined a CPA meeting online and was overwhelmed by the sheer friendliness of all those attending, who were clearly struggling themselves with a variety of chronic conditions. I immediately felt at home and made some amazing connections with fellow members. It was a bit strange, but also comforting, that I was "hanging out" with people in different countries, of different ages, and from all walks of life—people I probably would never have encountered in any other situation.

In this moment, I will make an effort to connect with someone, remembering that "fellowship, rather than loneliness and isolation, will be present in our life."

I was fortunate to find a Sponsor very early in CPA and started working the Steps right away, but I was not quite ready. I was balancing many commitments outside CPA; it felt like too much. Also, I felt a bit out of place. It was clear that many members had previous program experience and were quite comfortable talking about concepts like a "Higher Power" and "powerlessness." As much as I tried to incorporate program principles, it felt inauthentic. I found the statements in the literature promising a better life hard to believe. In short, I didn't have much faith in the program.

I took a hiatus from CPA. I was offered the opportunity for a medical procedure that might significantly reduce my symptoms. It became all I could think about; I convinced myself it was my ticket to a pain-free life. I obsessed over it, reading about it online at every opportunity. I had the procedure; it did not go as well as planned. So far, it has not really helped, though I still have hope.

I returned to CPA and my Step work. I have a fresher outlook now. I notice I am applying program principles more easily. I find the Serenity Prayer an excellent tool. My physical pain continues, but my emotional response to it has significantly improved.

Applying the Twelve Steps to dealing with chronic pain is a work in progress for me, but I am learning to turn it over to my Higher Power. It is not easy, but I am clearly heading in the right direction.

In this moment, I will be comfortable moving at my own pace. I will do what feels right for me without judgment.

When faced with anything difficult in my life, habit sometimes causes me to become preoccupied with the worst possible outcome. In CPA, I'm working on a new habit: asking myself, "What's the best thing that could happen? What if it turns out really great?"

For instance: I needed to move. My health conditions cause me to have very specific needs in a living situation. For example, I can't use stairs, use shared laundry facilities, or be too close to certain types of businesses whose practices could compromise my breathing issues. It was easy to imagine having difficulty finding a place I liked and could afford that would meet my many physical and emotional needs.

I asked myself, "What's the best that could happen? What if it turned out really great?" Suppose a friend called from a seaside resort and said: "We're going on a very long trip. Could we pay you to stay at the mansion just so we know someone's there? You wouldn't have to do anything, just remind the swimming pool company to use only natural products while we're gone."

Is that what happened? No. But I did find an affordable place with no stairs, laundry machines inside, in a suitable location. And I didn't have to drive myself crazy to get there!

In this moment, I will place trust in my Higher Power and turn over what is troubling me.

Sometimes, when I'm having trouble "letting go," I imagine what it would be like if I *could* manage everything. What if I had that power? It's scary to think what I'd let loose upon the world. Just driving cross-town, in my mind I've visited capital punishment on those who drove too slowly or cut me off. What if I had that power at hand? What if we all did?

I have often needed to review the many times in my life when things went their own way and a better scenario emerged than what I'd tried so hard to arrange. And, as an adult, I manage as best I can those things that are within my sphere of influence.

I do this best when I invite a process of discernment into my decisions. I don't go it alone. I ask myself, my Higher Power, and trusted friends if what I'm currently doing is moving me toward more doubt, fear, and anger or toward greater faith, hope, and love.

In time, I'm usually shown what to do. Or, as I wait for direction, the innate way of things resolves the issue. When I don't seem to get an answer, and a deadline draws near, I make the best decision I can with the imperfect data I have. I do my best to release the outcome, secure in the knowledge that I've done what could be done at the time.

I've learned to say, "I've done what can be done about this today. God, remind me that this is no longer my job alone, that I was not constructed to manage all things perfectly. Direct my thinking to what you would have me do and be, now." Then I breathe, and repeat, as needed.

In this moment, I will release my expectations regarding specific outcomes.

My Sponsor kept telling me to practice self-care. It made sense, but I didn't have any idea as to what that would mean for me. She suggested I make a list of ways that I can provide myself with comfort.

That list has come in very handy. I've learned that self-care has many different aspects. When I practice it, I don't do so with any expectation of an outcome. It is just a way of loving myself.

When the pain is high, I can provide care to myself. I look at my list and see what appeals to me in that moment. Sometimes it is a hot bath or listening to a novel. I know it is an act of care, not an attempt to fix myself, make the pain go away, or feel better. Often, something positive does occur, but for me that is not the intention of self-care.

In this moment, I will make time for self-care. I will ask my body what it needs and allow myself the time it takes without feelings of shame or judgment.

When I *Act as If*, I am not being inauthentic. I am building my self-esteem.

If I am with an intimate friend or persons in CPA, I am open about what's going on with me and available to listen to them too. I try to talk, as often as possible, about the solution. But the solution grows out of the problem, which sometimes I need to discuss, as do others. *Acting as If* is *not* about denial or blind optimism.

Sometimes I may need to act as if I am patient and kind with others in fellowship, even if I'm not feeling that way. Or I may choose not to give my spouse or close friend one more rundown on the sorry state of the nation of me, opting to spare them feeling too much put-upon. That sort of *Acting as If* feels okay within the larger context of healthy intimacy—probably because it is a choice. I know I can, and do, share more with my intimate friends over time.

Whether it's as mundane as acting as if I want to take a shower when I'd rather not, or as complex as acting, to the best of my ability, as if I am a full-fledged member of CPA—working my program—*Acting as If* builds my self-esteem and keeps me safely on my given path.

In this moment, I will remember: Progress, Not Perfection. *I will* Act as If *until I have made progress I can be proud of.*

The loss of trust in Higher Power (HP) when things are looking grim...is the test spoken of by so many wise spiritual leaders, throughout time.

For me, it is the time to deepen my faith, to surrender more deeply than I have before, to let go of anything I expect and be present with what is in this moment. It's not easy; it truly pushes us beyond where we think we can go.

For me, I have an easier time with anger than trust. I know that HP can handle all of my anger. So I pray for HP to help me find peace, to help me trust, to help me accept the unacceptable. And so far, HP has answered my prayers—usually in unexpected ways. So I know HP is out there, and even if the world makes no sense to me, it does to my Higher Power.

I heard a story a long time ago that gives me strength and perspective. In needlepoint, the front of the fabric can have an intricate, clear, and beautiful image, such as a bouquet of flowers. It all makes sense and is coherent. But if you turn it over and see the back, it's a jumble of threads and knots and colors and makes no sense at all—it's a tangled mess. HP sees the flowers and knows what He is doing. We see the tangles and think nothing makes sense. That story helps me find trust.

In this moment, I will have faith. I will let go and let God, trusting He knows the whole picture.

I am going to talk about something that's rarely discussed aloud, but it matters to the full reality of being the woman I am.

Chronic pain and medical problems have all but robbed me of the desire to engage in "intercourse," which is of course a component of sexuality. What can I say in regard to sexuality? One thing is: "I'm done with that. I'm done with all of that."

For me, intimacy is what matters. I know in my heart and mind that my husband still sees sexuality as important, though we've been married for twenty-eight years. We are intimate—as close as two committed beings can be (this includes spooning). My husband holding me close to himself is such a comfort, such a reassurance that I matter to him, that I am still loved by him. My husband has not "stepped out" because of my infirmity. He has drawn himself even closer to me. I fear he is afraid that I may drop dead at any time because of age and illness. We are choicefully bound—spiritually, mentally, and physically.

I thank God every day for my dear husband, so committed to our vows and to me. How lucky can a girl be to love more deeply than I could have imagined, even at this time in my life? Despite chronic pain and illness, intimacy continues to be a precious gift in my life, with the love of my life.

In this moment, I will make time for intimacy. I will be willing to find new ways that work with how my body is in this moment.

I've always been a very impulsive person—take action and talk later. This skill served me well at times in my life. I wanted things fixed or done, quickly and yesterday. Patience was a foreign concept; I wasn't aware how problematic that could be.

Encountering chronic pain and chronic illness, I realized, after many failed attempts at fixing my situation, that it was only getting bigger the more I tried to fix it. A methodical approach was unknown to me.

In CPA, time and time again, fellow members would say, "Go slowly." I heard it so many times that finally the penny dropped. I could see where my impulsivity had made for poor decision-making. CPA is teaching me to slow down and talk things through before taking any action, or sometimes waiting when no clear path or direction is visible or wise to take at this moment.

I can see how I was trying to get to the finish line—to put myself back to how I used to be—but in the process of being impulsive and rushing, I made many mistakes. I was putting the cart before the horse in my approach. I learned by making these mistakes.

Now, through CPA, working with a Sponsor, attending meetings, and listening, I am cultivating patience and slowing down the pace of my mind and life. I have been able, with the help of my Higher Power and fellow travelers, to make better decisions. (Not all the time—*Progress, Not Perfection*.) I've found that the more I slow down, the more is revealed to me—things I would probably have missed had I been racing ahead.

In this moment, I will remember to be patient with myself and others. I will stop rushing to get things done and just enjoy the process.

Sometimes with chronic pain and illness, it feels like I keep bumping my head into a wall. Being referred to yet another specialist, filling another new prescription, paying another hospital bill, are parts of the game I play. I used to get angry over the rules of this seemingly unfair and endless "chronic pain game."

CPA has shown me that I am not a lone player in this game—the chronic illness playing field can look much the same for many of us. Certainly, the emotional aspects are a commonality. Working the Steps helped me to acknowledge and accept broader views of the ins and outs, the challenges and triumphs. In meetings and fellowship, I learn tactics from other members. My Sponsor helps me recognize how I have grown and encourages me to listen to my Higher Power's coaching. A recent Fourth Step inventory helped me to release some of my resentment with the medical system, my insurance provider, and a former doctor. This cleared a channel for me to be more open-minded and trusting with my medical team.

I think that before CPA, I was a well-informed and pleasant patient. But inside, I felt bitter and helpless because the doctors and treatments hadn't helped much. Now I see that even though my physical health has declined, I am getting better at playing this pain game. I think this is largely due to acceptance, to recognizing and releasing my expectations, and to turning over outcomes. These tools were all learned in CPA, and they are developing with regular practice. I am grateful for my CPA teammates who help me clear my head, and for my Higher Power who guides me on my path.

In this moment, I will realize I don't have to do this alone.

For me, part of the humility of Step Seven is remembering that it's God, not me, who manages the process of removing defects.

I told one of my early Sponsors I wanted to create a spreadsheet or a database and put all my character defects in it so I could track them. He didn't think it was a useful recovery idea, but he finally said, "If you really want to do it, go ahead."

I got off the phone and turned on my computer. Immediately, smoke started coming out of it. I'd never experienced that before. I hurriedly pulled the plug. I opened the computer and looked inside. The power supply had burned up.

I called my Sponsor and told him what had happened. He laughed and said, "Well, it looks like your Higher Power didn't want you to do that project." I said, "My power supply burned up. Now I'm really powerless!"

Since then, I've never tried to manage and track my character defects. Partly because I realize that it's God's job, and partly because I don't want another computer to burn up.

In this moment, I will be proud of my willingness to work the Steps. I have made progress in my recovery, and that deserves to be celebrated.

A list of what I am grateful for helps me become aware of the good that is already present. It helps me to change my perspective—rather than focusing on what I'm lacking and/or have lost, I acknowledge the abundance that exists in my daily life. This list can be done at any time during the day. I identify what I am grateful for in that moment. It can be short—three items for the day, or a longer list, even using each letter of the alphabet to name one thing I am grateful for. I also keep an ongoing list that I add to regularly. I love the tool of a gratitude list. Everyone can find what works best for them. It amazes me how quickly my perspective and mood change by focusing on what I have in life to be grateful for.

In this moment, I will acknowledge what I am grateful for.

I can set boundaries pretty well now because I don't have much choice. I must accept that I'm as ill as I am. For example, I can't be up and about for more than four hours. To do so means resorting to medications that have side effects that are bad for me. Life has set this boundary for me, and I've come to accept it. Acceptance, humility, and Step One are a big part of how I conceptualize boundaries today.

What's still troublesome though is the difficulty I have in dealing with the storm of emotions that follow when I decline an activity, a meeting, or even a phone call with someone who does not (innocently enough) grasp my condition. I suffer over their hurt feelings. My ego suffers, too: not wanting to be tagged a drip/weakling/malingerer/exaggerator/victim/fool...all the things I silently labeled others who seemed to me to be overdoing their problems. Understanding and forgiving my old, ignorant view of such things helps me not blame others when I notice these reactions coming my way.

The sense of loss I can feel troubles me, sometimes acutely. As my siblings and I age, I find it especially hard to say to myself, "Well, if they don't get it, then we probably are not going to know each other very well anymore." There's sadness at what seems an unkind boundary that life is setting upon me.

What can I do? Live as I am. State the truth; don't blame or defend. Don't judge; do ask God for acceptance of possible losses. Make sure my behavior is expressive of love, hope for the best, and give it to God.

In this moment, I will ask my Higher Power for help with something I am having trouble accepting.

Years ago, when I was first ill and didn't have any program tools, if I woke in the morning feeling miserable, I gave up on the entire day. I falsely believed the whole day was shot. I didn't understand: I was feeling awful in the moment, but that was not predictive of how the rest of the day would unfold.

Once I found Twelve Step recovery and heard that I could start my day over at any time, I began to pay attention. I realized that my symptoms waxed and waned throughout the day. I had been tossing out entire days because of how they started. I noticed that some days began with me feeling strong and able to function, and later in the day, I went downhill. There was no predicting from one moment to the next how I would feel at any point in my day.

When I had a bad night, which was frequent, I would decide the day ahead was lost and that I'd have to cancel my plans and not be able to do anything. But once I began to stop writing a story about the future based on the present moment, I found I was able to start my day over. And sometimes my symptoms didn't improve, but my attitude did, which made for a saner day.

I've had small moments of spiritual awakening. Coming to see that at any point I can start my day over was one of them. It's allowed me to be open to more possibilities than I'd believed were possible.

In this moment, I will remember that I can start my day at any time. How I feel will change throughout the day. I will not allow a negative feeling or situation to ruin the whole day.

The first part of Step Two—*Came to believe that a power greater than ourselves*—unfolds differently for each of us. Some have had a Higher Power in our lives for some time, so this is relatively easy. Some have had no experience with a Higher Power, so it will take some thought to work this out.

If we don't believe in any kind of Higher Power, we can open ourselves to become willing or identify a Higher Power that we're comfortable with. Some of us use the fellowship, others use nature. Some of us create our own. Another way to work this Step is to *Act as If*. We act as if we have a Higher Power and go forward, using this as a starting point. As time goes on, our own Higher Power naturally develops.

If we're already comfortable with a Higher Power, we can begin to use that power specifically in the area of chronic pain/chronic illness. We can turn to our Higher Power for guidance as we work through the Steps.

The second half of this Step—believing that our Higher Power *could restore us to sanity*—can bring us real relief. We now have a Power to turn to; we begin to believe that sanity can again be ours.

Sanity can mean peace and acceptance of our circumstances. Things happen in our lives that are beyond our control; our Higher Power can help us accept these things. We are not alone; we can trust, and surrender. It may be easier for some than for others, but it's possible for all of us if we are willing. Working this Step brings us hope for a better life.

In this moment, I will take comfort in my growing faith.

It's been my experience in the program that I do best when I'm sharing with a peer or Sponsor the ways that I'm specifically applying the principles, or to speak freely enough so that it's obvious I am not actually applying them.

I may contact fellow members of CPA to vent—surely, that is human and necessary and part of real fellowship. But I need to report on the *solutions* I'm engaging in and how they are working, and listen to fellow members' experience, strength, and hope.

Here's an example: I am going on about love and compassion, and I think my Sponsor doesn't seem to be following my comments very well because he interrupts to ask, "How is that playing out at home?" I reply, "Oh, at home? Well, you know my wife has been unhappy of late."

He mentions that when his partner is "out of sorts" with him, he consciously treats her with some of that love and compassion we've been discussing. *Ah,* I think, *yes, loving-kindness meditation or some love-thy-neighbor-prayers are in order.*

But he just says, "I'll start by doing the dishes without being asked."

Without being asked? That kind of stuns me. I think to myself: *Wouldn't that be some kind of grave tactical error?* (Especially for someone as truly ill as myself.)

He goes on, "Talking about love is important, but doing the little things that are loving is often what helps."

"No kidding?" I say. I chew on this a bit and then say, "Alright. I get it. I gotta go. I have dishes to do."

In this moment, I will do things differently by taking one small action that is in alignment with my recovery.

Sometimes a simple acronym like *HELP (Hungry, Exhausted, Lonely, Pain)* helps me see when I am overdoing. It is in my nature to overdo. I was taught to be a "human doing," not a human being, so I kept pushing until I could do no more.

When I am *hungry*, I get irritable. When I am *exhausted*, I am irritable. When I'm *lonely* and when my *pain* flares, I can become sad and irritable. *(Why me?)* The truth is, when these things happen, I need *HELP*. I can implement suggestions, try to rest, try to eat something, but if I can't do that, I need to reach out, let someone know, and get *HELP*.

I want to think I can do it all myself, but the reality is that it's okay to reach out for help. All that stuff I learned when I was able-bodied is simply untrue. There are many people who are happy to help me—lots of folks in the CPA fellowship who will listen when I reach out. I am not alone, ever, anymore, thanks to CPA. There are meetings every day that I can pop in on and hear stories of hope.

I learned in CPA too that *Rest Is an Action*. It makes sense to include rest in my daily activities. On days where there just doesn't seem to be time, it makes sense to add time the next day or to practice good sleep care that night.

Paying attention to when I'm hungry, exhausted, lonely, and in pain reminds me to ask for *HELP*. It takes time to unlearn the behaviors I spent a lifetime doing and replace them with the compassion and love my Higher Power promises me.

In this moment, I will ask for HELP *when I need it, and I will accept the* HELP *graciously.*

Am I moving toward or away from serenity? This question is a tool I have found that helps me a lot. In any given situation, I ask myself if what I am thinking or feeling or doing is moving me closer to serenity or farther away from it. This gauge helps me put the Serenity Prayer into action.

> *God, grant me the serenity*
> *to accept the things I cannot change,*
> *the courage to change the things I can,*
> *and the wisdom to know the difference.*
> *Thy will, not mine, be done.*

This question helps me shift my attitude. Last week, I was so angry when it seemed that all of the money, time, and energy I'd spent in physical therapy (PT) had done absolutely nothing to ease my pain—and may have made it worse. I was mad at myself for wasting money and mad at the therapist for possibly making my condition worse. When I posed the question: "Is being angry moving me toward serenity or away from serenity?" I was able to step back and see how I was hurting myself, letting my anger take over. When I asked my Higher Power what would move me toward serenity, the next indicated action was clear. I made an appointment to speak to the therapist in his office, rather than in the large PT room, so I could get my questions answered. I decided to discontinue the treatments for now.

Applying this question and the Serenity Prayer to real situations helps me make sound decisions for my life and well-being.

In this moment, I will put the Serenity Prayer into action. I will trust Higher Power to reveal the next indicated action.

I am a new member to CPA's online meetings. I've been unable to commit to outside meetings as I suffer from multiple chronic pain/illness issues. I'm unable to work outside my home and cannot leave my house in the evening because my level of exhaustion is tremendous. I feel isolated and alone. I am tired of repeating my story to whomever I am canceling plans with. So I'm grateful for our online meetings!

I used to be like the Energizer Bunny! I owned four businesses and ran my home like a business, my three daughters wanted for nothing, and I exercised religiously for at least an hour a day. The day it all came screeching to a halt was the day I was sitting at a stoplight and a truck rear-ended me while going forty miles an hour. It left me with chronic conditions.

I fell into a deep depression. I was forced to rest. I had no idea how to do that. I had been working in some way, shape, or form since I was ten years old. I tried to use pain medications but got hooked. Now I am unable to use them.

What has worked for me has been finally accepting my pain as part of my life. I am always going to have pain. It is me. I am a chronic pain sufferer who needs rest to feel better.

It's been a long process to accept the things I cannot change. I cannot change the pain and illness. But I can lead the best life possible, and that includes scheduled rest. It's just what the doctor ordered.

In this moment, I will slow down and listen to my body.

Step Three is one that's never completed; I do it every day, often many times throughout the day. Early in my recovery, it was not easy or familiar. I didn't see how turning over my will would help me. It wasn't a thought that occurred to me when I was struggling, and I really didn't understand my Higher Power (HP). It took time to develop the habit. First, I had to remember to do it, and then I needed to see a result to believe it was worth doing.

When I first worked this Step, I was *Acting as If*. Over time, I've experienced the power of this Step in my life and witnessed it working in the lives of my fellowship friends. Sometimes I have an attitude shift, feel relief, or get an answer quickly. Other times it takes longer.

For example, I turn over the difficulties I am having with someone in my life and ask for guidance. The next day, I hear about a book that has exactly the information I need to interact with the person in a new way. I leave for a trip in great pain. I turn myself over to my HP, and it becomes possible to manage the travel and truly enjoy my trip.

Long ago, someone in a meeting told me, "Don't quit five minutes before the miracle." Step Three is often where I experience miracles—from small to large. Things happen that I never dreamed possible. So I will continue to make the decision to turn my will and my life over.

In this moment, I will have faith in my Higher Power to do for me what I cannot do for myself.

Most often, *Doing The Next Indicated Thing* refers to the process of narrowing my *entire* life/chronic illness dilemma down to what needs attention right now.

What's indicated is governed by the next obvious need. Sometimes my actual needs—even which one to address next—are not obvious, or they may be choices of consequence. That's when I turn to my morning meditation practice, which suggests I ask my Higher Power for direction.

I find it helpful to ask, "Is this a God thought? If I were my loving parent, would I be suggesting this? If I go forward with this kind of suggestion, is it my experience that it will lead to greater clarity, peace, or connectivity with my fellows?" My intuitive sense of God's will for me reliably increases as it is matched with a willingness to listen to any answer that might come, including the seemingly harder suggestions. I need to listen, reflect, possibly discuss, and then act and let go, chalking up the outcome— whatever it may be—to experience helping me develop this God sense.

Knowing that when I am too spun up with worry to know what to do, I can just pick up the simple tasks of life, one after another, as they present themselves—that is a profound awareness, just as are periods of reflection, informed by my understanding of God, regarding seemingly more consequential acts.

In this moment, I will be still and ask my Higher Power for direction, having faith that my Higher Power cares for me and sees the whole picture.

When I first came to CPA, I had no experience, strength, or hope to share. I was a sponge, soaking up the stories of others who had what I wanted. They laughed, were happy, and thought life was worth living. I was depressed and hated my life. But I found a meeting close to my house, and I went.

Thank goodness for all who had messages of hope to share. They told me a better life was available—that even I, unable to function or envision life as anything other than miserable, had reason to hope. They told me to keep coming back, even when I saw no change and was sure they were wrong. They held hope for me until I could find it myself. They shared about how they were once miserable, how they worked their program, and how it changed their lives. They talked about the tools that made a difference: prayer, a God box, the Steps, the literature, living *One Day At A Time*. I was told God did not make junk, that I was a precious child of God, and all I had to do was the next indicated action.

Slowly, my attitude changed, my life changed, and one day I had my own experience, strength, and hope to share. I'd not thought this possible; my friends in CPA knew better.

Today, I'm grateful for all I have endured because now I get to pass along my own experience, strength, and hope as a lifeline to someone else. When I'm struggling and have lost my way, my Higher Power brings me a fellowship friend who shares their story, and I find my way back to sanity once again.

In this moment, I will Act as If *I have hope until I find it for myself.*

I have suffered chronic pain and illness for almost half of my life. Most of the symptoms are the result of childhood trauma and neglect. While I believe this was not God's "original design" for me (not sure how best to express that), this is what happened, and God can work through it. I still oscillate between acceptance—of what they did/did not do to me and the resulting health problems and disability—and anger. This is part of the process of recognizing my powerlessness over past events and people. I'm very grateful I can let this go and surrender it all to my loving, caring Higher Power I call God.

While I cannot control my symptoms, there is a balance between surrendering inappropriate control and taking steps for ultimate pain and illness management. I take many pills a day, with specific intervals and substrates. This requires a lot of planning and intent focus. I also have a home exercise program, pain management, appointment scheduling (and keeping), dependents' appointments and meds, home maintenance, and yard maintenance to plan. Social life? There's not much time or energy for that.

I have no ultimate control, and yet I am in "control" of how I plan and execute each task, each encounter, every day. Thanks to CPA, I practice inviting God's presence into each moment of planning and doing. I am learning to say, "Thy will be done, not mine," many times during the day. I am getting better and better at attaining this level of serenity.

I cannot control the outcomes, but I can take the Steps.

In this moment, I will turn over my thoughts and actions to the care of my Higher Power. I will have faith that I am doing the next indicated action toward my serenity.

One of my Sponsors told me: "Your character defects are like a big, black, beach umbrella. You built it back in childhood to protect you from the storms and have been holding it over you ever since. But now, the sun is shining." Steps Six and Seven are about folding that umbrella up, putting it away, and standing in the sunlight.

I suppose if I ever needed the old, big, black umbrella, I could pull it back out. Or maybe I can get a better one. That is: I can always go back to the old behaviors. But maybe I can develop some better responses, should any adverse situations come up. Like one of those new umbrellas that folds up into a small space—easy to carry, easy to pull out and use, easy to put away again.

That's the kind I carry now, thanks to the Steps, fellowship, and program of CPA.

In this moment, I will recognize and release my defects of character that no longer serve me or my Higher Power.

August

Who are the newcomers in CPA? Possibly someone who has been in another Twelve Step fellowship who's found CPA, or someone brand new to recovery. Sometimes it's me—who has been around for a while, but a new diagnosis has turned my life upside down and I feel like I'm starting at Step One again.

When I first arrived, I was miserable and could take in very little information. The thing I could receive was the members' kindness, acceptance, and willingness to reach out to me. The laughter and lightheartedness attracted me. I thought surely the other people were not as sick as I was, their lives not as filled with suffering. I soon discovered that some had situations more challenging than mine, yet they were not unhappy like I was. I wanted what they had.

In time, I became familiar with slogans such as *Easy Does It*. I didn't have to do everything all at once, even my CPA program. Eventually, I felt comfortable at meetings and even braved leading a meeting. Someone sat next to me and coached me through it.

When someone new comes to CPA, I remember the discomfort I felt when I first started and how the friendliness of members eased my anxiety. I do my best to let newcomers know I am available, that they are not alone. Today I am so grateful to have found CPA. Now I too laugh, and life is no longer so serious. We enter CPA with heavy hearts. I do my best to be a ray of hope and light for the newcomer.

In this moment, I will remember the feeling of belonging and will extend hope and light to the newcomer.

I first worked Step Four using a format in which one is instructed, when reviewing one's troubles, to ask, "Where was I to blame?" This was my first introduction to looking not at what needed changing in others but at *my part* in my difficulties.

In CPA, I found, once again, that this emphasis on *my part* was the doorway to emotional freedom. Looking at where I was wrong meant not only moral wrongs but inaccuracies in my thinking and expectations. Where had I tried to skip over processing my feelings? What traits do I have or have I developed because of chronic pain and/or illness that are harmful to myself and others?

I became resentful, I nurtured and fed it. I developed a bad case of self-pity that I believed was unavoidable, considering all I had experienced. I experienced depression. I believed I did not have resentment; I was "hurt."

My searching and fearless inventory revealed that while my life was dramatically different from that of my able-bodied fellows, I blamed them for not understanding me. They did not intentionally cause harm to me. I discovered I had an expectation that others owed me complete understanding and help with all matters. Getting it out on paper allowed me to see these fallacies in my thinking and, with God's help, to release them.

When I attend meetings, I listen for the principles I need to be reminded of instead of stewing in bitterness. This is just one concrete example of how, though I'd worked the Steps many times prior to CPA, I needed to work them here.

In this moment, I will adopt a teachable attitude.

236

Medications can be such a difficult topic, and one I tend to avoid specifically addressing at a meeting. The reason I avoid discussing them specifically is because what works for me might not be appropriate or acceptable to another member.

But that doesn't mean the topic doesn't come up at meetings and that I don't choose, from time to time, to share about medications in a general way. One of the most common things I share, especially if a newcomer is at the meeting, is a quick reminder that CPA has no opinion on medications. I might also share my gratitude that there are medications that help me. I have a Sponsor I can speak with directly and specifically about my medications. Together we can address any concerns I may have about how they impact me or my program.

I can listen when others share their experience, strength, and hope regarding medication. I was at a meeting where a member shared a technique she used when deciding whether or not to take medications. I liked this approach and use it now when dealing with my own medication decisions.

I choose not to take medications during a meeting, even a business meeting. It is a simple thing I can do to avoid upsetting or triggering another member, and it helps keep the meetings a safe place for all CPA members.

In this moment, I will choose to have healthy, respectful boundaries when it comes to listening and sharing about medications in CPA.

Because I live with chronic health conditions, bad days are inevitable. It is the nature of the beast to cycle through good and bad periods. For me, the intensity of time and misery varies, and because it's so unpredictable and uncontrollable, I would be a crazy person if I didn't have CPA to help me navigate through the rough waves.

In CPA, I've learned how to function, even on what I consider bad days. As I type, I am in pain and it's unpleasant. The pain rattles my brain, and it is hard to think clearly. Yet because of my program, I've learned that I really can think and function when I feel this uncomfortable. With the help of my Sponsor, friends and my Higher Power, I discovered that I don't have to stop everything just because it is a medium-pain day. I accept this is my reality today and make the necessary adjustments, but I no longer believe the entire day is lost.

I also know I need to pace myself—take a break, get a heating pad out, and choose a relaxing activity or nap. Yes, I can function, but I know there are limits, and I care about myself, so I will respect those limits.

In this moment, I will change my level of activity to suit my current needs, with my Higher Power's help.

As I practice the program, I learn more about my fears. My CPA fear inventories have shown that beneath the surface lie false beliefs: *I will be abandoned. I will not be okay. Love, even love of anything in life, is dangerous because loss and grief are unbearable.* Knowing these root fears helps remind me: they are only old ideas and emotions that I'm attaching to my present circumstances.

I find it helpful to write or say aloud whichever fears of mine are active and then refute them. It's as if I'm both a prosecuting and defense attorney. I counter, *You are not abandoned—unless you abandon yourself, throw yourself on the floor and wail, "I'm lost!"— you'll be okay.* I say, *You are no longer a helpless child today. You have God, a program, fellowship…*

Ultimately, I have to get with God. It's not always that easy. The Twelfth Step helps me prime the pump for that touch of spiritual consolation. I take the opportunity to try to be of genuine help to another who is struggling with their emotional and spiritual journey. When I do, I'm reminded of all the positive things I do believe that are a part of my experience, and so find that I too am consoled. I can trust my Higher Power to direct my thinking, knowing I'm a member of this fellowship. Practicing the connective language of the heart is a most powerful antidote to fear.

In this moment, I will face my fears and rely on my Higher Power to console me.

The slogan *Progress, Not Perfection* reminds me that when I am at my "baseline," I can probably do anything, but I can't do everything. That is progress. I look back at my too-busy life before chronic illness, and I realize that this type of perfection—the expectation that I can do *everything*—doesn't exist. Even if I run around "producing," twenty-four hours a day, there will still be things left to do.

Life has certainly slowed down for me, and at last, thanks to CPA, I've become okay with that. This slogan reminds me that the progress I make on any day is enough. It also reminds me that there are many activities that count as progress. I am currently recovering from a "mainstream" illness, and my doctor's orders are to rest as much as possible. Again, thanks to CPA, I know that resting *is* doing something. Sharing in meetings nurtures me, emotionally and spiritually, so it is also doing something: producing…progress.

Before CPA, I could not grasp the concept of pacing myself. I could not stop hurrying. I was always crashing. I've learned a lot since my first meeting, and pacing is now second nature to me.

I can add this slogan to my toolkit of things that make my life today easier, richer, and more comfortable on many levels.

In this moment, I will seek to practice Progress, Not Perfection.

I came to CPA with decades of success applying other Twelve Step principles, slogans, and literature. I knew the Steps could restore me to sanity around my chronic pain and chronic illness, so I leapt into *Action.* I then heard, *"Rest Is an Action,"* "We do half of what we think we can do," and *"Easy Does It."* Everything I heard was contrary to my Action-driven thinking.

The Set Aside Prayer (in which I *set aside* everything I think I know about the Twelve Steps, myself, and my Higher Power) became my greatest friend. What if I didn't act selfish and self-centered? What if I am enough, I have enough, I know enough, and I do enough? What if my Higher Power (HP) *was* tangibly caring and loving? What if self-acceptance, not self-recrimination, was the key? What if self-care wasn't selfish? What if self-love was HP's will for me? What if…

The Set Aside Prayer helped me adapt a newcomer's mind-set and attitude. By becoming teachable and emptying my cup of knowledge, space was made for my Higher Deeper Voice to speak. Freedom from my distorted thinking allowed for new experiences and ideas to take root. I realized I had been in my obsession to control, by using the Tenth Step, repeatedly. I saw my self-loathing and self-abuse.

Now, I apply *Easy Does It* to my relationship with myself. I relate to myself with compassion, tenderness, and patience. I am so grateful that CPA has given me the wisdom to know there are many things I don't know and the grace to trust my Higher Deeper Self instead of my distorted thinking. Every day is an opportunity for new beginnings.

In this moment, I will set aside what I think I know about myself, others, and especially my Higher Power.

Working Step Eight in CPA, I thought most of the harm I'd done was to myself. That I'd slipped into self-pity or resentment over my predicaments seemed only natural. I came to see that my attitude had caused harm and needed amends. But I did not readily see how it had harmed others.

As the main breadwinner, I worked while ill and, over time, had slipped into a behavior pattern that shouted—sometimes literally—"I am the sick one, you are able-bodied, handle your own problems! I rage about mine when I feel overwhelmed because I'm killing myself to support us." I thought little of pouring out my desperation on my spouse, unaware of how this left her feeling weighed down and alone.

Listening to my Sponsor and many shares in CPA helped me realize that just because I am in pain, I don't have a right to be a pain. It dawned on me that I'd been able to not be a pain to friends and coworkers while completely discounting my actions at home.

I became willing to make amends and had to keep my motives in mind: *Am I really looking for an opportunity to share my newfound hope, or was my past behavior the best I could have done at the time?*

It was the best I could do. But it was harmful and remained my responsibility to make amends as best I could. I needed to be willing to go on record about my part in things, to listen if she had something to say about her feelings. *Are there things I can do to make things right and to listen?*

In this moment, I will remember just because I'm in pain, doesn't mean I get to be a pain to others.

I'm so grateful to the Twelve Traditions for guidance when challenges arise in my meeting(s). A perfect example of this was when we were reading a book that wasn't Conference Approved Literature (CAL) in our weekly meeting. This book provided guidance through the Steps for our fellowship before we had our own Step book, *Recipe for Recovery*. Many of us didn't realize that the writer of the book, who had chronic illness, catered the language to people with a similar experience. Our friends with chronic pain, without an illness diagnosis, began to feel overlooked. Of course we had no intention of doing this when we made the decision to read this book.

The unfortunate problem grew, however. Another meeting heard we were reading this book and decided to follow us and do the same. Now there were two meetings where some of our members felt excluded. Tradition Four guides us to acknowledge that our meeting can make choices that affect more than just our small meeting.

This controversy over the book even sparked a few committee meetings where a proposal was written and then brought to the World Service Conference (WSC). This occurred to protect the message of CPA in every meeting. I'd never want a fellow member to feel left out.

Just like we all need to contribute whatever we can financially, and energetically, for our Seventh Tradition, so that our meeting and CPA as a whole can continue to function, we need to contribute to adhering to *all* the Traditions. All this is done to safeguard the future of CPA, so that all who want to find us have an *us* to find.

In this moment, when in doubt about how to get along with others, I will turn to the Twelve Traditions for guidance.

For many years, I had my diagnosis. I'd tried the medical fixes, accepted what I had to live with, grieved my losses. I knew my limitations, accepted them, and adapted. The period of constancy that ensued, though extremely difficult, had a certainty about it; I could often turn my attention away from my illness.

I came to CPA after new symptoms arose. I feel off-center a lot of the time. I'm cycling through fear of debilitation, mustering energy, bouncing between acceptance and overmanagement of my health, and then surrendering again.

One thing that's helped: when new symptoms arise, I work toward a diagnosis and solution slowly, *One Day At A Time*. Very often, the solution has been finding a way to be in the world with the new symptom, using some adaptation that emerges over time, as the days are lived.

It's important that I do not catastrophize when something new occurs. Either I find a way to get some improvement or I don't, but each time, I discover that somehow my life has been okay—is okay. And isn't that what causes the terror when a new symptom hits? "Oh God, here it is: the thing that's going to make life intolerable." I recall saying to God, in periods of relief, "Thank you, I did not go under. I'm okay now."

In this moment, I will believe that I am okay.

August 11

Before CPA, I'd used another Twelve Step program to help me with chronic illness. It was difficult, mostly "going it alone," but I had some program time under my belt prior to falling ill, and I used everything I could. I was grieving my losses, coming to accept my conditions, and learning to adapt and live authentically.

But finally, I was in so much physical and emotional pain that one day I admitted that my relationship with God, without the support of others, was no longer working. I did not want to believe this because I didn't think anything could be done about it. I asked my Higher Power for *people* with whom I could feel a kinship about lifelong pain and illness, people with whom I could recover my spirit.

I decided to look for one more "how to cope" book, which circuitously led me to CPA. I phoned into a meeting that very evening. I talked late into the night with a member, taking my first Step One, Two, and Three, as well as a small but vital stab at Four and Five. That long day was my first spiritual awakening in CPA; it was profound and unforgettable.

My spirit's greatest awakening is simply this: I am ill, but it's the only life I've got, so I want to try to love it. Most recently, I have begun to suspect that learning to love ever more effectively may be the core task of life. I also realize it is often the sharp pain of things—those little, insistent thorns of light—that spur me on toward the great, good meaning life offers.

In this moment, I will seek to be more loving and feel gratitude for the kinship I feel with people in CPA.

Setting appropriate boundaries is a helpful way for me to manage the stress that accompanies my chronic pain and illness. When I am exhausted and in a lot of pain, my response to a stressful situation is often different than if I am well-rested, fresh from a CPA meeting, or feeling spiritually connected. This is where boundaries come into play. Realistic boundaries limit the stressors I am exposed to, and I can then creatively implement more resources (program tools) to the remaining stressors.

When I was employed full time and trying unsuccessfully to manage my pain and illness, I frequently made phone calls to doctors' offices and insurance providers while commuting to work. There are a few spots near my office where cell phone coverage is lacking. I would get so frustrated by the time constraint I had placed on myself and by my inability to take notes while driving. I've found I have much more effective conversations when I am comfortably lying in my bed, with my computer spreadsheet in front of me to take notes. I don't worry about dropped calls. This is so much less stressful for me!

Many of my boundaries were unhealthy and harmful to my condition. I could not see this until I listened and learned from others in CPA. My condition is unpredictable. Using *One Day at a Time* helps me develop more reasonable boundaries, and as a result, my stress is much lower, which helps my pain levels.

In this moment, I will look for boundaries to implement that may help reduce my stress.

Rest is part of a balanced, healthy lifestyle. Some of us with previous experience in Twelve Step programs often ran to extremes, which may have resulted in, or at least contributed to, our now being in pain/illness.

For many of us, learning to be still can be quite challenging, especially in the beginning, because it goes against our basic nature or our compulsive need to be productive, contributing members. We may need to learn that our worth is not equal to our accomplishments. We are so much more than just what we do.

The essence of who we are exists in just being uniquely ourselves—and in sharing this experience with others. This is our purpose, and no one else is more qualified. Yes, this version of ourselves is much more sedentary than perhaps we once were. But in CPA, we find creative ways of being—right now—rather than always going and doing.

In this moment, I will seek to be uniquely myself.

My Step Nine process has been revealing many things I don't want to see. It feels difficult—both to hold on to my old ways *and* to choose new, unknown ones. The fact that instead of going down old roads of panic and depression, I have come here, to CPA, is a Step Nine amends to myself. Sometimes I read just one paragraph of another person's story, and my recovery is renewed.

For most of my life, I walked side by side with my Higher Power. After I became sick, disabled, and wracked with constant pain, I gave up completely on God. Without that connection, I let out my anger more often and more intensely ("Who cares, anyway?"), but truthfully, I punished myself more harshly than others. It's been painful to discover that the choices I made to protect myself resulted in isolation and created a self-fulfilling prophecy.

My experience, strength, and hope is this: I'm writing from my "bottom." I have no cool philosophy or teaching to impart… but instead of going into loneliness and isolation, this time, I am sharing.

Others' recovery stories really challenge my "desire" to feel and be alone in this drama. *How could anyone understand the suffering I experience, every day?* I can see how one cannot make changes from the same logic and habits that one seeks to change from. That's why we need others and need this fellowship. I forget this, over and over again, and each time, I find my way back into isolation and more of the illness. By prioritizing my recovery, I can find a place, even in these darker moments, to keep working at it and keep moving forward.

In this moment, I will keep moving forward so I do not I slide back into misery.

I Sponsor others as my Sponsors have Sponsored me and as my Higher Power guides me and my Sponsee. Over and over again, I am amazed how the Steps can work without rigid rules or formats. Steps can be poetic, written in journals; there can be ceremonies when we burn a list of those things we no longer require in our lives. We talk, we cry, we identify, we share, we read, we pray, we answer questions.

I have worked with people who have no ability to write, and they too were able to work the Steps—reciting their entire Fifth Step aloud after having come to clear awareness of each item in their Fourth Step. I have come to realize that where there is willingness, there is always a way, if we are open to it.

Then comes the day a Sponsee asks me if they can Sponsor. They may be concerned because someone has asked them, so they ask if they are ready. We turn to Step Twelve in *Recipe for Recovery* and confirm: yes, the time has come. I am there for them still, when questions arise, and we may pray together or talk it through.

Those I journey with through the Steps change, and our relationship changes as well. Someone I barely knew becomes a close friend, a confidant, someone I can turn to at any time. It's a beautiful thing to experience.

For me, the miracles of working this program just keep happening. I truly believe the only way for them to stop would be for me to stop sharing, to stop working with others, one-to-one, heart-to-heart, with Higher Power at the helm.

In this moment, I will trust the Sponsorship process and appreciate its rich rewards.

I used to think about all that was taken from me through chronic illness. But working the Steps in CPA, I'm blessed to be able to look at my life with a healthier perspective. Most everything I've ever cared about, known, or believed in has been changed. It is now lived with and loved on at a level I never knew existed.

I always knew the loving relationship I have with my husband was possible, but I didn't think I would find it for myself in this lifetime. I'm happy to say that at the tender age of fifty-something, I actually found that person—that relationship. I'd been diagnosed with a chronic illness years before, but my husband always saw me as whole. Chronic illness was merely part of "the details," as he saw it. He helped me see this. CPA helps me continue to see that, and to not forget it, in all aspects of my life.

After a few years of marriage, my husband was diagnosed with a chronic illness. He's not a member of CPA but says he benefits from it. We all know that chronic pain and illness are hard on a marriage. With both of us being sick…well, it's kind of a circus at times. Sometimes it feels like we're a house of cards, each leaning on the other, holding one another up…taking turns being the cared-for or the caregiver.

Most of our decisions are made around our medical conditions. We deal with it all using humor, honesty…and sometimes just expressing our frustration. Through it all, we know how blessed we are, and we're grateful most of the time.

In this moment, I will be supportive of the people in my life regardless of their condition.

CPA has helped me learn how to respect myself by setting boundaries, and I am still learning.

I do this by saying no: to negative self-talk, to harsh judgment of myself and others, to not stopping to breathe in the moment, to not pausing to connect to my Source. I say no to autopilot, automatic reactions, and lashing out rather than circling inward to calm appreciation of what there is to let go of and learn in the moment.

I spend time feeling appreciation for the blessings in my life. And sometimes I need to rest and not feel appreciation for anything other than the sensation of the bedsheets against my skin. Healthy boundaries mean I trust myself and my own judgment , believing that I know what I need and will express it. Ideally, this expression comes with kindness and compassion. But if that doesn't immediately happen, I can always choose other words and ideas and try again later.

In CPA, I am becoming better at meeting my own needs. I now have acceptance that I cannot control unforeseen circumstances or anyone else's actions or tone of voice. I have to turn over that old habitual desire to control. Reaching out to my Source, appreciation of nature, and being connected to Love helps. So does sharing in the collective wisdom of my Sponsor and the CPA community.

In this moment, I will practice boundaries. I am modeling for myself and others the importance of treating myself with loving respect.

When I first came to CPA, I was dealing with the utter disappointment and despair of having to stop my art career mid-flight. As I got sicker and sicker, I could spend less and less time in the studio. Eventually, I had to give up my space altogether. I couldn't even pick up a paintbrush, my body rejected the motion. I was heartbroken.

My negative attitude almost kept me from staying in CPA. I heard a share: someone was trying to adapt to their new life and picked up painting to pass the time and express their creativity. I used this story as a way to separate myself from others. *See? They don't understand! They can still paint!* Jealousy took over; I found it hard to relate. I was busy comparing myself right out the door.

I'm so glad I stayed. When I look past the details of what a person is sharing, there are always things I can relate to. The person sharing the joy they found with paint could be an inspiration for me to find the joys that my body will allow. I talked to others and realized I needed to work through my grief about my career. The Steps helped me do just that.

I have begun learning how to make art digitally. I'm an artist whether I am painting, sculpting, or my artwork is only in my head. My illness, my pain, can never take that away from me.

My human "being-ness," instead of "doing-ness" is what I'm learning about in CPA. I am learning how to be the best version of myself. All of me is of value, making art or not. Even in my limitations, I can find joy.

In this moment, I will look for the nuggets of joy that surround me.

I became ill in my early thirties. At that age, I expected to have a strong, capable body. Instead, I found myself living in the body of an eighty-year-old.

Before CPA, I was at war with my body. It did not do what I wanted. It failed me. It was not like other people's bodies. It made me different and unable to keep up with my friends. I was ashamed of it. I didn't want anyone to know how poorly it functioned. I felt guilty—believing it was all my fault. This negative thinking led to feelings of depression and despair. There was no escape from my body and all the ways it was unreliable. I didn't see how I could go on living like this.

Through working the Steps and going to meetings, my attitude changed. I was able to see the ways in which my thinking, not my body, was causing me so much misery. I learned that my illness was not my fault; I am not defective. Though there were many things my body could not do, once I opened to a wider perspective, I saw all that it could do.

I replaced the rage and attacks toward myself with compassion. I learned that being gentle with myself, rather than pushing myself hard, resulted in more sanity, and that everything did get done.

The more I turned myself and my body over to my Higher Power, the more I discovered what was possible. Over the years, I saw that my body kept changing—some things got better, some things got worse, and some new things showed up. So I learned: this too shall pass.

In this moment, I will be grateful to my friends in CPA who showed me how to love my body and love myself.

Compassion is to care about someone's suffering and want to alleviate it. I'm quite good at giving this to other people. In CPA, I've learned that I am also worthy of compassion and that I can give it to myself.

This was a new concept for me. Mostly what I offered myself was a harsh tone of voice, demands for improvement, and belittlement of my efforts. I would accuse myself of being lazy, an idler, not trying hard enough. Never would I consider having compassion for the way I was suffering and how hard it was to be so dependent on others.

Over time, I have learned how to stop and notice that I am having a difficult time and that berating myself will not help me. Recently, I was bedridden and unable to walk without assistance. I didn't blame myself for making this happen, as I have in the past. I treated myself like a dear friend or loved one. *Oh, sweetie, it's so hard to lose your ability to function today. This is not easy, and it's not fun. I am so sorry it's such a hard day.* Then, as part of my shift of attitude, I accepted that I was staying in bed until this passed. There was no need to do anything other than rest. This was self-compassion in action.

Practicing self-compassion is part of the amends I made to myself in Step Nine. It is something that is ongoing, as I live with an unpredictable health condition. I use whatever energy I have available to practice gentleness, tenderness, and warmth toward myself.

In this moment, I will practice self-compassion, and when I falter, I shall recognize it and try again.

You'd think that, as an adult, I "should" be brave, not scared, when I go for a procedure or see a doctor about my health concerns. In CPA, I've learned that all my feelings are legitimate and that there are times I feel like a small, scared child. I don't have to pretend that I feel otherwise.

It takes courage to go see a new doctor or go to a facility for a procedure, to hear a new diagnosis or receive test results. I need to recognize both that I am afraid and that I can find courage when I'm in medical settings.

Turning to other people helps me feel courage. I reach out and ask others for support. This reminds me that it's okay to feel scared; my courage will be there when I need it. And even if it's not, I'll still be okay and get through whatever is scaring me.

Courage means to feel the fear and do it anyway. It's a great concept but hard to do at times. How can I take care of myself so I feel safe enough to "do it anyway"? I can bring a touchstone into a doctor's office or bring a supportive friend. I can use prayer or meditation as I prepare to leave the house. I may have a reward planned for myself afterward as something to look forward to.

I am an adult, and I'm human. My mind and body experience fear; courage does not always come easily. Thanks to CPA, I give myself permission for a full range of feelings and let go of shame when I cry or shake in fear. Being authentically me is courageous.

In this moment, I will face fear, be it small or ginormous, and I shall use the tools given to me by CPA.

For me, anonymity means keeping my mouth shut when I otherwise might not. I once was known as a "talker." We are often taught in recovery programs that we must talk to our Sponsors, speak up at meetings, share in fellowship. I was taught it was necessary to speak my truth to learn to live my truth. But my truth does not include other people's truths; there can be a fine line between gossip and caring loving-kindness.

I come from a family where no one's space was held sacred. In fact, knowing everybody else's business was a competitive contest. I used to hold my own in such conversations. Thanks to recovery, today, I choose not to—not in my home, with my family, or in CPA.

Breaking anonymity in the form of gossip is cruel and destroys relationships. I value the sacred space I'm discovering in CPA. We don't do that here. We show love for each other by respecting each other's trust and building a safe community for all to share.

On a spiritual level, anonymity also brings me closer to God. Learning to restrain my negative thoughts about others is teaching me to refrain from criticizing myself. Only God hears those thoughts, and with the help of a Sponsor and friends, I can learn to speak respectfully and kindly of others in every situation.

There is no need for me to reveal anything spoken in confidence to another. That is only stroking my ego and blocking myself from the joy, happiness, and freedom available in the sacred trust we hold for each other in CPA.

In this moment, I will keep confidences shared with me. In doing so, I respect myself as well as others.

When I am not feeling well, I get grouchy and irritable. My best self is not in charge. When my energy is low, my ability to think is compromised, I'm angry at the world, and it is hard to be a nice person.

Being reminded that "just because I am in pain doesn't mean I have the right to be a pain" has been helpful. I learned the hard way that people, even those who love me, don't want to be bossed around or yelled at when they are doing their best to help me. When I feel decent and am in my right mind, it makes sense to treat others with gratitude and kindness. But when symptoms show up intensely, I can forget what I know.

I've not found one perfect way to deal with my inability to be decent at my lowest moments, but there are some ways that help me regain my sanity. First, I recognize that the beast is coming out and that I may not have the inner strength to be nice. At those times, I do my best to separate myself from others when possible. I call my Sponsor and say all the negative thoughts in my mind so the energy is released. Often, once that happens, I can adjust my attitude.

There are times I make a mess of things, despite all my best efforts, and need to make amends. This means accepting myself as an imperfect being. It calls for compassion for the person I harmed and willingness to repair the pain I have caused. Then I let it go and work at doing it better next time.

In this moment, I will treat others with kindness. If I harm others, I shall make amends.

Today, self-compassion meant sleeping until 3:00 p.m. after a rough night of no sleep. I was awake, every hour on the hour, until I heard the creak of my neighbor's pipes as she began her day. Then I slept, maybe in the comfort of knowing I was not alone. This was clearly what my body needed and a gift I could give it without shame, guilt, or remorse.

I've often had difficulty sleeping: difficulty falling asleep, difficulty staying asleep, and, subsequently, difficulty waking up. In the past, before CPA, I sought the help of four specialists, each with their own unique sleep study protocols and devices. I tried every medication prescribed, some suggested by caring friends, forcing myself to bed at sunset and up at sunrise. None of these brought me relief.

In CPA, I found within myself the kindness to forgive myself for sleeping in or staying up all night while others slept. I have a nighttime ritual that works for me most of the time: With twelve hours in bed, I get nine hours of sleep, with an opportunity for a nap at any time that works. On nights I don't sleep, I often listen to audiobooks. Even if I only sleep a few minutes here and there, I learn something, often on repeat. I forgive myself for not sleeping and embrace the words.

With the self-compassion I've learned in CPA, I let my body tell me what it needs—sometimes that's a cool day sleeping in the comfort of my soft sheets and cozy blankets, with an electric throw blanket wrapped around my most painful parts—to the sounds of others' busy days.

In this moment, I will appreciate the rest and sleep I have been given.

Fear is my primary character defect and drives most all the others. When I was very young, I learned incorrectly that I was the only one I could trust. Any security to be had in this world, I would have to provide. I became an excellent planner, possessed with responsibility and prudence. I also lived in fear, and honestly, I still live with it.

Of course, with that background and the costs of living with chronic pain and illness, I would find finances especially scary. My ongoing version of fear of financial insecurity cycles through me like this: My spouse is showing signs of memory loss; I don't see our nest egg being able to meet their long-term care needs. Who is indifferent to those they love, their fate in life? Yet, would I have chosen to miss love to avoid this dread I have now? No.

What do I do when I'm afraid about money? I remind myself how irrational it is to think I could ever have enough cash to plug every failing dike possible in the future or that doing so in the way I imagine would even be the best solution. And wouldn't I still imagine horrific outcomes for my partner, or for that matter myself, no matter how much money there was?

I can no more be my spouse's Higher Power than I can be my own. I must return again and again to the God of my understanding for a more balanced view of things, a more hopeful one, for the ability to let go, to surrender and know, once more, the emotional and spiritual consolation that always follows.

In this moment, I will turn to my Higher Power when my brain is concocting negativity.

When I first became sick, I would compare my body to an abusive partner. It was unpredictable, caused physical and emotional pain, and ignored my protests to stop hurting me. Looking at my body this way was triggering; it brought up a history I thought I had worked through.

While working Step One, I discovered that although my body is in pain and causing difficult circumstances, it was also doing a lot of things correctly. I was digesting food, getting fuel; my heart was beating and pumping my blood; I was breathing in and out and absorbing oxygen. My body was doing all these things without any direction from me. It was a softer approach—to see my body as working for me rather than as the enemy.

I still wake up not knowing how I will feel and can't predict what my day will look like. My body, my pain, my illness, can shift on a dime—go from feeling okay to feeling wretched. Even with the unpredictable nature of living with chronic conditions, I now feel like my body is on my side. I see it as a strong warrior, withstanding the most difficult of circumstances. I'm proud of my body for being so determined to keep me alive.

One tool I have developed to keep my head in the most helpful space is listening to my body's messages and warning signs. I pause and ask, several times throughout the day, "How am I feeling, and what do I need?" Along with asking Higher Power for guidance, I can get through those really tough days, knowing that this too shall pass.

In this moment, I will pay attention to the messages I am being given about my body.

Over time, my description of God has evolved. When I first arrived at CPA, God was "Good Orderly Direction" and "Great OutDoors."

Several years ago, a surgical procedure went awry, leaving me in pain for the rest of my life. I was devastated. I felt alone, angry, and fearful. About that time, my husband was having procedures to correct his heart issues. While he was in the hospital, I was pacing the floor at home, scared that his heart might not restart. The "what ifs" kept going through my mind. What would I do if he didn't recover and come home? How would I manage on my own?

He is my best friend, full of love for me, and he is my support system. As I was pacing, I received a message—as clear as if someone in the room had spoken to me. The voice said, "Do not be afraid, you will never be alone, I am always with you." I was stunned. Immediately, warmth and love flowed through my body, and I was comforted. I fully trusted those words.

From that moment to now, I know that to be true. I feel God's love and support every day. I take time every day to nurture and deepen our relationship. I'm not much for formal prayer; rather, I talk to God throughout the day, asking for guidance to do the next healthy thing. I ask to align my will with God's will.

In CPA, connecting with others and hearing their stories, my attitudes about pain are changing. I'm becoming a much more accepting, compassionate, understanding, and loving woman. My definition of God is changing. I see God everywhere I look.

In this moment, I will see God as I go about each day, asking for guidance to do the next healthy thing.

My number one act of dishonesty is lying to myself, and subsequently others, about the true nature of my illness, disability, and the chronic pain I live with daily.

I was told by medical providers at a very young age that "children do not have migraines." My first symptom of chronic illness came upon me at age five, after I cracked my skull roughhousing with my friends. I was stitched up, but the concept of traumatic brain injury just wasn't investigated at that time.

I was taught to minimize my symptoms—minimizing is lying. Dishonesty has consequences. I started searching, behind my parents' back, for relief from the pain. I turned to drugs and alcohol, which are not a fit substitute for genuine medical care. At twenty-three, I gave them up so I could face the reality of my condition.

Since then, I have obsessively sought solutions for my medical conditions. By being honest, I found that some medical care is available, and it is my responsibility to seek it out.

Since coming to CPA, I have been able to drop a lot of blame. I blamed myself, my parents, and the world. One day at a time, one hour at a time, I try to check in with myself: *Am I being as honest as I can right now?*

The consequences of hiding my symptoms to please others has had devastating effects on my body, self-esteem, and spirituality. I've even tried to please doctors by diminishing my truth. I no longer do that. Today, I get better medical care, I have a loving Sponsor, and working the Step in CPA is setting me free of the guilt I carried for far too long.

In this moment, I will choose honesty with all those caring for me.

When I came into CPA, I had recently left an abusive relationship that closely mirrored my childhood experiences. I don't like the word "victim." I am one of millions of people who experienced or are now experiencing emotional, physical, and sexual trauma in life. What I wasn't aware of was how those experiences intersected with the illnesses and chronic pain I have lived with since childhood.

In a meeting, I heard the term "medical trauma." Currently, I am experiencing ongoing "medical trauma." The solution, for me, is practicing the CPA program. We all face medical providers who don't understand. They are not malicious. They simply don't know what this feels like. Most haven't been trained to treat the complexities or multiple diagnoses our bodies endure. Oftentimes, treatments are ineffective or have surprising side effects. The providers are just as discouraged as we are.

When I cannot cope, I turn to the CPA friendships I've developed through regular attendance at meetings, working with my Sponsor to apply the Steps, reaching out to others, and doing service when I am able.

I never thought I could look in the mirror and love the person I see, just as I am today. Every day, I wake up in this body. I come into it slowly. I check the date, time, and weather on my phone. I reach out by text to another CPA member as I wait for my foggy brain and stiff jaw to coordinate. I ask my Higher Power for direction.

Not everyone needs to know the specifics of my trauma, but a kind word, a gentle suggestion, and the program of CPA comfort me, carrying me through.

In this moment, I will notice the comfort I receive from applying the CPA program.

Step Two has been called the hope step: whenever I lose hope, I can come back to Step Two. This step was my springboard to first identifying and later trusting my Higher Power. I don't question the unconditional existence of a spiritual force, as my experiences have proven this beyond doubt.

At first, this required a monumental change in my thinking. One thing I had skipped over somehow in early recovery was the word "care" in Step Three. Today I am grateful to feel cared for in spite of chronic pain and illness. I try to relax in the caring arms of my Higher Power. At those times when my spiritual connection fizzles, the care that CPA members express warms my heart and soothes my pain.

Love, connection, and understanding are things greater than me that delight me and my Higher Power. I can't do these things alone. I share myself with another person, and spiritual guidance sparkles in the air. With CPA and my Higher Power, I know there is always a helping hand, there is always a solution, and there is always hope.

In this moment, I will look for hope by connecting to my Higher Power and CPA fellows.

Obsession means being preoccupied with an idea or desire. For decades, I spent a lot of energy obsessing about my pain and what I could do to stop it. I lived in fear, trying every kind of modality imaginable.

Should I see another doctor? Take a different medication? Or possibly have another surgery? Even the smallest movements could trigger symptoms lasting weeks. I responded with anger, sadness, and the idea that something was terribly wrong with my body.

I have a very strong faith in my Higher Power, and I consistently surrendered my life over to God. I prayed for help with my pain, turned it over, and put it in my God box. Then I found Chronic Pain Anonymous, and my life changed.

My attitude and relationship to my pain changed when I started going to meetings, reading the literature, and working the Twelve Steps with my Sponsor. This attitude shift was transformative and profound. I started practicing self-compassion. I learned to honor my body; I accepted pain as normal for my chronic condition. My anxiety and obsession decreased when I was not battling against my chronic pain and chronic illness. In fact, my pain even decreased and became more manageable.

I am finally learning to live peacefully, joyfully, and comfortably with myself and others. I still have many limitations and challenges due to my illness and need a lot of rest, but I am able to do so much now that I never thought possible. Today, I live with serenity and hope.

In this moment, I will find acceptance so that I may live peacefully, joyfully, and comfortably with myself and others.

September

When I first came to CPA, I didn't understand that my life was unmanageable. Before I became ill, I managed many different areas in my life, and I was good at it. I was sure I could manage my illness, fix it, and get back to my "real" life. The concept of being powerless over chronic illness made no sense. Of course I could find solutions and have control over my body.

I didn't recognize that no matter what I did, I was not going to get rid of my illness, and I was not going to return to what I believed was normal. Even though this reality was in my face, I did not see it. I was obsessed with trying to control my body, the people around me, and my healthcare providers. I was sure I'd just not looked under the right rock yet, and I desperately kept digging.

It was an awakening to finally understand that my life was unmanageable. My relationships with family and friends were filled with tension. I had the erroneous belief that if they just didn't ask so much of me, or held a party at the time of day I wanted, or didn't open windows, I could prevent symptoms from showing up. It was exhausting and ineffective.

It wasn't until I came to CPA that I could see this. Once I did, it was a huge relief. Learning from my Sponsor and hearing others share in meetings showed me my life was unmanageable. And not only that—I wasn't expected to manage it. The skills of a lifetime to manage at work and in my busy life were not the skills I needed to live with chronic illness.

In this moment, I will be patient with myself as I let go of my past and unrealistic expectations.

Today, I have a dreaded project I need to tackle that I wish I would have completed a year ago. It requires concentration, and I am only able to work at it in increments. I could be irresponsible and not do it all. I could push myself to work hard at it until the task is completed and I am a total wreck. I don't believe either of these options would bring me serenity. As a person who loves productivity, I resist how long it is taking me to accomplish this task.

How am I addressing this task by applying my CPA program? I have turned this project over to God numerous times. *Step Two.* Today, I will tackle another piece of it. *One moment at a time.* I don't have to finish it today. *Progress, Not Perfection.* I will do what I can do and then rest. *Rest Is an Action.* But I do need to take the next step. *Keep It Simple.* And that is all I need to do, each day— take the next step. *I have enough, I know enough, I do enough, I am enough.*

In this moment, I will turn to CPA slogans to reduce my overwhelming anxiety and dread.

In Step Nine, my first amends were to myself. Before I could approach others, I had to acknowledge the ways I had harmed myself and make amends by relating to myself differently. Then I would be able to speak to others from a healthy mind-set.

Beating myself up had to stop. *"Why did you eat that food when you knew it would make you sick?" "You stupidly went to that party and now you are paying the price!"* The harsh voice in my head had caused me much harm. Part of making amends was to begin to speak to myself as I would to a dear friend who was suffering.

I now use a tone of voice that is gentle, I give myself with an attitude that is loving and kind, and I shower myself with lots of forgiveness. I now forgive myself for choosing to push beyond my limits at times. It was okay to make this choice. I treat myself with compassion when the time comes to pay the energy debt I have incurred. After doing my inventory, I understood that kicking myself when I was down was no longer acceptable.

After making amends to myself, I proceeded to make amends to others. It was with a relaxed attitude of forgiveness of my imperfection—not laden with shame, blame, or guilt. It was a slow effort, guided by my Higher Power (HP), to behave and speak in new ways. Some amends to family and friends were a change of behavior, a "living amends," and required no words or explanations. My HP, my Sponsor, and I knew what I was doing, and that was good enough.

In this moment, I will begin the amends process by forgiving myself and adopting compassionate self-talk.

In the past, I believed that if I wasn't busy and doing something productive, I was being lazy and a slacker. People rested when they went to bed at night; rest was not a daytime activity. My narrow definition of rest didn't allow me to do the exact thing I needed to do to take care of myself.

When I first heard in CPA that I have permission and encouragement to rest during the day, I was surprised and delighted. It took me a while to adjust my thinking and begin to truly accept that it was okay to rest, to go to bed in the middle of the day and do nothing. At first, it felt like I was going to get caught, that I was somehow being "naughty." I had to let go of the judgment of myself that said I was doing something wrong or thinking I should be ashamed of myself.

As I began to include rest in my daily life, I experienced the benefits and realized it was not a *bad* thing but a very good thing. I felt better when I took periodic rests throughout the day. I found I had less pain and more energy when I was active for a short time, then returned to bed or the couch for a while. This pacing—alternating action with inaction—made me less cranky, and much to my surprise, higher functioning!

Today I am a pro at resting. Sometimes this means I take thirty minutes in my lounge chair, watching TV; sometimes it means I take three days in bed, barely moving. I've learned that taking the time to rest is a gift to myself and to those around me.

In this moment, I will remember I am not being "naughty" when I rest.

CPA, and all that is offered, along with the members who understand fully what it's like to live this way, have changed my life. Sharing openly at meetings and with CPA members takes strength and shows faith. Reading and hearing others share what lifted them up and how prayers were answered gets me through the day and gives me great hope for the future. We may have different health issues, but when we share our experiences, we have so much in common.

Living with chronic pain or illness does not mean our lives are void of all happiness. We may struggle physically but can heal mentally, emotionally, and spiritually.

Believing in a Higher Power (HP) greater than myself, one I cannot see, has helped me in this healing, more than I could ever have imagined. When I took that leap of faith and started trusting in my HP, I let go of my control. I began believing in what cannot be seen. When needing help and unable to take physical action, I instead can choose to take *spiritual action* and trust fully in my Higher Power. As time went on, my faith became trust. I saw tangible results of the Great Unseen taking care of me in ways I never dreamed possible.

Previously unescorted, I now have fellows and friends, and my Higher Power, who is only a whisper away. From being alone to belonging, CPA holds my hand as I take life *One Day At A Time*.

In this moment, I will celebrate my CPA participation and consider taking spiritual action to deepen my conscious contact with HP.

To prepare for a procedure I had recently, I began to turn over my anxiety about it at my regular CPA morning meeting. I brought up the procedure in fellowship and asked members to share their experience, strength, and hope about how they had managed their fear and anxiety and different aspects of this procedure. The connection with others who had used CPA tools helped me enormously. I learned that it would be a good idea to rest the day before, to take sunglasses for the bright lights, and take my own earplugs for the very loud machine.

The day of the procedure, I said the Serenity Prayer a number of times and practiced breathing exercises in the waiting room. I messaged my Co-sponsor and asked for her prayers. I was nervous about using my own earplugs and asked the technician if it was okay. He said I didn't need them, so I put them in my locker and went in. I again said the Serenity Prayer a few times as I lay on the table. The noise was awful; the headphones the technician provided were not quieting enough. I got through it without panicking by asking my Higher Power to be there with me. I felt surrounded by loving light.

Afterward, I talked with my CPA fellowship about the experience and was able to let go of any frustration about the noise level that had been so agitating. I made a mental note that next time (and there most likely will be a next time), I will bring and use my own earplugs. I don't need permission to do that, just my Higher Power's guidance.

In this moment, I will recognize all that I am doing to support myself. I do have choices regarding my healthcare needs.

Before CPA, I had spent decades in other Twelve Step fellowships. I utilized a technique learned from Sponsors and program friends, where I sit quietly with my indecision and ask Higher Power (HP) for guidance. I use my emotions to interpret my HP's will. If irritation overwhelms me, that is not HP's will. If I feel calm and have a sense of ease, then I am aligning with my Higher Power's will for me.

In CPA, this hasn't worked for all things. Often, I am faced with choosing between one painful action and another. Neither decision feels all that calm or easy. So I added another step in my process. I pray:

HP, help me welcome these difficult emotions. Help me to stop struggling against things that scare me or things that cause me discomfort. Help me learn to be in harmony with my feelings and honor them as valid.

I understand that life doesn't always leave me feeling great. I can become extremely frustrated when my doctor doesn't have anything else for me to try. I get upset that my meds aren't curbing my pain today. Those feelings are valid, but I don't stay there.

I find I can get through difficult, painful, irritating times by doing these simple things:

1. Acknowledge my emotions and sensations with validation (Step One).
2. Ask HP for comfort and guidance (Step Two).
3. Listen for action to be taken and take that action (even when that's challenging) (Step Three).
4. Repeat, if necessary.

In this moment, I will experiment with prayer and the first three Steps.

The Doctor's Opinion in *Recipe for Recovery* speaks of CPA's role of "listening to suffering individuals with compassion and understanding, offering hope and support." I want to be there with the loving hand of CPA for every member and give back what was so freely given to me, but some days I just can't.

It has taken many hours with my Sponsor and hours of trial and error to learn how to draw self-loving boundaries. In the beginning, I believed I had to pick up every call, respond to every text. If I didn't, I was somehow being selfish, or I was afraid they would pile up. I was overwhelmed. I had forgotten that *I* was among the suffering individuals of CPA.

Today I can give members the space to express what they need to on my electronic devices without any direct response from me. Thanks to CPA, I can reply to a twenty-minute message by texting, "I love you, you're not alone, and I just can't talk now." Or simply send a heart or praying hands emoji. And "as if by magic", all my CPA friends still love me. We have an unspoken agreement not to take things personally. If we don't respond, it is not because we don't want to—it's because it would cause us harm to do so. I constantly remind myself that others have a Higher Power (HP) and I'm not it. I even tell my Sponsees to "call" their HP before they call me, then call and let me know what HP said. When I pause and ask my Higher, Deeper Self if and when I should "pick up," I find unknown resources of cognition and energy when the answer is yes.

In this moment, I will honor my energy and apply my "oxygen mask first."

Regarding the Ninth Step: it can be a good idea to vet my amends with a trusted advisor before proceeding. I've done it in writing or by role-playing. My experience has shown, both as Sponsor and Sponsee, that it is very easy to slip into something other than acknowledging my part in past behaviors, along with a willingness to change.

My Sponsor or trusted friend might help me ask: Am I really trying to get the other person to somehow acknowledge his or her part in things? Am I trying to rekindle an old, inappropriate romance? Am I looking for an opportunity to shine as the new, improved Captain Spirituality? Do I wish to take the fact that the person is willing to have an intimate conversation as a chance to offer some advice or to talk, once again, about my illness and pain, once more trying to get another to understand it fully?

Because the Ninth Step is about my part only, it's certainly not another opportunity to turn things back into "all about me." It's about me in terms of cleaning up that which was *my part*, devoid of any subtle insinuation that the other played a role in how I behaved, nor indulging in windy explanations about my illness, my new spirituality, my new requirement to make amends, and so on.

With care and the help of my Sponsor, I prepare myself properly. Making amends focused solely on my part, I am unburdened and so able to move forward, free to meet the world, once more, squarely.

In this moment, I will commit to reflecting on my words, actions, and choices. I will continue learning and take responsibility where I ought to and aim to keep my side of the street clean.

Finding the best time to do a Tenth Step inventory has been a process for me. By the end of the day, I am often tired and foggy. In addition to not having an accurate memory of the events of the day, I'm also harder on myself when I'm tired, which is not so productive.

I've recently started to take short inventories throughout the day, especially when I've just finished something that usually brings out my character defects. For example, when I have dinner with family members, while I'm on the way home I'll take a quick inventory of the time I spent with them. Taking inventory of shorter spans of time has helped me to not get overwhelmed trying to remember details of the day. It also helps me to spot when I need to surrender something to my Higher Power.

I find it very important to take an inventory when I'm uncomfortable. When feelings of shame, fear, or anger start to crop up, I try to pause and track down what thoughts or behaviors are driving these feelings before I blame them on someone else.

In this moment, I will honor my physical and emotional states and be as creative as I can with my Step Ten inventory process.

As strange as it sounds, it's been easier for me to practice acceptance when I am mostly bedbound. That's when the internal war between my mind, my body, and my chronic illness reaches a peace arrangement, a deal or truce if you will. Acceptance grows and then plateaus when I know what to expect each day.

The war begins again during the weeks where I feel much better. It's like having a little taste of normalcy, and that activates an intense longing for things to be different.

Oscillating between fight mode and acceptance, it can seem as if I am constantly at odds. But on a deeper level, I know they can coexist. I can keep trying to get better while simultaneously accepting my reality.

People in CPA recovery share that some days they have to take it one minute at a time. I can relate to the unpredictability they speak of, since I don't know what condition I will wake up in each morning.

I no longer think of acceptance as a final destination. For me, it is a tool or a practice that I keep circling back to at different stages of my illness and healing. Acceptance is always available to me, right where I am—in this moment.

In this moment, I will practice acceptance as something to do, *like breathing. I can accept being here, right where I am, in this body, as it is right now.*

I found CPA through other groups. I was in recovery, but deep down, I knew there had to be more. One of the support groups I was in started a CPA group, and I went along for the ride.

I have many angels in my life, and they often show up as people in my meetings. One convinced me to get a Sponsor and work the Steps in *Recipe for Recovery*. So I opened my heart and got a Sponsor. I started Step One again. And this time, it was different.

The decision to act, to become a member of CPA, even if I didn't know it at the time, would finally bring me some peace. The fellowship I feel so connected to was something I didn't even know I was missing until I was there. With my fellow CPA members' support, I worked the Steps every day and incorporated them into my life. I have learned to forgive myself and my crumbling body. I have discovered that I have a huge heart, soul, and mind. I have found a place for regeneration and a continuation of that process. I have joy, love, kindness, and mindfulness thanks to being an active member of CPA.

In this moment, I will express my gratitude for CPA by sharing information with others who are interested.

Having boundaries is an important aspect of my self-care, especially as it relates to living with chronic pain and chronic illness.

My boundaries are situational and contextual. Creating them starts with me becoming aware of what I need: understanding what's important to my self-care in a given situation. Then, I express this to others in a way that honors them, remembering this is a two-way street—I need to listen to others and respect their boundaries too.

My boundaries can be emotional, physical, or mental. They're guidelines that keep me safe; they outline the ways I will behave toward others and what is acceptable in how they behave toward me. They can be rigid or flexible. Boundaries allow me to establish what's important to me so that I'm not ignoring my own needs and letting others control me, nor am I being self-centered and insensitive to the needs of others, thereby dominating the situation. This is a balancing act and takes practice. I can have specific boundaries or be more open. I give myself permission to say, "No," at any time.

For me, setting boundaries in a relationship is a collaborative process. They often require my flexibility, self-awareness, and willingness to practice this skill, knowing it is *Progress, Not Perfection*. Identifying my boundaries and having the self-agency to communicate them is empowering. Ultimately, they lead to mutual trust and respect in my relationships, whether with friends, family, or healthcare practitioners.

In this moment, I will honor my boundaries and try to express them clearly and compassionately.

I was going to have a frightening procedure, and I wasn't sure I wanted to go through with it. With the help of CPA, I became empowered to allow myself to stop the procedure at any moment, even when they were about to begin. Giving myself permission to say, "No," to set a boundary in the moment was liberating.

I need to set boundaries with myself and others. It helps to set limits on how much energy I expend daily. This means scheduling periods of time each day to rest, not answer the phone, not work at my desk.

I have set limits with my spouse. For example, I've asked him to respect this boundary: "When you are awake and ready to get out of bed, please try not to wake me up."

I set limits with my friends: "I don't go out at night, so can we get together during the day?"

Sometimes, my boundaries are set in advance; sometimes, in the moment. My flares are unpredictable, and it takes self-awareness to not harm myself further. For example: My daughter phones me, is upset and wants to talk. If it's been a long day and I don't have anything more to give, it's important to give myself permission to say, "No," in a respectful way. I can tell her I am sorry it's been a rough day, I wish I had more to give. I can say: "I can listen for five minutes," or "I can't listen now, but maybe in an hour." I can even say, "I love you and I want to hear about it, but I just don't have it in me to give you the attention and comfort you deserve."

In this moment, I will remember that saying, "No," in a loving way is still being loving.

When I'm feeling poorly, I can get irritable and easily blame another person. I'm learning to express boundaries using "I" statements, not "you" statements.

My husband puts our dirty dishes straight into the dishwasher. I'm often too tired to keep up with them, so I put them in the sink. When I have more energy, I deal with them, which might mean they get loaded tomorrow. This drives him crazy, and I can get nasty in response. "Stop bugging me! If you want the dishes in the dishwasher, *you* do it." But, thanks to CPA, I now say: "I'm tired. Thank you for your patience with me. I will put the dishes in the dishwasher as soon as I am able." And wow, his whole attitude shifts to one of understanding and compassion. When I used "you" statements, he immediately went on the defensive. When I use "I" statements, it becomes clear to him that I'm not shirking my responsibility, just honoring my pain and fatigue. And nine times out of ten, not only does he load the dishes I was supposed to take care of, he asks if there is anything else he can do to help me.

Boundary setting is an ongoing and imperfect process. It has taken me years to understand that I can take responsibility for keeping myself safe and asking for what I need and that others shouldn't have to walk on eggshells around me. *Easy Does It* and *One Day At A Time* are good slogans to keep in mind.

Setting boundaries, in advance and in the moment, is a part of my program that I never get perfectly.

In this moment, I will stick to "I" statements and avoid putting my loved ones on the defensive.

When I found CPA, I had no previous Twelve Step experience. Some of the Twelve Step language, as well as the meeting format, felt strange to me. But I felt welcome and understood. It was refreshing, and I felt hopeful. I heard working the Steps was beneficial, but I couldn't grasp what was impressive about them. For a while, I just attended the meetings and enjoyed the support and fellowship I found there. After a number of months, I began working the Steps with a Sponsor. I learned this is a program of action and to discover the positive impact of the Steps, I would have to practice them.

For me, Step One is about honesty. Admitting powerlessness made me face my denial—I couldn't make my illness go away. Trying harder wasn't working and wishing didn't help either. I blamed myself for somehow causing my illness. To acknowledge my powerlessness, I had to let go of that self-blame.

My life had become unmanageable. I often ignored what my body was telling me and pushed ahead, resulting in an endless cycle of fatigue, pain, and stress. I frequently set unrealistic goals and felt defeated because I couldn't reach them. I wanted to be in control, to keep everyone around me happy, and to get all my work done.

CPA suggests that to find peace, serenity, and joy in our lives, we are going to have to change—to do things differently—and that we can't make this change alone. It took time for me to become willing, but with guidance and support from God, my Sponsor, program friends—and applying the Steps—I did change. For me, working the Steps led to deep insights, personal growth, and maturity.

In this moment, I will be grateful for my Honesty, Open-Mindedness, and Willingness (HOW).

I was explaining Step Two to a Sponsee once, and it hit me: Being restored to sanity/clarity is not a one-time thing. It has to be continually renewed.

The core of my sanity maintenance is made of meetings and fellowship, Steps, and service. If I get away from one or more of these, my insanity can start to creep back in. I begin minutely tracking my symptoms, thinking I'll discover the triggers and eliminate them. I think I've found the magic trigger—then a few days later, I think it's something else. Next, I think I am going to get better, and then I won't need these people anymore, thinking I'm not qualified to be in CPA because my symptoms aren't severe enough. And finally I "know" I'm worse than other people here, nobody understands me, and there is nothing left to live for. For me, this is the definition of distorted thinking and insanity.

Add a touch of grandiosity, resentment, and codependence (all of which I suffer from), and I am truly insane. I know it and so does everyone else! Time again for Step Two!

"Higher Power, restore me to sanity. Give me clarity of thought, word, and action." This is a prayer I return to again and again. *I can't, God can. Let God.* Step One, Step Two, and Step Three. My "123 waltz."

I'm not a great dancer, but I remember that it's *Progress, Not Perfection*.

In this moment, I will ask my Higher Power to restore me to sanity, clarity, and humor.

The slogan *Just for Today* has brought me closer to the ideal of living *One Day At A Time*. I can look at any experience I am having and know I will be okay, *Just for Today*. And it invokes a sense of my Higher Power (HP) every time I say it.

In my first years in CPA, my concept of a Higher Power was that HP got some of the credit for my successes but disappeared when things got difficult. Somehow, saying, "Just for today," reminded me I was not alone; I was getting through this day with my Higher Power, whatever kind of day it might be.

Recently, I was working on a complicated project for CPA. It became too much for my brain to organize. It had been due the day before, but deadlines in CPA are generally flexible. I called the committee chair and acknowledged I was late. I told them I had done what I could, *just for today*. I was done, *just for today*. I hadn't failed. I was simply *done for today*. As a member of CPA, they understood.

By acknowledging my limitation and by trusting things will get done in Higher Power's time, I didn't push too far. I now feel capable of looking at the project again and doing what I can, *just for today*. It is amazing, and things get done this way: little by little, step by step. *Just for Today*.

This slogan (and others like *Easy Does It* and *Keep It Simple*) remind me that all things change, and with my Higher Power, I am capable of addressing whatever comes my way with more grace, serenity, and peace than before. *(Just for Today!)*

In this moment, I will experiment with Just for Today.

When I especially need help, I'm often unable to see, right away, what kind of help I need. Taking quiet time in the morning and reviewing what will happen that day with my Higher Power helps me see where I will benefit from assistance.

I only have an aide two days a week. There are always lots of things that need doing, and I can't always think of them on the spot. So I make "quiet" time to compile a task list. If it does not seem complete, I may visualize the house as I recall it, going room by room, to see what needs to be done.

On the days when there is not an aide, I consider what I can do and cannot do, given the state of my body. I know I may only do half of what I plan, but half is progress. My Higher Power will see to ensuring that the key things get done. If I am stressed and feel frozen, I ease into that feeling for a while to see if it will pass. If it does not, I reach out to a CPA member. I may not necessarily share the specific issue I'm facing; just reaching out relieves stress and reminds me I am not alone, even if I am physically by myself.

In this moment, I will remind myself that, with my Higher Power and the CPA fellowship, I am not alone.

I've discovered that one of the most powerful things I can do is let someone know I love them.

The most influential discovery in my life was that my Higher Power (HP) loves me. When I ask HP throughout the day, *"What would you have me do?"* I hear lots of things. Some are my own thoughts, and then there is the warm thought, *"I love you,"* expressed by my Higher Power.

I have missed the chance to tell so many, person-to-person, that I loved them. Even though they "know" how much I love them, I also tell them I appreciate them and am grateful for them. When another person leaves my life, I hope I'd made sure they knew how much I loved them.

I am practicing. My family and relatives all say, "I love you," at the end of a phone or face-to-face online call. I tell people who might not expect it—doctors and my mail woman (who is always so kindly putting packages on a table outside the door so I do not have to bend to pick them up). When I tell them and express my love, they smile or tear up. I smile too. And just like that, I feel that same warmth and love that my Higher Power extends to me every day.

My life once felt dark; pain and illness changed its course forever. HP's love helps me through. Not just barely, but with moments of joy, adding up and up and up, when I take the time to say, "I love you."

In this moment, I will commit to expressing love to people or creatures every chance I get.

Recovery in CPA is defined as the ability to live peacefully, joyfully, and comfortably with ourselves and others. Joy does not come easily when I am feeling physically miserable. But it helps my spirit when I take a moment to find it. I ask myself, "Where is the good?" And I've discovered that something good can always be found.

I'm not bypassing my suffering or sugarcoating it. Looking for the good broadens my perspective. I see the suffering, but I am not laser-focused on that one thing (the loud ringing in my ear, the pain in my hands). Seeing beyond my pain lifts me out of obsessive attention to my body.

I find that joys come in many flavors and intensities. Experiencing joy brings a smile to my body, along with a moment of relaxation and ease. I was in bed the other day, with the kind of fatigue that doesn't go away by being prone and resting. There was so much that needed doing, and I wasn't going to be able to do any of it. My eyes and head hurt, so I couldn't read or watch TV. I found a podcast someone had told me about, on my cell phone. It was just what I needed. Grateful, I stopped, and reminded myself to see the good. The big AAAHHHH I felt in my body, listening to something that didn't hurt my ears or head, was satisfying, and a distraction from my discomfort.

This habit of finding the good helps me see that every minute of every day is not terrible—something I used to believe. Even on my worst days, there are moments that fill my heart with joy .

In this moment, I will endeavor to find something that fills my heart with joy.

What is my relationship with my body? For many years, the answer would have been, *"What body?"* Before I had chronic health conditions, I had no awareness of sensations and was not connected to my feelings. I was a head, floating around, with no contact to my body.

I did not begin with a kind attitude. I was always at war with my body, trying to force solutions. I was not feeling well, but I'd ignore the messages I was receiving through pain, fatigue, and cognitive lapses. I did not know how to listen to the communication I was receiving from my body.

It was through working the Twelve Steps that I was able to identify how I was treating myself. I felt held and gently guided toward a mindful relationship with my physical self. There were many ways I had abused myself that went on my Step Four inventory, and, in Step Nine, I was able to begin to make amends. This meant that I had compassion toward myself, I treated myself tenderly, and I learned ways to practice self-care. I could rest when my body was tired. Such a novel concept. I could say no to an activity that was putting a strain on my physical resources.

It seems so basic to take good care of oneself. However, this was not something I knew how to do until I learned from my friends in CPA what it looked like in practice.

In this moment, I will open my mind and heart to a more mindful relationship with my body.

I have an autoimmune disorder that manifests in poor sleep. Some days, I awaken exhausted and ill. Other days, I awake refreshed and function very well for about three, sometimes four, hours.

Prior to CPA, I took medications that allowed me to override my dysfunction. The meds did not give me energy I did not have; they sapped my innate reserves and, over time, accelerated my overall decline. In CPA, I saw that I had to accept my condition. I released the medications that were harming me and accepted that I would have much less "energy." The great upside is that I am no longer getting sicker every day by fueling my power drives with what was, for me, toxic fuel. I feel more grounded and in touch with life.

I have discovered that for me, there is a direct correlation to exhaustion and distorted thinking. I've found it especially helpful to practice an ongoing, spot-check inventory of my thinking, and when it's inaccurate, I amend it.

Specifically, and sometimes, I'll say aloud: "No, these things don't just happen to you. Remember, your life is meaningful, still filled with opportunities for love and service and the appreciation of beauty."

Then, I lie down and rest.

In this moment, I will remember that my life is meaningful and still full of opportunities for love and service.

Just Do the Next Indicated Action. When my mind is spinning, trying to solve problems in the future, this slogan comes to mind. I don't have to figure out the rest of my life at this moment.

Whenever I ask myself, "What is the next indicated action?" I find it's something simple and manageable. There are dishes in the sink—I can go wash them. I am feeling poorly—I can lie down. I've fallen into a dark emotional hole—I can pick up the phone and call my Sponsor. When I live life in each moment, guided by this slogan, I don't feel overwhelmed by the thoughts swirling in my head. I am no longer paralyzed by fears and doubts. I can take just one action and move forward.

The other day, I woke up and there was no gas in my tank. Energetically, I was on empty. I was powerless over this situation. There were many things on my to-do list. I was awash in feelings of disappointment, anger, and confusion. I tried to plan the rest of the day; that just made me feel worse. I remembered: all I had to do was the next indicated action. At that moment, it was to get out of bed and go to the bathroom. This, I could manage. That is how I went through the entire day. I moved slowly, I dealt with each moment.

This slogan reminds me that I can only live in this moment, and I am always shown the next right action. Little by little, with each choice, the next one appears. This is how I live now, in serenity and ease.

In this moment, I will do the next indicated action *as slowly as needed.*

I always felt smart, capable, and strong. I had fear, even neurotic fear, but I had plenty of resources to face my fears and take action. When I fell ill, over three decades ago, I responded well. With nothing to lose, I followed my passions and did things I'd have never risked doing when I was well. I could have been a poster boy for how to cope with chronic illness and win! So I thought.

After many years of pushing on, I reached my limits and fell into a major depression. It was profound, and it took a long time to come out of it. Subsequently, whenever too many things come at me with too great a frequency, I feel myself sliding, without much prompting, into another of those terrible bouts.

Knowing I must shepherd my limited energies very carefully has resulted in constant, persistent background fear. I feel weak and afraid of life. My go-to fear-buster of diving *INTO ACTION* is impossible.

What helps? First, I affirm that, to acknowledge this outsized, pernicious fear is not to give in to it. This means, for me, that I acknowledge that it is there, that I have lived with it for many years now, and that it has not taken me out. Then, it quickly becomes obvious that I need to ask my God for the courage needed this day. I am somehow always granted this, when I've asked. I have "come to believe." I also believe that my friends in CPA are direct expressions of God, so I often seek their company, sometimes their counsel, and always their spirit.

In this moment, I will accept that fear is normal, and I will "come to believe" that my fears are not too big for me and my God to handle.

I spilled a supplement on my bedspread because my hands are weak and painful. It's a brutal reminder of the things I can no longer do, and that makes me angry. My mind viciously responds with negative self-talk. I lash out against parts of my body I feel have betrayed me.

CPA has taught me to recognize and address negative emotions. First, I name the feelings: I feel *frustrated* that my hands are weak; I feel physical *pain* using them. I feel *isolated*. I am *sad* that I am unable to do my job and resentful that I'm not healthy. I don't accept help because I am *full of shame*.

Examining these negative emotions, feeling them, and then giving them to God clears the way for positive emotions to come in. Self-compassion is key. I know from my CPA friends that these kinds of things happen all the time! It's normal. I bet healthy people get upset with themselves when they spill something on the bedspread!

It takes effort, but I can take a self-compassion break with supportive and caring self-talk. Sometimes these words come from a friend, a Sponsor, or my God. Eventually, they come from my own lips. *"Dear, you are doing okay. Your hands are tired, but they are still beautiful. You can spill things all over the house, and I will still love you. It's okay to feel weak, it's okay to feel pain. You are not a failure, you are capable, and you are competent. This one event does not define you. It illustrates your common humanity. You can set it aside when you are ready. You are loved just the way you are."*

In this moment, I will face my feelings with creative, compassionate, and caring self-talk.

The first time I read the Twelve Steps hanging on the wall of a CPA meeting, I balked at the word "God" in Step Three. Fortunately for me, the program itself certainly qualified as a "Power greater than," so I tiptoed in, with a tiny bit of willingness, and set my God fears aside. Frankly, I didn't feel too much of anything, just awkward and uncertain.

My perception of a Higher Power has evolved since joining CPA. I've started to notice the word *care* in Step Three. The spiritual richness I gain by asking for and accepting guidance while in *the care of God* has been profound. I have begun to feel that I have a new purpose, and I feel serene (until doubt or fear creep in, since I am only human).

On high-pain days, I try to picture myself being comforted and enveloped by my Higher Power. This new practice has replaced old behaviors of self-deprecation and self-imposed neglect. My caring Higher Power has made these things possible. I am also grateful to be in *the care of* CPA.

Step Three has become the backbone of my CPA recovery. I have made turning over my will (my thoughts) and my life (my actions) a regular practice, and I am blessed to do this together with other CPA members. Often, I find that others are turning over the same thing, or, after hearing another person's share, I recognize something more that I can put into God's care.

In this moment, I will remember one of the ways I can come to believe I am in the care of loving Higher Power is by listening to other members' experiences.

I love Step Eleven because it helps me to keep in touch with God. I like to spend time on this Step in the mornings. It helps me feel grounded and organized, and it's a way to open myself up to God's guidance.

There's a difference between the days when I just plow ahead without thinking and the days when I contemplate and ask for God to be in control. If I do not purposely do this, I easily slip back into my obsession to control and direct. It does not have to take long or be complicated, but I do like to take a few minutes to start the day this way and see how it goes.

I notice that this Step instructs me to pray only for knowledge of God's will for me and for the power to carry it out. I do communicate with God about other things, but I try to always come back to God's will. God knows more than I do. I may think one thing would be good, but maybe there are things that I do not know but that God does. I'll be honest, I don't always want God's will. I want what I want. But experience has shown me that when they differ, I am better off in the long run with God's will instead of my own.

Step Eleven is a Step that adds a lot to my life for a relatively small investment of time, on a regular basis.

In this moment, I will make time to improve my conscious contact with God throughout my day.

I heard someone say that the opposite of fear is faith. This has become a vital tool in my recovery.

There are different kinds of fears. The ones in my mind—when I'm fixating on worst-case scenarios like: *What if my eyes get so bad, I can't see any more? What if my hands get so bad, I can't write or hold things?* I face these with program tools. I call my Sponsor, pray, and get to a meeting.

Then there are the fears that overwhelm my body. These are quite challenging. Attitude shifts don't seem to alter them. I'm unable to think clearly, and there's a clutching in my gut, shortness of breath, shakiness, and instability. This is when faith is all I have to grab on to. It's like a scary roller coaster ride; I just have to sit in my seat until the car comes to a stop.

And this is when my program and recovery get strengthened. That is the upside of fear in my life. Facing everything means I observe my body, my emotions, my thinking—I am a compassionate witness to my suffering. I can experience this fear and keep living my life. I reach out to my Higher Power (HP) constantly and have faith that I'll be given strength and courage. I remind myself that *this too will pass.* Faith that my HP is there is what keeps me sane and able to sit in the roller coaster car until the ride ends.

I am powerless over fears arising, but my HP can handle them. All I have to do is to keep turning it over. I need to keep my HP very close, which deepens my recovery.

In this moment, I will notice my fears and turn them over to God.

I woke up the other day in greater pain than usual. My first thoughts were about what hurt, how much it hurt, and how it was going to impact me. Then I imagined all the things that would be harder. My thoughts were spiraling away.

Suddenly I realized: I hadn't started the day with my usual routine. Normally, when I wake up in the morning, I thank my Higher Power and share some gratitude. I paused, smiled a little bit and said, "Hi," to my Higher Power. I thanked my Higher Power for having this day to live. I remembered that it is part of being human to adapt and overcome problems. These are challenges, not barriers, that I am called to face.

I decided to cancel my planned excursion and use the time as an opportunity for self-care. I declared it a Day of Compassion. As I pampered myself, my obsession with why I was in more pain or whether I was the cause of my pain melted away.

That day, I went to several CPA meetings. It was safe to be my authentic self. I shared this miraculous story of how my day started on a slippery slope and how my Higher Power gave me traction and the ability to stop and choose a different route for my day.

In this moment, I will declare that "today is a Day of Compassion."

October

When it was suggested I attend a recovery program, I thought that meant drug addiction recovery. I immediately felt I was being denied my experience as someone who has suffered with chronic pain for nearly twenty years. My attitude was the polar opposite of acceptance.

I worked hard in my career, and then I had to leave periodically due to my health. By increasing or decreasing my medications, and with discipline and focus, I would sometimes improve enough to return to work. I did this many times. I was constantly fighting for my old life—anything other than being in this state. I thought I was in control. But in fact, my pain had never been completely manageable and controllable by me, my doctors, or anyone else.

My career counselor kept suggesting that I come to CPA. I did. I learned, after a few days, that it wasn't as I'd feared: a call to give up and give in to my illness and pain. Working Step One in CPA, I learned to accept that I do not have total control over my pain; I never did and never will.

My spiritual path has always been about seeking peace, and yet my body has been in chaos. I learn more and more that it is a choice whether my mind is part of this chaos. I am seeing that to choose acceptance is not about buying into a concept; it's about letting go enough to see the truth. Acceptance seems the most courageous and spiritual approach to truly living this life each day.

In this moment, I will ask how I can apply Step One to the circumstances of my chronic pain and illness today.

I am not good at boundaries, but thanks to CPA, I am learning. I am learning to tell people no, and it's not easy. However, as I practice doing it, I am seeing that the world does not come to an end. I am having to adjust my job, and my role in my family (especially around babysitting grandchildren and providing holiday dinners). I worry about what people will think. I want to please everyone, but I am beginning to practice setting boundaries for myself in a way that is loving to all.

I have an illness that is not apparent a lot of the time. Others do not realize the physical struggles and pain I have because they can't necessarily see it. I do fear being judged as lazy or not willing to do my part. When these thoughts come, I remember the saying, "What others think of me is none of my business," and that is enormously helpful. When I set boundaries, I remain thoughtful of others and compassionate with myself.

Sometimes I choose to overdo it, and that is okay, too. It is my decision. If something comes up that I know will cause me extra pain, I can still choose to do it. I don't want to live my life only to prevent extra pain; I want to find a serene balance between doing and not doing. CPA gives me tools to help me set boundaries when it is the right thing for me. I am gifted the freedom and wisdom to not let my fear unnecessarily narrow my living.

In this moment, I will set boundaries that are thoughtful and compassionate to myself and others.

I thought I was committed to faith and that CPA's Step Two would be simple for me. It has proven more difficult than I imagined.

In my chaotic childhood, I was determined to fight for independence. I took great responsibility for my siblings and myself. As an adult, I wanted to be the creator, controller, and the hero of my life story. One tool I used was a heady, academic faith.

I always prided myself on staying calm and strong in the face of crisis in my career and personal life. Then I became sick. Life became confusing and disordered. I couldn't figure out how to be "well," and I couldn't muscle my way through problems without physical repercussions.

Practicing Step Two taught me to stay open to a less intellectualized spiritual path, and I encountered a loving, caring Higher Power. Instead of depending on self-sufficiency, I could find humility in releasing my idea of how life should be. At first, letting go can feel like giving up, but it's actually the first step to making room for a Higher Power's involvement. By remembering to make space for my Higher Power and stay out of the way, I've discovered sanity inside the truest part of myself.

If I pause when I'm activated, I often receive spiritual guidance. In this process, I have learned to cherish myself and find purpose, releasing myself into an ocean of wisdom that is always present in a Power greater than myself.

In this moment, I will let go and give my Higher Power space in my life.

My chronic pain and illness were the root of innumerable fears that existed long before coming to CPA. Near the top of the list: fear of economic insecurity. I clung to my career, long past the point where most people would have let go. Fear was the thing that blocked making a change. I had surgeries, received workplace modifications, and shared some of my tasks with others. These actions kept me functioning for a few years, but I knew it was unsustainable. Fear held me hostage in a job that was very fulfilling but physically beyond my capacity.

It's no coincidence that my last day of work was ten days after my first CPA meeting. Willingness to face this problem was simply not available before. CPA miraculously gave me tools to face the previously unfaceable.

While applying for disability, I faced my insanity and my anger and sorrow over the loss of my vibrant body that used to fly up the office stairs two at a time. I reviewed the entirety of my situation and then turned the outcome over to my Higher Power. I shared my emotions with CPA friends who had traveled this path before me. Over time, recovery seeped in, displacing the former fear.

My Sponsor accompanied me, step by step, throughout this journey. I am so grateful for the insight I got through Step work, as well as the support of many Co-travelers. *Facing Everything and Recovering (FEAR)* helps me live peacefully, joyfully, and comfortably thanks to the care of my Higher Power, and is mirrored in the faces of the fellowship.

In this moment, I will remember that nothing is too frightening to face with the help of my Higher Power and my CPA Co-travelers.

One of the gifts of recovery is the practice of taking the focus off others' faults and putting it on myself, where, with God's help, I can address *my part* in things.

For me, in Step Ten, *Where am I wrong?* has become: *What's inaccurate and unhelpful in my thinking and behavior? What thoughts or emotions or behaviors are distorted, exaggerated, or obsessive? Where is my ego seeking power of some kind? Am I indulging in negative emotions rather than letting them arise and pass? Am I repeating to myself things that make me miserable and that, upon close examination, are distortions caused by fatigue and pain? Where have I strayed into obsessing over things I know are beyond my control this day? What is it I'm unwilling to accept? What do I need to let go of?* And always: *What do I need to do to promote deeper trust and surrender?*

In CPA, amending these ills is a major way I can treat the debilitating effects of chronic pain and illness because most often it is in these ways that I harm myself and then others. Awakening to them is facilitated by the Tenth Step.

When I examine things that are vexing, I look for how my perspective may be contributing to the problem. I amend my attitude where needed and promptly make amends to anyone I may have harmed while I was stuck in the problem rather than moving into the solution. I'm glad for this Step. It allows for the fact that in CPA, I'm engaged in a process of self-appraisal and amendment that is ongoing; it was created for ever-imperfect persons, of which I am one.

In this moment, I will remember Step Ten helps me see my part in that which causes me misery.

I am still pretty new to CPA, having arrived at CPA bewildered, despairing, and despondent.

Prior to CPA, medical appointments filled me with guilt and shame. I felt too sick to bear the physicality of a medical visit and feared encountering another dismissal, another shameful, and visit with no solution. Granted, I tended to waited until I was in crisis before I went to doctors and would then overwhelm them with information and requests for help. It is unreasonable to expect anyone to see the horizon while being hit by a tsunami.

My growth in CPA has given me a new relationship with medical professionals. I now know the serenity that comes from preparing in writing what I need them to know and pausing to pray before appointments. I cannot overemphasize how helpful this has been for both me and my doctors.

With the help of loving guidance from a Higher Power and a Sponsor who walked me through all Twelve Steps, daily meetings, literature, tear- and laughter-filled conversations with members, and following practical suggestions, I am finding a stronger, shameless, blameless voice in *every* area of my life.

In this moment, I will honestly say I am a grateful member of CPA, learning to live differently with chronic pain and illness, and for the first time in years, be excited about the future instead of dreading it.

There's a slogan I heard when I first arrived in recovery: *Don't Quit Five Minutes before the Miracle.* Although I was working the Steps, going to meetings, and reading the literature, it didn't seem like anything was happening. My life was not getting better. My prayers to my Higher Power were in my God box, but they weren't being answered. Everyone kept telling me to "keep coming back" and that the program "worked if you worked it." Well, I was working it—why was I still so miserable?

Impatience and wanting immediate, dramatic results hindered my ability to see the progress I was making. Someone in a meeting reached out to me, and we began to talk on the phone. It helped to have a caring person to share the challenges of living with my chronic condition and who understood and was a good listener. I'd been isolated; now, I was no longer alone.

This was my dramatic miracle, but looking back, I realize how many small ones I missed along the way.

In this moment, I will not quit "five minutes before the miracle."

I love working the Twelve Steps with another person as a shared journey. Although each person's path is unique along the road of recovery, I often find there are some common wonders and obstacles we meet along the way. I enjoy sharing what I've learned as well as guiding someone through their own, unique exploration and discovery. We're not in a hurry; the pace is up to our Higher Powers.

My Sponsor has helped me to trust, and that made it possible for me to learn to trust others. She modeled how to communicate clearly and directly, taking care of her own needs. I was afraid to call when I was struggling, but when I called, she'd let me know she had fifteen minutes or that she could not speak at that time. I learned it was safe to reach out, something I'd not experienced before. And it is this experience, strength, and hope that I in turn get to share with the people I Sponsor. I can be a mirror in which someone else can see their own strengths, successes, and inner wisdom. These are some of my closest relationships because we each share our mind and heart, with honesty, vulnerability, and courage.

In this moment, I will be grateful for the shared joy and growth I receive in Sponsorship.

It's easier for me to *talk* about willingness than to practice it in all my affairs. Until I admit that a life lived on self-sufficiency isn't working, I won't become willing to depend on a Higher Power (which may mean depending on my CPA group).

I was not thrilled about working the Steps. I needed the "gift of desperation" to prod me to do so. I have realized that those who are practicing recovery are sharing about how they work the Steps; they are talking about reliance on a Higher Power.

I qualified for membership because I had the desire to treat the debilitating effects of chronic pain and illness, but the willingness to get busy eluded me. After a period of complacency and duress, I began this business of living as fully as possible—by allowing the healing of the CPA program experience, the Twelve Steps, and the literature into my process.

I needed to leave behind "being around" CPA and become willing to be "a part of" CPA, as much as my body and mind allows. I needed empathy—to be heard and understood. And most of all, I needed my own internalized, *workable* contact with a God of my understanding. For that, I needed the specific, time-proven efficacy of the Twelve Steps.

In this moment, I will choose recovery. It's the attitude of willingness that turns the key.

I've heard it said that Step Ten is the first of the "maintenance Steps." Having worked Steps One through Nine, I have seen beneficial recovery changes in myself, in my relationships, and in how I react to my chronic pain and chronic illness. But I'm human and imperfect. Step Ten acknowledges that I will fall back into old habits and will make mistakes. The good news is none of that is problematic. There is a solution. I can become aware of my thoughts and actions, and when I notice that I've not been in alignment with my recovery, I can take steps to repair that.

The *CPA Step Ten Inventory* shows me ways I may be moving away from my program. One question that stood out for me was, *"Did I project negatively into the future?"* This habit gets me into trouble. My fear stokes my active imagination, and my mind generates stories of horror and doom. Why make myself miserable about something that has not happened and likely will never happen? As I await tests and treatment options, I am reminded to live in this day and not project my fears into the future. I choose instead to return to faith and trust that my Higher Power is in charge and that whatever happens, I will have all that I need to get through the days ahead. I don't want to waste the joys of this moment by living in an imagined scenario about the future. Practicing Step Ten helps me maintain my serenity.

In this moment, I will remember that although my conditions and humanness can knock me down, it is possible to get back up by applying Step Ten.

My good times and bad times can be unpredictable, and I find that disconcerting, to say the least. If I'm having some good days, I may be tempted to put off things I need to get done and do something fun instead. So I do some fun things, and then BAM! I hit an unexpected bad time and lose the time I thought I had to get things done. I don't always have to get everything that is due in the near future done before I can do fun things. But when I don't and bad days come, I can feel like such a loser. Guilt and shame become associated with "having fun."

Sometimes when bad days happen, whether it's because of pain or fatigue, I can begin to sink into depression. If it lasts longer than I expect, I begin to experience fear—to believe it will never get better. After all these years in CPA, sometimes I forget my program! Again, more erroneous guilt and shame.

But at some point, I remember: Oh yes, I have tools I can use. I have literature I can read. I can visit the awesome CPA website. I have people I can text or email or call. I can go to a meeting. Most importantly, I remember my Higher Power is always there, waiting for me to pray to ask for the best possible day under the circumstances. This is one of my favorite things to do on good and bad days.

In this moment, I will remember all that is available as a CPA member to help me get through life with chronic pain and chronic illness. CPA helps me with the bad days.

I have lived through situations when I felt completely disconnected after an unkind word or action from someone. I default to a trauma response in which I feel unsafe and lose trust in my own intuition and sanity. An old belief looms large that I'm in this life alone and can't trust anyone.

For much of my life, I've been hypervigilant in controlling and directing everything and everyone, and I believed that if I did that perfectly, I would be safe. Step One in CPA was easy for me because I had decades of evidence that my best efforts to make myself feel safe had only made my life more unmanageable. I had turned myself into a chameleon in order to survive. It was suggested that the Twelve Steps could restore me to my Higher, Deeper, Authentic Self and give me a sense of refuge from the volatility of others. I asked for the courage to change the things I could and find a Sponsor—one person I could share the "real" me with.

Thanks to my Sponsor and the spiritual awakening promised in Step Twelve, I am finally living "as me"—for the first time in fifty-five years—and the sense of freedom and well-being is indescribable. I love myself exactly as I am at any given moment and can accept life and others peacefully and comfortably. When I'm the object of someone else's ire, I don't get completely derailed because there are people I can trust who will give me support if my feelings are hurt. Thanks to CPA, I now seek the wisdom that traumatic life experiences have to offer me.

In this moment, I will remember that other peoples' unskillful words do not minimize my truth or compromise my emotional safety.

It takes courage to say, "I need help to get to the bathroom." It takes courage to say, "I'm sorry, I can't." It takes courage to just lie in bed. It takes courage to go to yet another medical appointment. It takes courage to cry, let alone laugh. Of my own volition, I didn't have that kind courage. I had to find something greater than my mind to come to believe that it wasn't up to me alone.

CPA and the Twelve Steps guided me toward releasing what society conditioned me to believe—that it was all *Up to Me*—and gave me the courage to ask for help and to set aside all I thought I knew about myself, my abilities, and my life.

Now I see the profound courage present when I say, "Help," or "No," or "I can't," and, most importantly, when I say "Yes!" I will try something new. "Yes, I can be extremely creative and adaptive." "Yes, I will use the Steps." "Yes, I will ask for the courage to change the things I can."

In this moment, I will remember just how courageous I am.

Before I worked Step Four, it loomed over me. I thought it would be a lot of hard work and be unpleasant. I don't know why I had these negative ideas. I think sometimes Step Four gets a bad rap.

One thing I did have right: it was work, and it was not something I could do quickly if I wanted to do it justice. I found it to be a process that I did a little at a time, working slowly, along my chosen method. I just needed to start and then continue taking steps, spending time on it in chunks and thoughtfully working through it.

My Sponsor and I did Steps Four and Five together. I learned I was carrying blame for things that were not my fault. These were things I had not been able to see, but my Sponsor could see past my emotions to the truth of different circumstances. It was a relief to be rid of unwarranted guilt. A greater awareness of who I was grew, and my weaknesses and strengths became more apparent to me. This awareness came into play, working subsequent Steps. Because I had faced and identified my faults, I was better able to notice them when they were active. This in turn made it easier for me to let go and allow my Higher Power to remove them.

Recognizing my strengths was also beneficial and led to greater self-esteem.

I am grateful for a wise and loving Sponsor who guided me through Step Four. It's an important part of working the Steps, and it's right where it belongs in the progression.

In this moment, I will remember that the Twelve Steps are an amazing resource and that Step Four is a great gift.

When I was working my Steps, one of the people I discovered I had harmed was myself. When it came time to make amends, one of the ways I did this was to practice self-compassion. This meant new behaviors and new attitudes for me to learn. This took time; none of it came naturally at first.

When having a hard day, rather than berating myself for something I believed I'd done wrong that made my symptoms worse, I'd find a way to soothe myself. It didn't make the discomforts go away, but it allowed me to be kind and loving to myself. A cup of tea, a call to a friend, putting on music—these were ways I acted on my compassion.

There were times I was stuck in a movie I was creating in my head. My mind was in a future in which I was writing a story of disaster; it never had a happy ending. With kindness, I would let go of the story I believed to be the "truth" and return to the present moment. I would focus on the question, "What do I need right now?" and take steps to care for myself.

Being kind to myself, treating myself the way I would a friend who was in pain, was new for me; it's still something I need to remember to include as a tool of recovery. I used to think being easy on myself would let me off the hook, that I need to push myself hard. I've found that just the opposite is true. Being compassionate and tender toward myself is what gives me strength and courage.

In this moment, I will be compassionate toward the way my mind tends to become negative and obsess on the worst outcomes.

"One Day At A Time—I will ask for help when I need it. I will accept assistance graciously and be thankful. I will appreciate the people in my life who support me."

I will accept assistance graciously and be thankful. I was not good at before I came to CPA. I was frustrated that there was much I could not do myself and generally unhappy with the way others did things. I was a demanding perfectionist toward myself and others. In CPA, this became an area in which I had to make many amends, and still do.

For example, during the years I could no longer manage the family finances and my husband took over these responsibilities, instead of being grateful he was paying our bills—with whatever system worked for him—I criticized him for what he missed, how he did it wrong, how the files weren't kept up to my satisfaction. I was anything but gracious!

Today, there are still moments I will slip into old behaviors. I can be in bed, unable to make something to eat, and my husband will bring me some toast. It won't be the bread I wanted or he puts too much butter on it. I feel that twinge of frustration, and most times I catch myself and simply say, "Thank you," and gratefully eat what is provided. This is an act of humility and gratitude. It increases my sense of well-being and the enjoyment of my relationships.

In this moment, I will accept help. I will find a simple way to graciously express my appreciation.

In CPA, the parts of me that felt neglected and pushed aside for so many years have become the focus of my spiritual work. Before CPA, I disregarded how I felt, physically and emotionally. I did not even consider these to be "parts of my life." My focus and struggle were to keep up and somehow fit into a world where that was becoming increasingly impossible and actually threatening.

Since childhood, I had problems sharing how I felt with others. There was no room for my grieving and all the painful emotions and mental anguish that accompanied my physical problems. I tended to be quite stoic, focusing on others and their needs first as I'd been brought up to do. My own needs were uncharted territory. By taking responsibility for the work I needed to do to allow my spirit to heal and open myself to others, I've learned to share myself fully in the fellowship of CPA.

These days, I easily reach for the phone, send a text or email to another member, or go to a meeting. I call my Sponsor on a regular basis, and this sharing, one with another, is how my healing takes place. Some of the most important people in my life today are members of CPA. We may have vastly different personalities, but we have so much in common that the differences don't matter to me as much as they used to.

In this moment, I will remember that sharing my pain and difficulties may be exactly the thing that helps another member. Every part of who I am has value.

In making a searching and fearless moral inventory, my Sponsor helped me see that Step Four was the dawning of a real relationship with myself. This was when I first started showing pieces of myself to others. I started sharing experiences I wouldn't have previously. I came into CPA with a wall built around myself, so strong that no one could hurt me emotionally or physically.

In CPA, I was gently given space to be in a place of honesty, which is now how I live. It was okay to be vulnerable. I see that I am powerless, and always was, and that I'm going to be okay regardless of outcomes. The loving eyes of my Sponsor and fellow members of the program watched, and I was patiently guided. It all started with willingness.

The time spent on myself seemed to be counterintuitive at first, but then I began to see an old friend: myself. I had lived under the impression that knowledge, success, outward appearances, and living on others' terms were just how life was. Then my goals got crushed by chronic pain and chronic illness. All that was left was surrender.

All of this helped me see that my wall needed to come down. Fear of knowing myself was keeping me from being able to move forward. I had a deep sense that there was more. I am now able to sit with myself as I am. I like who I am, and I feel blessed.

In this moment, I will release my protective walls, trusting that I know enough, I have enough, I do enough, and I am enough just as I am.

I used to think of my body as something separate from who I am—a sort of flesh prison that my mind had to live in. I treated it badly, as if to punish it for the way it was. I wanted no pain, so I wanted no body. I used to hit my head on the wall when it hurt; I used to yell at my body parts, insulting my legs, my back, my head—not understanding that by yelling at my body, I was yelling at myself because my body is not just part of me, it *is* me.

In CPA, I'm learning to be gentle with myself. Myself includes my body. I'm learning to say, *"Hey legs, you're not feeling okay? Okay, we will rest today. Or I will use my cane. Would that help?"* instead of screaming, *"You useless legs, I hate you."* I'm learning to say, *"Poor little back...here is a heating pad,"* when I've done a little too much, instead of thinking, *"Why must my back punish me like this?"*

By accepting that my body (me) is different and has different needs, I can live in harmony and serenity. Existing as a human is having a body; the great human illusion is that I have a mind that is separate from it. I am learning how to live fully today rather than hoping my body will feel better later and planning for a life in a body I don't have.

In this moment, I will accept that my body might be different, but that doesn't mean it's weak, inadequate, or wrong.

My Sponsor shared with me about using code words to communicate with loved ones when she's not okay. If the code word is funny or silly, she suggested, it lightens the moment.

I broached the topic with my children. I've been telling them for years, "Mom doesn't feel very well today." But how can they possibly differentiate between times when I'm a little unwell, or very unwell, when it's physical (I can't go somewhere with them) or more emotional (I need some time alone and can't be available for a little while)? My younger son suggested a red code word: "The fox is in the box." I laugh every time I think of it.

This code word reminds me that it's good to laugh, and I don't have to take my illnesses so seriously. It puts *me* on warning, too—reminding me to try to be considerate.

Just the other night. I was exhausted and in pain. My son did a magic trick and wanted to do many more. I knew I could not watch even one more. I said, "The fox is in the box." He accepted that in a moment. No long argument with him not understanding, me getting frustrated and speaking harshly, both of us feeling badly afterward—which would happen in the past. It's a miracle that I'm learning to laugh about my situation. I find that the more I accept what my situation is and what my needs are, the easier things get.

In this moment, I will feel blessed to have a program where I can learn from others and not take myself too seriously.

In CPA, I was taught that we share our *Experience, Strength, and Hope.* It was pointedly noted that we don't share our unsolicited advice, push our political opinions, dispense marriage or psychological counseling, or play at being any kind of medical or legal professional. As a member of CPA, I'm qualified and free only to share my own experience, strength, and hope as it has evolved out of my active participation in CPA. Even if I were certified and qualified to provide something other, that's not what I do in CPA.

This distinction saves me from a host of pitfalls. It saves me from grandiosity and possibly grave errors. If I'm chatting with a friend who's also a CPA member and share complaints, talk of medications, specific therapies, or whatever else we may know about, as trusted friends, we are, of course, free to do so.

In meetings, I share what drove me to CPA, what has happened as a result of my participation, and what my life is like now—any part of that which is in my experience. When a newcomer, peer, Sponsee, or any member reaches out for help, I share what is offered here: a Twelve Step program of action that really works—in fair weather and in foul.

This slogan helps keep me honest. If I have no program experience with something, I say, "My experience with that is limited…" What I consider when asked for help: *Am I sharing my actual experience, strength, and hope found in my Twelve Step recovery program, or something else? Am I practicing the patient compassion others show me when I reach out, wanting help with the CPA solution?*

In this moment, I will be mindful of how and what I share in CPA.

I have lived with chronic conditions most of my life, and I had long ago accepted the nature and chronicity of my illnesses. What I hadn't done, prior to CPA, was look at the cruelty I continued to use on myself—even using recovery language and fearless moral inventories, service to others, and more. My brand of denial came in the form of: dissociation, diversion, and drivenness.

These can be ways to make things seemingly easier and less painful. When living with chronic pain and illness, even blaming and shaming myself seems easier than the vulnerability of being powerless over things that hurt me.

Working the Steps in CPA, I became aware of this added layer of denial and self-abuse, accepted it, and became able to take the next indicated action. One day at a time, I've arrived at a deeper level of acceptance, surrender, self-compassion, and freedom than I've ever known before.

In this moment, I will be aware of my self-abusive habits and change the things I can.

In CPA, what I'm powerless over is *with* me—my body and the pain and suffering it causes me. I can't separate these things from me. What I can do is recognize my powerlessness: I have an illness that is not curable. This was a hard pill to swallow. I relentlessly sought the right doctor, procedure, pill, miracle supplement—to cure what I had, to relieve my pain.

Today, my powerlessness is evident—I cannot control the pain and suffering. But I can look at myself with compassion. I can rest, eat right, take my medications responsibly, take advice from doctors and other practitioners, and apply what makes sense for me. My power today comes from a loving God who only wants me to live in peace and security.

Step One is a challenging Step to take. I know now I can't do it perfectly or do it one time only. I need to take this Step every day, sometimes every minute, and pray to God to give me strength. My life is getting better because of CPA. I am so grateful for this program and the people who have supported me along the way.

In this moment, I will remember I am powerless over my body and my pain, but I do have power over how I relate to my God.

Working Step Seven in CPA, my Sponsor helped me see that *I* do not have to remove my defects of character myself. I only need to become willing to let go of my defects of character—issues, behaviors, grief—all beliefs that are blocking me from serenity and joy. I only need to be willing to let go and be changed by something greater than myself. And I do this by humbly requesting willingness for something different and new.

As I look back at my story, I can see that my Higher Power (HP) has been helping me the whole time. Humility sets in when I ask my HP what's next and follow the breadcrumbs. I trust my HP to do for me what I cannot do for myself.

My Higher Power cares about me deeply, and that includes my hopes and dreams. When I work Step Seven, I humbly wait for what is next to keep my serenity and access to joy.

In this moment, I will believe that my Higher Power is doing for me what I cannot do for myself.

Before CPA, I suppressed all feelings. I suppressed joy—waiting for "the next shoe to drop." I suppressed anger—terrified by the thought that, once released, it would be all-consuming. I tried to force myself out of sadness. With an unskillful "Pollyanna" routine, I denied the fact that I was in emotional pain. Thanks to CPA, I now know that suppressed feelings only increase stress and anxiety, exacerbating my physical pain and therefore my emotional turmoil as well.

After experiencing the spiritual awakening promised in Step Twelve, I have been living *Peacefully, Joyfully, and Comfortably* regardless of my physical condition. But a new, unexpected health challenge has thrown me for a loop, and I am angry. I am fighting reality. I am done! I am back at Step One. And I am loving myself, even in the midst of my misery.

Thanks to my surrender in CPA, I know that hope exists and that Higher Power (HP) will restore me to clarity, and that for now, I am honoring my struggle and anger by practicing outrageous self-care. Today, distracting myself with below-par TV is self-care. Today, staying in my room with my door closed and phone off is self-care. And I remember that what is self-care today may be self-harm tomorrow.

Today, I can honor all that accompanies my present reality with self-love and compassion. I remember that *This Too Shall Pass* and give myself needed comfort, in whatever inspired form it appears.

In this moment, I will remember my HP is fine with my impatience and my choices. Self-acceptance gives me the ability to love myself exactly as I am.

The CPA tools I have learned to use over the last few years have given me the ability to be proactive in starting my day over, any time I want. Living with chronic illness and pain, I need to be able to use that thought of starting over, throughout the day.

Sometimes (more often than I like) things come at me so fast that I can't comprehend what's happening. I am growing, every day, to help myself see past behaviors and learn that I can use what I notice to benefit myself. I've learned to take breaths and quiet myself. I am listening to my Higher Power. I can take this moment to try to understand, problem-solve, or just process. A moment of gratitude doesn't hurt and brings me into the present.

Being able to check myself as the day goes on is much better than contributing to my illness and pain. I can start my day over at any time; it's up to me to use the tools of CPA.

In this moment, I will open my CPA toolbox and apply what is needed to begin my day again.

One of the first things that made a deep impact on me in CPA was a reading that said something to the effect of: *I have value and my Higher Power loves me, even if I can't get out of bed that day.* I immediately teared up and thought, *No way, they can't actually say that!* I certainly was not raised to think anything like that. But I immediately felt in my soul that it was the truth. That led to my new belief that resting is okay, it is healthy, and it is often the thing I need to do. And my Higher Power (HP) supports me resting by guiding me to it.

I had a real flare-up and ended up resting the whole day. I was angry at my HP for the way I was feeling. I didn't have the energy to attend my son's baseball game. My other son came home from school and wanted to talk. I realized that if I could put my problems aside and listen to my son, validate his concerns and needs, I could truly be of service that day. My resting and subsequent acceptance of my situation provided me with the patience to listen to my son's problems.

I've learned in CPA to stop viewing my pain as punishment from my HP or a sign that I am less-than. I am no more and no less than others. I don't know why I have this pain, but I do know that we each have our own journey. I am a good, loving person. I deserve good things and to take time for myself and have fun.

In this moment, I will be grateful. Many of the lessons I've learned in CPA could only be learned by being still and willing to feel and hold my pain.

Over the years, I've written fear inventories about surgeries, appointments with new doctors, finances, and more. Recently, in my Fourth Step work, something arose that I was afraid to look at—grief. I grieved my formerly healthy body and active lifestyle, the loss of my career, and the ability to be independent. I prayed for willingness and gave it time, but I was making little progress with my Step work, so I asked my Sponsor if she had any suggestions. Her suggestion: a fear inventory! So I wrote my answers to a series of questions: 1) What am I afraid of? 2) If that came true, what am I afraid of then? 3) Repeat question two until there is no more fear.

Doing this simple exercise revealed why I was afraid to look at my grief: I might find I am still in grief…which might cause despair and depression…which might cause me to not be able to function…which might cause me to give up. Wow. I had been afraid of the menacing tip of a "grief iceberg" and guessing what dreadfulness was hidden beneath the surface. It was too scary for me to face, and I balked. Doing my inventory like this let me see my deeper fears clearly. And, as is often the case, I saw that they were not entirely based in reality.

There are many unknowns when living with chronic illness and pain, and I am grateful to have this powerful fear inventory tool to break through my fears and restore me to sanity. It can be an opportunity to ask my Higher Power to remove my fear and direct my thinking toward what God would have me be.

In this moment, I will humbly request the courage to inventory my fears.

It's not always simple to find Sponsorship, but it can be done. And for me, it is necessary.

Why? Because, after all, CPA is a Twelve Step program designed to produce a spiritual solution. Most spiritual traditions advocate fellowship. I can't effectively work the Steps in isolation. It is one thing to speak in ethereal terms of matters spiritual but another to try to live out a spiritual life without discussing the specific nuts and bolts that make up the *practice* of that spirituality. This "road less traveled" is such because it is difficult and takes ongoing presence of mind, willingness, and courage on my part. I need others on this path.

I get and give this fortitude as a peer Sponsor or regular Sponsor. I share at meetings that regular moments of being Sponsored and Sponsoring are necessary, and I think of my official Sponsor as special, as the one to whom I tell all, to whom I've written a kind of blank check, certifying that he may speak freely to me too without hesitation, when that's what I really need.

It's been said, "You have to give it away to keep it," and written with certainty that, "The spiritual life is not a theory. We have to live it." It's in Sponsorship that I've found the sure-fire way to experience the warm feeling I get when I know I have truly helped another. I worked in a helping profession and know that I helped people there, but in Sponsorship I've been *certain* of it, and there is no finer feeling.

In this moment, I will be grateful for all my fellows who travel the CPA road to recovery.

I am grateful. The weather is cool, I have two beautiful puppies, and my home is shaping into a cozy nest where my body can relax and soothe itself through its hardship. In this space, I feel held and warm through this uncomfortable moment.

My thoughts are racing. I'm in pain. I can't breathe. It's been six years with no solution. And yet, amid this suffering, I can stay home, I can take a break. Thanks to CPA, I'm learning to communicate my needs with the world, express my difficulties, and ask for help in effective ways.

Amid the chaos of my illness, there's peace and quiet around me. I have found sanctuary. Supportive people and friends remind me to breathe or urge me forward when I don't think I can move— who empathize rather than fix.

I realize my mind can get as sick as my body, but I also know there's more to my life than illness. There's a place of stillness. There's a place where there is space around the pain, and in that space—that "loose-garment" embrace—is my Higher Power (HP). And with my HP is my quiet, the invitation to experience pain and accept it as what it is—an uncomfortable experience.

In this moment, I will relax and feel my HP's gift of serenity surrounding me in the stillness.

My holidays are different from they were before I became ill and chronic pain became a part of my life. One of the big keys to enjoying this time of year has been practicing acceptance, specifically the *Three As: Awareness, Acceptance, Action*. I am *aware* that my capabilities are reduced from what my family and I were accustomed to. I *accept* that, and I take the appropriate *action*. I accept that the holidays are not what they used to be, but they can still be joyful. Acceptance was not easy for me at first, but the more I practice it, the more it appears in and enhances my life.

I'm very fortunate that my husband is willing to do the lion's share of the work for holiday celebrations. I know not everyone has that help. There's still a bit of a problem with this, though. I have to let go of how I think everything should look and be willing to accept something different from what I would have done. That can be a struggle for me. When this problem pops up, I remember my program and apply the things I have learned in CPA. I don't always remember to do this right away, so I go to a meeting, read online posts of the fellowship or literature, and am reminded that I have tools to help me.

In this moment, I will be grateful for all the CPA tools that are a source of practical help in my life. The holidays are definitely a time when I see and experience the value of applying spiritual principles.

November

I love that in CPA, a Higher Power gets to be *my* Higher Power (HP). No one gets to tell me what it is or what I have to believe in. And I like that my relationship with this Power can develop over time. I don't have to know exactly what it is right now in order to work the Twelve Steps or to be a member of CPA.

Currently, this is my concept of HP: I think each of us has our own Higher Power. And, I believe there is an Ultimate Higher Power, greater than all of us, which I call UHP. I call *my* HP "Higher Power of Love" and "Spirit of Kindness and Compassion." My Higher Power is available to me to handle whatever the Ultimate Higher Power brings into my life. I may not know *exactly* what my HP is, but I am discovering what it wants for me.

My Higher Power:

- wants me to feel safe
- wants me to feel loved
- wants me to love myself
- wants me to accept myself exactly as I am
- wants me to live with ease
- wants to know me
- wants to be here for me
- wants me to believe that there is nothing wrong with me and there has never been anything wrong with me
- wants me to feel proud of myself
- wants me to be kind and gentle with myself and others

My HP wishes that I had all of these things when I was a kid growing up and felt so scared and alone. My HP wants all of this for me, and so much more.

In this moment, I will accept what HP means to me.

The actions of the first three Steps—*admitted, came to believe,* and *made a decision*—make me think of that wonderful brief description: *I can't, God can, I will let Him.* That *"I will let Him"* sounds pretty simple, and I think it might be, but it can surely also be daunting…to turn my will and my life over to something other than my own control? Whoa there.

I've found it can be challenging to let go of control and be at peace with trusting my Higher Power, and it can be easy. The easy times are when things look hopeless, when running my life has ended up causing more pain and maybe even a big mess. That's when I'm ready to wash my hands of it all and give my Higher Power a chance. A lot of the time, it's not easy because I want to be in control to be sure things turn out the way I want them to. Experience has shown me, however, that me being in control often does not end up with me having the result I want.

A tool that's helped me is the idea that I can try turning my will and life over, and if I don't like it, I can take it back. Often, I find I inadvertently have taken it back. In reality, I turn it over and take it back, often. This decision is growing and evolving as I continue to work the program and the Steps.

Yes, I have worked Step Three, but that does not mean it was perfect and will never change. I remember that it is *Progress, Not Perfection,* and I will keep doing my part.

In this moment, I will let go of control and turn to Higher Power.

Step Six is a gentle Step. I identified my defects of character in Step Four and shared them with my Sponsor in Step Five. Now, all I have to do is become willing to have them removed. I put the first three Steps into action: *"I can't, You can, I will let You."*

Step Six liberates me from my insanity of thinking that if I just work harder or smarter, I can change the aspects of my personality that create problems. It's no longer in my hands. In Step Seven, I will be giving my defects to my Higher Power (HP). But in Step Six, I'm merely getting ready to ask. My CPA program of recovery has built in baby steps because all I have to do in Step Six is get ready.

What I needed was a physical action for it to be transformative. I got ready by writing down all the things I was going to give up for removal. These were old habits; I was I was ready to release them. They are like one of the sweatshirts I've had since college. It's filled with holes, threadbare, and doesn't really keep me warm, but it's familiar and comfortable, and I wear it anyway. The day comes when I decide it is time to let it go. It does not serve me. I need to get psychologically ready to let go of my old friend, filled with many memories.

I do the same in Step Six. I get ready to let go of old behaviors that are not serving me and may be harmful. Step Six prepares me to let go and ask for my HP's help.

In this moment, I will ask for HP's help in letting go of all that does not serve me.

I've been ill for decades. For many years, all my days were "bad days." I was often overwhelmed, and that intensified the suffering.

What I find helpful is to separate, when I can, my physical pain from my emotional and spiritual maladies.

On days I acknowledge as extra tough, I vow to use the tools of the program so that, at day's end, I can say, "Well, it was a good day: I did not succumb to hopelessness, and I know from experience how suffering rightly accepted and responded to today brings me closer to my God and has moved me forward in my spiritual and emotional growth—even though it may not have felt that way this day."

CPA asserts that my emotional and spiritual issues are treatable. I decide to trust the process and believe it, or I quibble and balk and feel my spirit diminish. The more I can separate out my irrefutable pain from any distorted magnification of my emotional distress about that pain, my day improves. Certainly, I wouldn't choose suffering, nor do I have to like it, but I can accept it and be open-minded and teachable as to how to respond to it.

For sure, there are times when I'm so ill that I can't see anything of value in my day, yet I choose to stick to my program practices because my experience is that these habits pay dividends. The great adventure I've embarked upon is a spiritual one—that is the guiding principle of a good day—this day.

In this moment, I will focus on all that is positive.

My problem/obsession in CPA is that I think I have control over my health conditions. I'm sure that if I find the right doctor, the right treatment, the right procedure, it will go away and I won't have to deal with it anymore. Many in CPA have been focused on this for years—have been searching for "The Answer" for a long time. Despite all of our efforts of time, money, and research, our situation has not gotten better and may have even gotten worse. In Step One, we recognize we have been operating under an Illusion of control and need to surrender, to let go of our belief we can control our condition.

Step One invites us to do something different. It suggests we admit our desire to change our bodies, our desperate need to fix them, and surrender into powerlessness. In Steps Two and Three, we identify a Power greater than ourselves who can help us, and we turn our lives over to this Power. We start to give up obsessing and fixating. But we don't give up our hopes or actions to help ourselves. We learn to have confidence and trust in the guidance of our Higher Power; we follow the guidance rather than our self-will. Surrender allows us to be open to the idea of living in a different way and possibly even adopting a new belief system.

This is all we need to do as we begin our recovery journey. Acceptance is not asked of us in the Twelve Steps. Acceptance is what happens as a result of working the Steps. We grow toward acceptance of our reality.

In this moment, I will continue to have faith and work the CPA program.

Am I moving toward or away from serenity?

Serenity is such a fine "place." Sometimes I feel like I'm there, just for a moment, sometimes for maybe a few moments. Other times I wonder if it's even possible.

Today, I'm imagining it as the tip of a pin—a very tiny space, with a huge amount of space around it. And I see myself as moving away and then closer, and then away again, from the tip of the pin.

But I don't experience serenity itself as a destination or a goal; it is a moment-to-moment experience. When I work the Steps, I acquire tools to help me move closer to serenity. I am able to think more of others and be more honest with myself. I can ask for spiritual and others' help, and I can do service. I realize that though I might be powerless, my Higher Power is more than enough to get me through today, regardless of how much serenity I feel at any given moment.

Just knowing this moves me toward the tip of the pin. I don't have to beat myself up if I am not in a serene place. I can just turn to program tools and I will move closer to it. I don't think it is possible to force myself to be serene, but there are things I can do to move toward it.

As with anything, serenity comes and goes for me. All things pass. I think this is natural, and when I can accept this, I find myself even closer to that which I seek—serenity.

In this moment, I will accept that serenity can fluctuate.

Step Two required that I consider just how much my emotional and mental processes were skewed. I saw that I was not thinking clearly or effectively—I arrived at CPA in a dark place.

I was demoralized, depressed, and afraid; on some level, I knew my own resources were not up to the task of coping. I could buy that I needed to be *"restored to sanity."* I didn't understand then that my desperation brought with it the gift of humility.

I could sense that many in the fellowship had found a way out—they had what I wanted. It seemed logical that if I could bring myself to do what they suggested, I also could come out of the dark place I'd arrived at on my own. But I had lots of baggage when it came to God and a deep, irrational fear that I could only trust myself.

I was wisely told I might avoid thinking too much about a Higher Power. It was explained to me that I need not *first* understand this Power and then decide if it could restore me to sanity, but rather that this program of specific action would allow that Power to flow, and in experiencing it, I would know it was real and vital.

I needed the experience of finding this power. My Sponsor suggested I just get started and added that if it made things easier, I could address my petitions for help: To Whom It *May* Concern. And that if things didn't work out, the program would "refund my misery."

Today, I thank God for such forthright, kind, and sensible CPA members who brought me around. It became the great experiment of my life.

In this moment, I will appreciate the support and wisdom of CPA members.

When I came to CPA, I became aware of my brokenness of body, mind, and spirit as never before. I was defeated, licked, and could not deny it any longer. The process of accepting this brokenness was painful and difficult.

Surrender of body, mind, and spirit continues to be an important element of my spiritual growth. The actions that I take daily are in opposition to the dictates of my ego. They require me to open my mind and heart to the spiritual solution for my problems.

In CPA, I've learned how to open myself, just as I am, to be useful to my Higher Power. The Twelve Steps are my path, and as I travel, I am never alone. The unlikely way has become the true one. I have been given companions to walk with me along this spiritual path. We meet and share our ups and downs, and we help each other on the way when we become confused and weak. We offer each other spiritual nourishment and comfort as we journey to wholeness. We all walk the path of the Twelve Steps, and we try to stay together—that is where we find our safety and our strength.

In this moment, I will go to a meeting or connect with a friend in my CPA program, knowing that our togetherness yields comfort, nourishment, safety, and strength, and leads to spiritual growth.

Medications provoke an internal battle: the little child inside me doesn't want to "swallow any stupid pills!" When I first came to meetings and learned that CPA has no opinion on medications, it helped me to feel safe. I've had to make some difficult decisions in dealing with medications, but there are so many wonderful people in CPA with whom to speak privately about making these choices.

There was also an external battle for me to face. Because of shared past experiences with addiction, my partner had strong opinions about medications I should avoid. With the help of working the CPA Steps and talking to others in the program, I have been able to have honest conversations with my spouse about my choices. This is all really difficult for them, yet I know how important it is to include them in my recovery. CPA has made it so that I'm not relying on someone who, in this situation, is incapable of giving me the support I need.

Now, when new medication recommendations come up with my doctor, I feel prepared to deal with the proposition because of the meaningful experiences that are shared in CPA. I take my time to make decisions about new medications and treatments. And I always pray or meditate when I'm feeling doubts. I feel so grateful to have a community to help me through all these difficult decisions—leaving me feeling good about my choices and my life. I'm no longer alone on this journey

In this moment, I will use the resources and fellowship of CPA to support me in making healthcare choices I feel good about. I can involve my loved ones, as needed, with grace, ease, and honesty, knowing I have all the support I need.

My experience with Step Ten is that I easily forget about it, which results in not receiving its benefits—to help *"maintain our spiritual fitness."*

After I completed the Steps, I thought, *Okay, I'm done.* But the truth is that we are never finished working the Steps if we want to keep them active in our lives. Step Ten is crucial because when I continue to take personal inventory and admit when I'm wrong, I stay aware of the areas of my life that need improvement and those where I can acknowledge I have done well.

I use the Steps in my life often and apply them to things outside of CPA. Step Ten is such a clear way to continue to work my program. If I stay aware of my weaknesses and strengths as they come up in my life, I'm reminded to turn them over to God, and they can be removed or used.

Realizing I was not using this Step to its full potential, I thought about ways to make it more active in my life. I decided to find a Step Ten partner. We agreed to email or phone each other once a week to discuss our Tenth Step. Ideally every evening (but actually a few times a week), I reflect on my day. I become aware of character defects that show up and notice my strengths. Checking in with my Step Ten partner gives me accountability, and that encourages me to follow through. Not everyone needs that accountability, and I may not always need it, but for now it's working well.

I am keeping this Step active, and that's resulting in good changes in me.

In this moment, I will remind myself to take a personal inventory and reflect upon it.

Serenity happens when I practice Step Eleven.

My daily practice consists of morning meditation and prayer to ask for guidance on what my day could look like. I ask for my defects to be removed, to clear a way to hear my Higher Power (HP). The evenings are for journaling, reflecting, and praying about my day. I ask for the power to carry out my Higher Power's will.

The more I practice, the more love, joy, calmness, and self-compassion arises in me. I have better mental stability and emotional maturity. Emotional maturity has also resulted from keeping things simple. When I meditate, I feel peaceful and know I am connecting with my HP.

I find, as I come to forgive and love myself, that I am more able to give away what has been given. My relationships with those I love have grown, and I can see my emotional sobriety growing as I connect with myself and others.

I've learned to quiet myself when things come too fast; I pay attention to my breath during difficult situations. I gain serenity, being present in the moment, Presence is my power. There is a relief in finding acceptance within myself.

I've also discovered I am more than my chronic pain and chronic illness. I look at my past and see how I was always powerless in my life and that my HP was always there. Practicing every day has helped me recover.

My behaviors have been gradually changing as I work the Steps. Finding my inner power with prayer and meditation has changed my life. Today, I humbly ask to be used for the greater good of our fellowship and of the world.

In this moment, I will turn to prayer and meditation.

Just for Today is an important coping strategy for me. Often, I experiment with breaking down a calendar day into smaller chunks.

Sometimes *Just for Today* means *just for this moment*. *Just for now*, this is what I am feeling/experiencing. Reducing my perspective to "just for now" helps get me out of the rut of feeling overwhelmed by trying to figure out how I'm going to cope with a set of symptoms and circumstances for an indefinite period of time. When things cannot be fixed in the outer sense, using inner tools such as spirituality and coping strategies becomes essential for resilience and my quality of life.

Basic meditation practice helps me. I use breath as the anchor for meditation—the focus I return to, again and again, after the mind inevitably wanders elsewhere. Suggestions such as "there is nowhere else to be, nothing else to do" help me return to the present moment. Engaging in meditation practice that has a beginning and an ending is relaxing. There was a period of time when I needed to set a timer for four minutes at a time. Even though my goal was to meditate for twenty minutes, that was an inconceivably unendurable amount of time. So I gave myself permission to go for smaller chunks. For those meditations, my "days" were four minutes long.

Just for Today helps me cope with living with chronic illness and pain in skillful ways. I don't have to figure out how I am going to cope with five or ten or twenty more years of this with unknown but anticipated additional challenges. Using this slogan, I can let go of that uncertain future and focus on the now.

In this moment, I will appreciate the wisdom of CPA slogans, especially Just for Today.

Normal sex is out of the question in my marriage. Before CPA, I viewed this as yet another pleasure I'd been robbed of—my body had betrayed me with illness and pain. Later, my husband experienced similar losses—pain, medications, fatigue, limited movement, and difficulty breathing. Not "being able to" have sex was a blow to the ego and self-image. Surprisingly though, not as much as I would have assumed.

I no longer look at the unfolding of my life through a dark and desolate lens. I see now that my body has not betrayed me. In reality, it works very hard to keep me alive and able to love, to live, and to connect with others. There are laws of nature, and illness is part of that law. It's a fact of my life. Accepting that fact has freed me up to choose how I will live the rest of my life instead of being angry about how I think it "should have been." I can trust the process.

Today I believe things are unfolding as they "should" by divine standards, not mine.

Life and love have meanings that I could not grasp before chronic illness. It isn't the illness that gives me all I have today; it's the spiritual program I work due to that illness.

Connection and honest communication feed the intimacy in all my relationships, particularly my marriage. Touch is more meaningful and important to me now that sex is not in the picture. Romance is sweeter. I know without a doubt that I am loved, that my touch is desired, and that I have a connection with my best friend and lover that I never thought I would find in this lifetime.

In this moment, I will receive and give love to myself and others.

When I am having a really grateful day, I realize that there are more things that work right in my body than things that malfunction. I have come to recognize and live by the fact that my body works very hard for me. When I first got sick, I saw the situation as: my body broke down on me—it let me down. Now I realize that even while Laws of Nature are behind some parts of my body and its systems malfunctioning, the rest of my body works very hard to compensate for those malfunctions.

I didn't come to have these more positive beliefs overnight, for sure! And CPA has never suggested I ignore what brings on sadness or concern. That is not compassionate or kind. I have to grieve my losses. The loss of physical health and the impact of having chronic pain are huge. Grieving is necessary. Also necessary is that I understand and accept that for chronically ill, disabled people, grief comes and goes. Gratitude for what is good in my life helps balance the grief; it carries me through grieving and onto the other side of it.

One constant gratitude I have is for the fellowship of CPA. I do not grieve alone, nor do I have to be grateful alone.

In this moment, I will accept my evolving grief and the support of the CPA fellowship.

When I first came to CPA, I struggled to understand the idea of surrendering. I didn't want to give up. I was in my early forties, and my eleven-year-old son needed me. I had been his homeschool teacher his whole life. I was fighting for my health so that I could be a mom and a wife. I was involved with advocacy for people with my illness, which I found very rewarding.

In CPA, surrender doesn't mean we stop medications, treatments, or therapies. We don't have to stop advocating for ourselves or others. It took me a while to understand that surrender doesn't mean giving up. In the past, when one of my doctors recommended a new medication to try, my hopes would soar. And if the side effects were too much or the medicine didn't help as much as I had hoped, my whole attitude would plummet. I would be depressed and overwhelmingly disappointed. It would stretch out to affect my whole life, including my relationships with my family.

After working through the Steps and right-sizing my attitude toward my pain and illness, I have found some freedom. People with my illness still need to make some noise in order to create change. But the difference for me now is that I'm not so invested in the outcomes that my spirit lives or dies with each step forward or back.

I have "given up" the struggle. I'm proud of my body and all that it does correctly, especially with all of life's obstacles. I never know what scientific advancement may come or what limitations might improve or simply go away. Today, I surrender: I accept myself, my body, my illness exactly as I am right now.

In this moment, I will let go of outcomes and turn toward acceptance.

My Step Four began with some dread. I expected it to be hard and unpleasant. I do not know where I got that perception, but it turned out not to be true. Step Four, for me, was simply a methodical and careful look at myself. I discovered things that were hiding, and I recognized things that were in the open. I spent time looking at myself in a way I don't think I ever would have otherwise.

This Step helped me to know myself—to see my weaknesses and strengths. Step Four is a building block to the next Steps. Becoming aware of my weaknesses was key to Steps Six through Nine. Spending time exploring these helped me to see and recognize when character defects popped up, giving me the chance to turn them over to my Higher Power to remove at the right time.

I think the Twelve Steps are a wonderful gift to us and that they're in the order they are in for a reason. Step Four is in the perfect spot in the progression. The knowledge and insights that working Step Four has given me have been invaluable.

It's suggested that we find a way to work the Steps that fits each of us—there are several to choose from—and that we work them at our own pace. It may seem like a big job, but…how do you eat a large, nutritious meal? One bite at a time. We can take our time, enjoy the process, and let our Higher Power guide us. Working this Step with a Sponsor's guidance and support was essential for me. It kept me on track. Working this Step has been a wonderful blessing in my life.

In this moment, I will recognize my own courage in working each CPA Step.

When I first came into CPA, I had recently resigned from the position that financially supported both my husband and myself. I thought letting go of my high-powered job would allow me to get better. I had enormous fear of financial insecurity but enough savings to cover a year's worth of living expenses. I assumed I'd be able to work again.

My husband had retired ten years prior and taken over as a "house husband" and renovator of our fixer-upper home. After three months, I'd gotten worse physically; it became clearer and clearer that I wouldn't be able to work, even from home. I balked at applying for disability, as I had no clear diagnoses to explain the daily debilitating fatigue I was experiencing. I told my father we were going to lose our home soon, and he began to financially support us. At first, I felt shame, but I began to see that my Higher Power had stepped in to keep a roof over our heads.

I am now able to work a few hours a month, and my husband is making small amounts of income here and there. I've been able to let go of shame and gracefully accept food every week from our local food bank. We are by no means financially secure. What has changed for me is this: by working the Steps, I've moved from fear of financial insecurity to trusting that my Higher Power has a plan for me. I don't know what that plan is in the bigger picture, so as long as I focus on today—the here and now—and do God's will for me, I know I am okay. God is my employer.

In this moment, I will turn to my faith in a Higher Power, especially when I feel afraid.

It's a blustery fall day, with gentle rains moving from fall into winter. The apartment is cold. My will today is to stay in bed, my head wrapped in heat and ice at the same time, to wallow a little in the frustration of my chronic illness. I have things to do. I'll be moving soon to a more accessible apartment that meets my physical and emotional needs. I want to wallow in the sadness of leaving, grieving that my body cannot maintain a rural lifestyle through another winter.

I made a service commitment to CPA for today; I want to be present for that more than I want to be in bed. This is a simple example of recognizing God's will for me.

Today, I try not to get caught up in word choices for my Higher Power. I'm okay with slipping between "God" and "Higher Power," whom I find most strongly in Nature. But for me, God is everywhere.

When I resist God's will, I feel, live, and experience the consequences. God wants me comfortable and rested, not emotionally, physically, and mentally wrung out from pain and illness. I'm learning how to bring my will in alignment with my Higher Power's will for me, a day at a time, an hour at a time, a minute at a time, a second at a time.

Right now, that means being kind to myself, indulging a couple of more hours in bed before I come face-to-face with the friends I've made and am making in CPA, avoiding loneliness and isolation, and letting God work through me and my fellow members.

In this moment, I will rest and take the time I need.

Using CPA tools before surgery:

As soon as I am made aware I need a surgery, I contact my Sponsor. I had a major surgery this year. I knew three months ahead of time when it would happen. I asked for support in my various recovery communities, local and international. I also sought assistance from the religious society of which I am a participating member. A woman younger than I intersected these circles of support, organized a flow chart for rides to and from the hospital two hours away, and made a regular schedule of visitors and helpers including a soup train.

Using CPA tools during surgery:

At the hospital, I arrived perky and ready for surgery. I tried my best, even during trying times with staff, to be kind, considerate, and generous in thought and action. This surgery has only been performed there twice this year, and there was much confusion once I left the operating theater. I spent a lot of time breathing, hiding my swollen head under the sheets to protect myself from the bright lights and too frequent, seemingly harsh intrusions of nurses and doctors. I prayed, and prayed some more.

I turned the entire experience over to my Higher Power and asked for help. I did not once go without what I needed.

In this moment, I will be strategic about who I ask for support and then turn this over to God.

Before CPA, it felt like I was just trudging through a miserable life that I could not wait to end. Everywhere I turned, there were new problems, new diagnoses, new pain. Looking into the abyss of ever-increasing illness, I saw no joy—just suffering.

Then I came to CPA. And now, I laugh—a lot. I am able to share my experiences, both in meetings and in fellowship. In meetings, I share in a general way; when I'm hanging out with the friends I've made, I share more specifically. Since I'm able to say things out loud to people who really get it, it feels like I don't have to carry that awful weight around anymore. Not only have I begun to enjoy my life, my outlook for the future has become more joyful also.

For me, joy occurs in fleeting moments. And when I am in one of those moments, I soak it in. I remember how it feels and put it away for a rainy day. To be honest, there is "rain" every day. But there is also joy in every day.

Even though I have pain and illness, I have a good life. I have an active social life. It doesn't look like the lives of most people in the world. It looks like my friends and I getting together online and hanging out. We watch TV, we laugh and joke and share deep, painful truths.

I don't have to do this alone. And with the people I've met in CPA, it's not bad at all. That's where my joy comes from.

In this moment, I will appreciate my connection with CPA members and using humor as a tool.

I used to think I had to do everything perfectly. I'd feel bad if I turned one problem over to my Higher Power today only to obsess and try to fix another tomorrow. If I had a period of serenity and was miserable and in a dark hole a week later, I thought: *What's wrong with me? Why aren't I getting it?*

My Sponsor pointed out that I'm human. I'm never going to work a "perfect" program. It's not possible to have serenity twenty-four hours a day. I had an unrealistic expectation of myself and how a successful program was supposed to look, so I kept feeling like I was failing. The old thoughts that said, *I am never good enough,* kept appearing.

It took time and practice for me to become gentler toward myself, to learn slowly and make mistakes along the way. I attributed my success in life based on working hard and being perfect. It was a revelation that I could not do my program perfectly 100 percent of the time,

What I've come to understand is: my recovery is about small changes, not quick, major overhauls. Harmful patterns didn't disappear. I became more aware of how and when they showed up and noticed them sooner than last time. This gave me freedom to make new choices. When I found myself in a depression, I would cycle out of it just a bit quicker, maybe remember to use a few of my program tools when I was in it. It took me years to consistently remember I have a Higher Power to turn to when I'm struggling, unhappy, or confused.

Perfectionism still appears, but today I notice it and then tell it I'm okay just as I am.

In this moment, I will accept that I am perfectly imperfect.

I use Step Eleven on a daily, sometimes hourly, basis. Each part has challenged me.

Prayer and meditation were not skills I had when I first arrived in CPA. I thought prayer meant telling God what I wanted. I thought meditation meant sitting in an uncomfortable position, making my thoughts stop. Now, I have a broader understanding. Today, I regularly speak to Higher Power (HP). Just knowing I am not alone helps me. I've learned many methods of meditation. A favorite is simply focusing on my breath, feeling it flow in and out of my nostrils. This shifts my mind and helps me pause and redirect my attention.

As we understood Him. No one in CPA tells me what my HP is supposed to be. I don't have to follow any religious traditions or use the word God, a male pronoun, or any other description someone else believes in. This is personal. It's like any relationship: sometimes I move away, then come close again. I have to put some effort into maintaining it, hence the *conscious contact* part of this Step. As I deepen my connection, my love and trust in HP gets stronger.

*Praying only for knowledge of His will for us and the power to carry that out...*this was so hard for me at first. What about my will—what I want? Being so ill, I didn't like what seemed to be HP's will. What I've found is that often my HP's will for me is far better than what I'd imagined. Sometimes it's a gift I'd rather return. That's when I need to pray for *the power to carry that out.*

The miracle is that HP always gives me what is needed.

In this moment, I will focus on my breath and deepening my trust in HP's bigger plan.

Anger is an emotion I find challenging. I want to suppress it or push the feelings aside. When I do, it can leak out in ways that hurt others or myself. In recovery, I've learned that anger is part of being a human being.

Angry feelings are triggered by a need, but I'm not always aware that's what's happening. If I can stop and identify what I'm trying to fix with my anger, I can more easily determine how to move forward. Often, anger is a reaction to fear, or a person who's not met my expectations, an increase in my pain and symptoms, or feeling frustrated by a situation that's not going the way I want it to. When I feel helpless, anger can show up. Blaming others or trying to force a solution are not productive.

When I feel anger, I can practice *First Things First*—beginning with self-care. I may call my Sponsor or a friend, which often leads to calming down as the energy gets vented. Then I can think more clearly and discover the next indicated action. I've learned that anger is useful if I use it wisely, not destructively.

When anger arises, I am not rational. I can raise my voice, say things I later regret, attack or try to control others, or turn it toward myself. I discovered these behaviors in my Step Four inventory.

My practice today (which I do not do perfectly) is to pay attention to my anger as a clear message that something is needed. With the guidance of my Higher Power (HP), I can focus the energy toward effective and appropriate action.

In this moment, I will pay attention to and honor all my feelings, especially anger, when it arises and then turn to HP.

How do I say what I mean without being mean, or say no to people I love? Giving *others* the option to say no without explanation, conditions, or hurt feelings has taught me to allow myself the same privilege. I can say, "No," "Not now," or "Not today." Some are hard nos—there are some people I have nothing to offer. I gently direct them to others who might be more qualified to meet their needs.

Because speaking is physically difficult for me, I manage the amount of energy I put into speaking daily. I encourage others to reach out to me via text first. Then we choose a time that mutually works. I am not an emergency crisis helpline. I can only listen to so much resentment in others before I become emotionally and physically exhausted. In that situation, no one is getting my best attention.

Within a conversation, I listen, and then I gently stop and ask questions about solutions. "What solution might work for you right now, in this hour, in this day? Is there anything about tomorrow that needs to be handled today? Can we pray together on finding a solution?"

I have reached out to several others to create a support circle within CPA that I can go to when my Sponsor is not available. Not everyone is responsive. I don't take this personally. With so many seemingly unmanageable and conflicting health conditions between any two CPA members, it takes effort to set time boundaries, establish times to communicate, discover what form of communication works, and then open up. Taking the risk to reach out while setting healthy limits for myself and honoring others' healthy limits take time and attention, and are worth it.

In this moment, I will set limits when I need to, releasing any lingering guilt.

FEAR: Face Everything And Recover. Reading these words triggered that part of me who feels she has to push herself beyond her limits—with no right to say (or even think), "No, I can't do that." One of the most challenging things I've learned to face is the experience of suicidality. For me, remembering the distinction between experiencing suicidality and acting suicidal is very important. Being suicidal is taking concrete actions toward ending one's own life. Whereas suicidality refers to thoughts and feelings related to wanting to die or ending one's life. As I've faced such thoughts and feelings, I've learned about how and why they occur and how to respond differently than I used to.

Thoughts of suicide often arise when I'm feeling overwhelmed. Noting how frequent, fast, and intense such thoughts are aids me in understanding that something unexpected must have happened. My inner world got shaken, and I am experiencing the aftershocks. This recognition can cue me to review what has happened and identify the trigger.

Depending on how overwhelmed I feel, I can take a break for self-care. This may mean taking three deep breaths. It may mean praying to my Higher/Deeper Power for love and care, help, and guidance. Meditation has significantly helped, both in the moment and over time.

Life always comes from unexpected directions. Learning how to better navigate through those times is a worthy endeavor. Part of that is learning the anatomy of how I respond and react. Facing difficult issues and engaging them directly and courageously has deepened my understanding of what works and makes sense for me and increased my quality of life.

In this moment, I will recognize that facing my greatest fears and my deepest suffering has helped me recover.

Prior to CPA, gratitude was not something that I thought of often.

I'd been in pain and sick for twelve years before finding CPA. I had allowed my condition to take over my life, my wellness, my sense of self, and my zest for life. All of this led to hitting a dramatic life-altering rock bottom that I'm lucky to have escaped from alive.

This was the direct result of not working on the emotional pain and turmoil that a life with chronic pain had caused. I was broken—a far cry from the previously social person I once was. At the time, I felt that I had nothing to be grateful for.

When I found CPA and began attending regular meetings, I started to have hope where I'd once thought my life was over. I saw a light at the end of the tunnel—the promise of a joyful and fulfilling life, simply by following these Twelve Steps.

That's when my immense sense of gratitude began to bubble to the surface.

I realized that the day of my rock bottom was actually something to be grateful for. I escaped alive and was given a second chance at life! Why *wouldn't* I be grateful for that?

That day that was once the worst day of my life has now become the best day of my life and the basis for the life of gratitude I live today. When I think back to the misery and despair I was in that day, I realize that *anything* is better than that.

With the help of CPA and an attitude of gratitude, I have found a life of hope and possibilities.

In this moment, I will express gratitude for the blessings in my life and all around me.

I thought that in CPA, I'd stop making unrealistic, self-imposed demands of myself. The stark facts are these: at any given time, I have a deficiency in my intellectual needs, exercise needs, artistic needs, social needs, sleep needs, etc. Surprisingly, as a CPA member, I began to think I ought to be able to have all these things in a way that met my specifications.

Because I give great weight to the remarks and examples of those who are ill, seemingly more than I am, yet are clearly program "winners," I slipped into a pernicious trap of my own unconscious fashioning: *"He is doing this, she, that. What's wrong with my character that I can't seem to do so too?"* I engaged in my old motivational style—"tough love."

With time and effort in CPA, I'm learning that my chronic pain and illness "normal" is mine, and yours is yours. I'm beginning to refuse to reject myself via comparison with others. I understand our oft-repeated phrase, *"Here I don't have to explain, you get me,"* to mean, *"I don't know your specifics nor will I question them. If you say, ' I can't,' I understand, and I don't question you."* Never has anyone in CPA not accepted when I had to do less than we'd hoped I could. If they ask, it's about my health concern rather than judgment.

Of course, as I move forward in recovery, I slip back a little, too. So I won't be surprised if there's a moment when I say to myself: *"Just snap out of it!"* If that happens, I'll accept myself as I am and look forward to my next CPA meeting.

In this moment, I will notice when I'm comparing myself to others and offer myself compassion instead.

Since joining CPA, I've found that I am more at peace while waiting for a flare to calm down. When my symptoms flare up and I have already done the things I can control—taken my medication or supplements, applied the ice or heat packs, or done whatever therapy is indicated—all that is left for me to do is rest and wait.

Before CPA, I was not good at waiting. I didn't have the ability to rest and let the indicated actions take effect. Instead, I would panic, unable to withstand the flare, and, five minutes into it, decide that what I'd already done wasn't going to work, and then try other medications or treatments. I would run around, changing my mind over and over again about what was going to work and put my body through more stress.

Now I find that, during a flare, I no longer panic after doing the indicated actions. I trust that the treatment will work, whether it's quickly or slowly. And in the meantime, what my body calls for in those moments of waiting is rest, and I do my best to honor my body's needs.

In this moment, I will rest, patiently accept Divine timing, and consider the next indicated action.

There are times when I get lost in my misery and self-pity and forget that I have a choice—about my attitude. Focusing my attention on what's not working—the obstacles I face, what I don't have—makes me unhappy, depressed, and angry. I want to live in serenity, yet discontent with my situation does not cultivate peace.

When I remember to practice gratitude, I see what is working in my life, what blessings there are, and all that I have. It doesn't mean I ignore the challenges. It means that I see the balance. And generally, what works, what is good, and what I have far outweigh what I believe is lacking.

I notice I have a roof over my head; I have running water in my home. Although some of my senses are diminished or absent, I stop and remember the ones that work. I notice the people in my life: the mail person, the checkout clerk at the grocery store, the friend who drops off a meal. I notice nature: a blue sky, trees in the wind, and birds singing.

This practice of noticing the good in my life fills me with joy. Making the conscious decision to become aware of all the ways in which my world is filled with support, kindness, and beauty means I am not spending that time fixated on the pain in my body, anxiety about the procedure next week, or the person who let me down.

Gratitude is the attitude that allows me to choose how I live. It is not the external world that makes my life happy or miserable. It's my internal world—through the lens of gratitude—that makes it possible to be happy, no matter the situation. This is freedom.

In this moment, I will notice what I feel grateful for.

I was once shown a method for understanding if one is lost in one's own will or moving toward God's. I used it when I was struggling to understand if a medication I'd been using successfully for many years was still a good fit for me. I used it when I needed to know if I had to stop spending my time in a way that had, for years, been the right adaptation to my life with chronic pain and illness but which had become too taxing. It recently helped me move away from a relationship that I'd held dear but which I suspected had become irrevocably toxic. Here is the general idea:

<u>What I am doing may not be God's will if it:</u>

- tends to drain me of hope, making my motivation flag
- prompts me to give up on activities that were once very important
- seems to be pushing me more and more into negative feelings
- increases my self-absorption
- erases from my mind the spiritual and emotional milestones I have known
- draws me away from my fellows

<u>It may be in the direction of God's will if it:</u>

- inspires me to have new ideas
- tends to balance my emotions
- reminds me of times I have been led by my Higher Power
- sparks a new flame in me
- realigns my focus to that which is beyond myself
- refreshes my spirit
- opens me to the heartaches and joys of others

This is something that has helped me. I share it here to be used or discarded, in part or in whole, by you, given your own life experience in finding your Higher Power's will for you.

In this moment, I will use the tools that work for me.

December

Anonymity supports recovery. It helps me feel I am a "part of" instead of feeling different from others.

Some of the titles and roles I had before chronic pain and illness don't apply to me anymore. CPA has taught me how to release my past and process the emotions that come with letting go, so I'm free to define myself in a new way.

Anonymity helps me to see my inherent worth as a human being. Importantly, it has helped me be more aware of where I am judgmental and allows me to release those preconceptions. When sharing in a meeting, I no longer get hung up on details of my illness or treatments. Instead, speaking in general terms about these things focuses my attention on my feelings and actions as I learn to adapt to my reality and apply the Twelve Steps of CPA. Experience, strength, and hope are what we have in common.

Learning to speak in general terms took practice. Before, I was very caught up in details and oftentimes blind to the bigger picture. Anonymity reminds me that I am not healthier or sicker or more able-bodied or more disabled than anyone else. How I grow and change my attitude is through listening to everyone, without letting my opinion of their situation (which is definitely incomplete and inaccurate) block any messages of experience, strength, and hope. Anonymity supports unity and equality—two principles that I strive to practice in all my affairs.

In this moment, I will apply the CPA principles of anonymity, unity, and equality in all my affairs.

I've gone through almost four years without a single day of morning-to-night wellness. I've had maybe four or five days of wellness over the past several months—just enough energy to dress, or sit in the car for a drive, or maybe go for a very short walk.

In my new life with chronic pain and illness, the times I've been able to get out have felt miraculous—literally. I feel full of grace, of gratitude, and of love. There is access to an inner experience of a lightness of heart toward being and staying alive. But most days, walking outside, just to force myself to sit outside, is all I can do before I get too dizzy and weak and need to come back in and lie down. Not accepting that and desperately wanting more is nothing short of excruciating. I need the support, wisdom, compassion, and understanding of my fellows in CPA. They help me relax into a new relationship with faith and hope .

I thank my fellow CPA warriors for answering my call for help and giving so much compassion and love, which was sorely missing in my life. My prayer today is that I will continue to learn and to grow into the whole-hearted person God has always intended me to be.

In this moment, I will find gratitude where I can, accept all that I can, and relax into my growing faith.

After attending my first CPA meeting, I realized I needed to really start working these Twelve Steps. Lately, I have been practicing Step One every day.

It has been difficult to admit that I have a chronic illness. For years, I denied the fact that I was living with it. I was out of tune with my body and the signals it was trying to give me. It's been almost ten years since I was first diagnosed with my chronic illness. I fought against the diagnosis and never allowed myself to believe I was powerless over the pain.

Admitting powerlessness didn't come easy, but today I know: I am indeed powerless over the pain. Reading the CPA literature provided to me at my first meeting helped me recognize that my life had become unmanageable.

By working Step One, I have been able to admit I have a chronic illness, to admit that I am powerless over it, and to realize how unmanageable my life is when I try to control it or ignore it. I've begun listening to my body again and using self-care when needed.

In this moment, I will find courage to listen to my body's wisdom and respond in self-loving care.

A long time ago I asked three fellows what it meant to surrender, to truly take Step Three. All three said, you just let it go. Well, that wasn't very helpful to me. But then the third person added, and sometimes you have to walk away. Well, in CPA I can't always physically get up and leave the room, but as another fellow pointed out, I can distract myself. I can switch gears and do something else.

I am currently working Step Three in CPA. My Sponsor suggested that I start with something easy, something safe to practice surrendering. For example, choosing when to brush my teeth or which shirt to wear. I was thinking I would be able to practice on which TV show to watch next. It turns out I am practicing on my breakfast. I have about 6 different items on my breakfast plate. I turn over what order I am going to eat them in. For someone who craves routine and sameness, I would have always eaten them in the same order. But now I let Higher Power guide me in my selection, and I am often surprised at HP's choices.

Now that I am practicing that with something "easy," I look forward to trusting HP with more meaningful decisions in the future.

In this moment, I will ask HP for the next indicated action, and I will pause and wait for an answer.

Coming to Step Two, over the years, I've always said to myself, *"Oh, sure, a Power greater than myself—yeah, yeah, yeah, I got that. I believe in God."* Then I'd look at the second part and focus on that. I knew I was "insane" and needed to find clarity.

As I think about it today and reflect on its deeper meaning, it's not just about finding a God. It's about finding a God and believing He/She/They/It has the ability to *do* something for me and in me. In Step Two, that something is restoring me to clarity.

What does clarity look like for me today?

- God is there for me, holding my hand, tangibly showing me support and care.
- I have stopped the endless searching for the right treatment, pill, therapy, doctor, and procedure. I no longer expect perfection in anything or anyone, especially myself.
- I think before I act and calmly make decisions, understanding the benefits and the consequences.
- I can't be afraid to take care of myself. And I do not have to feel guilty when I do.
- By accepting that I have chronic pain and illness and by making peace with that fact, I am inviting joy and serenity into my days.

As I continue to pray and listen, God continues to reveal itself to me in new and powerful ways.

In this moment, I will come to believe that I can be restored to clarity and serenity.

What I learned about rest in CPA was life-changing for me. I was raised in an atmosphere of always completing everything that had to be done before I did anything relaxing or fun. I was considered "bad" if I wasn't being productive, if there were tasks waiting to be completed. When chronic pain/illness became part of my life, this mind-set no longer served me. I found myself pushing to get things done that I thought had to be done until the pain increased to the point where I could no longer continue. I overdid it, and that resulted in me needing more time to recover.

It did not come naturally to me to rest without guilt. It took effort, but I taught myself that rest is doing something important—not being lazy. Rest is being a good steward of a valuable asset: my energy and ability to function in day-to-day life. If I look at rest as wisely using my time to extend my energy and capacity and to have a more pleasant life, it becomes an extremely positive activity.

It is helpful for me to look at the things I think need to get done compassionately. What will happen if they don't get done until a few hours later or tomorrow, or longer? I've learned to let things go and develop a more laid-back, lenient mind-set.

I now view resting as constructive and learned to not let guilt and shame control me. Taking a break actually gives me more time in the long run. Resting is now an accepted and pleasant part of my life, something that improves and enhances it significantly.

In this moment, I will view rest as a constructive and productive activity.

When my condition first grounded me, I thought my life had shrunk down to the size of my house. So much of the time I was unable to leave the house, or even my bedroom. I believed I would never have fun or play again. It was a dark time. All I saw was a dismal future ahead.

Then one day I realized that the world is wherever I am. It doesn't matter that I can't travel to the grocery store, let alone to Paris. Wherever I am is my universe. I can always, only, be right where I am. And at that time, that was in my home. When I became willing to be creative and see the abundance right at my doorstep, I discovered many ways to play and find enjoyment.

I live in the desert, and there are many creatures that come to visit—coyotes, javelinas, bobcats, lizards, and birds. Soon I had a stack of books about desert life and a new pair of binoculars. I could sit at my big picture window and be entertained. I learned about wildlife and felt soothed by nature.

This shift of attitude and perspective opened many new avenues of play and creativity for me. I started to write and found writing to be a wonderful way to channel my creative energy. Soon I found opportunities to travel the world online and never had to leave my bed to visit a museum in another country. I found people to interact with at various online sites and made close friends with people all over the world.

Given the technology available to me, I know today that the only thing that keeps me a prisoner in my house is my mind.

In this moment, I will find creative ways to enjoy life and limits.

This year, we had to once again cancel our annual Holiday Hootenanny. We used to share our music, home, and festive spirit with many people in our communities—singing with friends, playing instruments, and going to all hours. It is one of many absences that are now part of our new holiday season. Last year, its loss seemed yet another way the world was "punishing" us. This year, what has changed is that my family and I have been using CPA recovery tools to face the holidays. Instead of counting the "things we can't do anymore," we collectively decided to refocus, and our holiday season was simple, pleasant, and one of the best in many years.

It can be hard to hear, as the holidays come around, people telling us about missing our once-great parties, but I try to point to the essence of those gatherings: connection. These days, though gatherings need to be smaller for me to handle, smaller gatherings aid intimacy. I am not wasting all my energy or saving it for one big blow-out each year. My daughter and I recommitted to our connection this year, and it feels like the holiday spirit is a part of every day, not just for certain times of the year, because our focus is now on what the holidays might bring, that love and feeling of pure presence. Through program tools, those aspects become alive more and more, each day.

In this moment, I will make a list of the things I most value during times of communal celebration; I will take a moment to notice where those things already exist in my life.

After my divorce, finances were a big concern. I was not able to work. I was very careful with money, spending the least amount I could as I figured out how to survive.

Somehow, the funds I needed always came in. A family member paid for a large repair. Someone offered to cut my hair for free. A loan I thought would have to be paid off was excused. This is how I learned that my Higher Power is in charge of my finances, along with everything else in my life. I had to do the footwork and manage my funds, but I didn't need to spend sleepless nights worrying.

Then, an old friend asked me to work at his company. I explained that I lived with a chronic illness and that I didn't think I was dependable but needed the money. I thanked him for the offer and said yes. To my surprise, I was able to do the work. I worked from home, on my own schedule. The job grew, and my ability to do it grew as well. The service work I'd done in CPA had given me the confidence to say yes, as I had been able to take on tasks I'd thought were impossible for me. I was able to support myself for the first time since becoming ill, in a field very different from the one I trained in, and I was good at it.

This was a blessing from my Higher Power. It reminded me of the slogan: *Don't Quit Five Minutes Before the Miracle.* Being asked to work just when I needed the money, being able to actually do the job, and earning enough to support myself was that miracle.

In this moment, I will consider that service work in CPA may have unexpected, miraculous ripples.

I arrived in CPA mostly relying on myself. I used my natural gift for prudent planning to the degree that it became an obsession. I believed: *If some planning is good, more is better, and constant planning is best. Of course I have to have plans for every possible problem. I need an infinite series of safety nets.* It was, literally, a sickening endeavor.

This self-imposed obsession to control leads only to more pain in the future when my plan does not go to specification. My expectations, unmet, cause my disappointment and fear to grow greater. Overwhelmed by my false belief that I can and must control everything, I conclude and my feelings of despair confirm: there is no hope.

This is my emotional and spiritual debilitation. And it's treatable.

If I trust in the wisdom of the Serenity Prayer, changing what my God directs me to change, accepting what I can't change, and trusting the wisdom to discern the difference, I save myself much physical and emotional wear and tear. I come into the present, where I can learn to live as I go. I can take appropriate action, trusting I've done what can be done, and accept that the world will do what it will. Much of life will remain a mystery to be lived rather than a problem to solve. Today is my given day, and it's worthy of my best care.

In this moment, I will accept that my ultimate powerlessness is the portal into moving out of the problem and into living, even savoring, my daily emotional and spiritual recovery.

Just Do the Next Right Thing. Early in recovery, I often didn't know what that meant. How am I supposed to be the judge of what the next right thing is?

When I came to CPA, the literature and members said, *Just Do the Next Indicated Action,* rather than, *Just Do the Next Right Thing.* That was something I could grasp much more easily. Since I had already some Twelve Step background, I knew what doing the next indicated action felt like. In CPA, I've learned that I have to let go of the obsessive thoughts I have about my illness to see things more clearly. Often, I just have to take a step back and listen to the experience, strength, and hope of others to fully comprehend this concept.

I came into CPA with a compulsion to overdo anything and everything in order to fix my health problem. I thought micromanaging my life would heal my pain and illness. What I came to find out was something very different: I had to heal from my emotional pain to recover.

Today, I listen to my intuition and the voice of recovery/reason. When I'm struggling to find the next indicated action, I go to a meeting, talk to my Sponsor, and reach out to my network for guidance.

In this moment, I will continue to take the next indicated action, and I will trust my intuition and gut feelings. I know that if I continue to follow the voice of reason, I will maintain my recovery, One Day At A Time.

It is an amazing journey that leads to Step Twelve. I now can see I have changed dramatically. Others see it too, and they seem to very much appreciate the "new" me.

Who am I now? Well, I no longer resent or fear my condition. Neither do I deny it. It is part of my life. All the fear-based questions that used to live in my brain have subsided or become fleeting. Questions like, *How do I fix this?* or *What is my purpose?* or *How will I live like this?* or even *Am I faking this?* which used to barrage my brain, have fizzled out. I see purpose in every day, and I am grateful for each sunrise.

This is certainly not how I came into CPA. An amazing transformation has happened, and I am grateful to my Sponsor, who helped me to work each Step until I felt it in my heart, until they were really a part of my daily life. Now, I no longer fear a newcomer reaching out to me and asking, "Would you be my Sponsor?" I welcome the request.

At one time, I feared the number of people I might be asked to take through the Steps. But today, I trust that my Higher Power will not overwhelm me with too many requests. I trust my Higher Power will guide me to those I am to journey through the Steps with again. That is how it is for me, another journey through the Steps. I did it once, I can do it again, and now I am just doing it with someone new.

In this moment, I will remember that as I Sponsor, I too am journeying through the Steps.

Recently, I needed a procedure that is fairly common, but it was new to me, and I was scared. I prayed, asking God for courage and strength. I contacted my Sponsor and shared all my fears. I worked Steps Six through Nine with her. As an amends to myself, I gave myself permission to be scared. I didn't have to pretend to be brave when I was not feeling brave. I determined that if at any point I decided to change my mind, I could.

On the day of the procedure, I bookended the experience with my Sponsor. Before I left the house, I called and shared anything that was blocking my faith and trust. Then I contacted her afterward. I felt held by her love and compassion while I was at the facility.

My prayers that day included asking that the medical staff be guided by God. I prayed for serenity and turned myself and the outcome over to my Higher Power (HP). I was surprised at how calm I felt. I felt the presence of my HP every step of the way. And though there were mishaps as they prepared me, I just kept reminding myself that I was safe—no matter what happened, my God was there.

The outcome was not what I expected, but my worst nightmare did not come to pass. My Sponsor reminded me to keep surrendering; that my HP will show me the next indicated action. I went home and did nothing. I didn't answer the phone. Nothing! I simply rested and had gratitude for the love of my Higher Power and my Sponsor.

In this moment, I will share my fears with a trusted CPA friend and turn any upcoming procedures over to the loving care of my Higher Power.

Before CPA, I could never find real hope. In the past, I felt short bursts of hope because of promised results from a new doctor, treatment, or medication. The rabbit trails I went down ultimately ended in failed results and feeling disappointed.

One day, while searching for the real solution, after numerous attempts, I felt real hope when I found CPA. I believe my Higher Power led me to you. From my first meeting, I felt a mustard seed of hope, although CPA was not what I had expected. I felt as though my eyes and my heart were open to living a different way. To experience chronic pain and chronic illness, not looking for the cure. To really live despite the situation and recover from the emotional and spiritual debilitation.

Hope came flooding in as I experienced further contact with you, who I lovingly refer to as "my people." Members were not going on and on about disease cures but instead, you gave me real heartfelt solution to my emotional and spiritual pain. And I found my body responded. I felt lighter and more connected to the world.

I now view my life l as a glass half full. I do what I can and have hope for my future. CPA freed me from my obsession with pain and illness.

In this moment, I will be grateful for my faith, even if it is the size of a mustard seed.

When I'm tired, things seem to be more overwhelming than they truly are.

I recently had to be away from my email for a couple of days, taking care of a family member who'd had minor surgery. When I returned home, I had a long list of emails to return—from CPA, my job, and other things. I felt vulnerable and frustrated as I read through all of these and perceived them as demands. I found myself feeling resentful, like quitting, because: *there's no way I can do all of this.*

My negative feelings created more stress and exhaustion. When I used the slogan, *HELP*, I realized what was happening. I wasn't Hungry or Lonely or in significant Pain, but I was Exhausted. It was helpful to become aware of that; it helped me put things in perspective. I did not have to respond to everyone right away, and when I looked at it logically, instead of emotionally, I found I did have time to do it, that I could and would do it. I would schedule the tasks in an order that made sense.

HELP reminds me to notice when I am tired—and therefore reacting with negative emotions. Then I see: maybe this is not the best time to get caught up on everything. I take care of my tiredness with rest, then I'll be able to do what I need to do. I turn the moment over to my Higher Power and give myself a break.

In this moment, I will ask myself if I am Hungry, Exhausted, Lonely, or in Pain? If I answer yes to any, I will address those self-care needs immediately. First Things First!

I am so grateful that the slogan *Just for Today* seems to be one of my CPA Sponsor's favorites—which means I hear it a lot and it's starting to seep in. For me, it has created a major shift in my sanity and serenity. Today, as the holidays and an upcoming move approach, I've had a lot of fear. I can look around my house, see how everything is nice and settled and orderly, and think, *Just for Today, I get to enjoy that everything is settled right now, just for this moment.* Next week, it won't be quite as according-to-plan, but that's not today. And next week, when the house starts to look chaotic with all the boxes and such, I can tell myself it's *just for today, it's not forever.* I can get through it, one day at a time.

If the moment starts to become overwhelming, I can choose to shift my focus onto positive things—like the excitement of being together with my children again. In the past, the only thoughts that would be taking center stage would be worry and fear, negativity about the chaos to come during the move, and wondering, *How will I have the energy for that?* There would also be so much fear that very little serenity would be present during all the chaos.

Today I can enjoy what is right in front of me, with faith that God will help me deal with what is to come. And if I can hold on to my sanity, just for today, then perhaps I can have some serenity the next day as well, just for *that* day, and so on.

In this moment, I will shift my thinking and live just for today, one day at a time.

From the day I was born, my mother said I ate twelve hours and slept twelve hours, and this was true. Then came chronic pain and illness. My appetite disappeared and nighttime became my most symptomatic time of day. I began to dread the sun going down, as I knew the discomfort and pain that were to come.

Sanity and serenity came in CPA's Step Seven, when I asked my Higher Power (HP) to give me a new relationship with food and sleep. My part was to stop the negative thinking and attachment to twelve hours each for food and nighttime, by repeatedly saying, "Thy will, not my taste buds', be done," or "Help me not to judge this night before it even happens." I became open to a new experience of both by setting aside all I thought I knew about myself and asking HP to change my beliefs and give me new thoughts and actions regarding self-care.

Through experimentation with this new, open attitude, I've found that when I stay in the present moment, I am able to accomplish HP's will for me, regardless of the number of hours or meals I get. Step Four really showed me the damage I was causing myself in my need to label things as good or bad (a "good" night's sleep is only good if it equals twelve hours). My HP and CPA have freed me from self-imposed, self-harming labeling and opened me to a life of peace, joy, and a comfortableness in being me, by letting go of who I "think" I am.

In this moment, I will open my mind and let go of what I think is "good/bad" for me. I am willing to have new experiences that may prove my thinking wrong.

CPA has returned the wonder for life that my chronic conditions robbed from me. My vision of the world was gray, bleak, and dull, but CPA taught me that wonder can be cultivated by experiencing gratitude and noticing beauty around and within myself. CPA and dialogue with my Sponsor help me do more of that. Now, one day at a time, I try to cultivate that awareness and deepen my connection to Source.

And the more I do, the more peaceful I am. If I'm not feeling peaceful, which can happen to humans living with chronic pain and illness, I try to remember to pay attention to my five senses, as much as I am able in this moment: the warm cup of tea in my hand, the soft fur of my cat, the sound of her dinner howl, the sight of a plant I'm managing to keep alive, the taste and smell of the mint tea grown in the yard, and so on.

In this moment, I will wonder at the pleasant things my five senses are experiencing amid my pain.

I am grateful I released my resentments against the healthcare system when doing my Fourth and Fifth Steps. I had a chance to vent about the many exhausting surgeries and to bemoan the extra conditions I now have. It was good to get these out and not be judged, just as it was extremely helpful to look at the only part I could change—my attitude about my past experience.

I am chronically ill, in pain, and must continue to interact with modern medicine. I need to continue using the Steps and program tools to deal with issues unpleasant and common to healthcare. I often do a Tenth Step to review my fears and the part I sometimes play in my distress. Sometimes, I am refusing to accept that all persons and systems are imperfect. I am having unrealistic expectations—expecting that doctors can fix all my ills and that all medical staff will be loving, kind, and patient all the time.

If it's a major appointment or procedure, I will bookend my visit with calls to my Sponsor. I commit to keeping my interactions simple while talking to the doctor, not spilling out all my emotional angst, nor being overly nice (thinking that will get me better treatment). I reaffirm the knowledge that I can't control outcomes. I express appreciation when appropriate. When I ask God to direct my thinking before each appointment, my experience is consistently less stressful and bountiful

In this moment, I will be grateful that my time in CPA has indeed changed my attitude, outlook, and experiences.

All manner of physical issues affect my sexuality. Pain, medication side effects, limited movement, fatigue, actually *having* a headache! My list goes on and on.

Emotional concerns can tax my ability for sexual expression—a sharp or brittle persona too often finding ascendance over my softer, gentler, genuine self and souring the times I might be trying to "set the mood." My emotional blocks and flat affects because I've too many things that have not had the chance for healthy expression show through. My unresolved anger, fear, and erroneous shame are often tangible.

The CPA program is effective because it is real. I am encouraged to privately "get real" about such delicate topics with my Sponsor and trusted friends. Talking about the notions we have about physical intimacy, sharing our experience, strength, and hope in this area, in a place where we know it's safe to do so, helps open us to fresh possibilities in an area that matters. Have you found adaptations for this fundamental need? Have you let go of any old ideas that stymied your chances for experiencing touch? Have you any luck in helping your partner adjust? What ideas helped you? I am so grateful I was granted the courage to explore this area of my life that I believed was gone forever. I love how real indeed I am encouraged to get in CPA recovery!

In this moment, I will pray for the courage to investigate that which I fear the most with people I trust the most.

The tool of rest is a significant resource in my life. I get cranky and irritable when I've overextended myself. My ability to function and think decreases. I feel like a wind-up doll that conks out, and I lose my ability to speak. When I am in energy debt, I can feel like a sixteen-wheeler truck running on the engine of a compact car.

Rest comes for me in many forms. It can look like pacing my activity throughout the day: I do an activity for twenty minutes, and then I head back to bed for as long as I need to recharge. I do that throughout the day. It can look like staying in bed for an entire day, including eating in bed and only leaving to go to the bathroom. It can look like spending the day away from the computer and cell phone, not having contact with other people. Interacting with others can be draining, and a day of rest can be a day of being quietly at home alone.

In CPA, I learn that only I can give myself permission for all these different ways of resting. I used to feel guilty and believed I should always be doing something. I accused myself of being lazy if I wasn't accomplishing something each day. Now I know that nothing gets accomplished if I don't take care of myself. If I get overtired, my symptoms will increase, and then I can be in bed for days, weeks, or months. I learned this the hard way over many years.

In this moment, I will know that being kind to myself means I rest my body and my mind for as long and in whatever ways allow me to return to homeostasis. Then I am able to return to the world.

You'd think that self-care would be easy. It's logical: we take care of ourselves. However, this simple skill is one I had to learn in CPA.

I have great compassion when someone else is struggling; I listen to them share their emotions and thoughts, without judgment. But on my recovery journey, I realized I did not offer the same empathy toward myself. When I was feeling ill, I would blame myself, or judge myself as lacking, attacking myself with words such as "lazy" or "irresponsible." I practiced self-violence rather than self-care.

Using the tools I've received in CPA, I now stop and practice kindness: "Oh, sweetie, you are having a bad day." I speak to myself in a soothing tone and might even wrap my arms around myself. I do something nice, like make a cup of tea or listen to music that calms me.

It turns out it is quite simple to practice self-care. And it feels so much better than berating myself or believing I did something wrong. All I need to do is the next indicated action, with a gentle attitude toward whatever I am experiencing in the moment. If I'm cold, I get a blanket. If I'm hungry, I get food. If I'm lonely, I reach out to someone. And I do it all with tenderness.

When my symptoms are making life miserable, I have a list of inner and outer resources. I wrote these down on a day I felt well. I need this list because I don't always remember there are ways to care for myself when I am in a bad state.

In this moment, I will turn toward actions that will soothe and comfort me.

When I first came to Twelve Step recovery, I thought anonymity meant that I didn't tell anyone my last name. Over time, my understanding of this spiritual principle grew to encompass so much more.

Anonymity helps our meetings feel inclusive. By not speaking about the specifics of my health condition, my diagnosis doesn't identify me or exclude me as a member of CPA. I focus on what I have in common with others, which is how the loss of my ability to function alters my life in profound and challenging ways. What matters are the feelings I share about how I judge myself as lazy or how much sadness I feel that I can no longer get out of bed early and go to the gym.

Anonymity creates an atmosphere of safety. I need a place where I can speak aloud my dark thoughts, as well as talk about my joys and my blessings. Articulating feelings and thoughts that are vulnerable, raw, and sometimes scary helps me become aware of my reality. Awareness leads to acceptance, and sometimes it is in the safety of a meeting that the first glimmer of my truth comes into the light.

Anonymity makes recovery possible for all and supports us as equals. I am not judged by whether I have money in the bank or none. There are no expectations because of the degrees I have earned or rejection because of the education I didn't receive. We are there because of chronic conditions; that is our only concern. This makes it possible for everyone, no matter what walk of life, religion, politics, or culture, to receive the benefits of our program.

In this moment, I will be grateful for my growing understanding of anonymity and its value to my recovery journey.

I used to believe that any kindness I showed myself was selfish. If I did even the smallest thing for myself—having a quiet cup of tea or painting my nails—I felt I was wasting time I could be spending serving others. I couldn't figure out why I felt so depleted. Part of it was my illness, but part of it was I was constantly doing for others and neglecting myself.

In CPA, I learned about self-compassion. I have begun practicing it. Not just physically—allowing my body to rest and not being angry because it needs extra rest—but also emotionally. My inner critic—the voice that always tells me how terrible I am, no matter how hard I try—is so much quieter now. It used to be the loudest thing in my head; it told me I was a failure. That's not true. I have challenges others don't have, but I am no less a person than anyone else. I'm learning to love myself, regardless of my bodily limitations. And the more I do it, the easier it becomes. Sometimes I'm compassionate with myself without even realizing it.

Self-compassion was the missing piece for me. It taught me I can love myself just as I am. Today, I am kind, I am gentle, and I love myself. I don't care if people call me selfish; it's okay to be a little bit selfish. I have to take care of me, or I won't have anything left for anyone else. Most of all, I want to take care of me because…I love me. That is such a gift.

In this moment, I will be kind to myself more than I am cruel, and I will care for myself as I would a friend or a child.

There are so many miracles that happen daily now that I am on the lookout for them.

Before CPA, my obsession with every physical sensation and uncomfortable feeling ruled my every waking moment. I could not get comfortable with myself or others, and Higher Power seemed so far away. I could not see beyond my misery.

It was when I made the decision, in Step Three, to turn my thoughts and actions over to the care of a loving god as I understood God that I heard the concept of investigating the *caring* nature of this Greater Power. I began looking for "caring" miracles. To my surprise, those miracles abounded: that perfect parking spot for my doctor's appointment; finding the last one of an item I needed at the store; a phone call from a CPA friend just when I needed to talk or had the energy to help a loved one. I began making a note of each one. My miracle journaling brought me closer to trusting my Greater Power to provide and care for me.

Today, when things are tough, I practice actively looking for the wisdom and the good in what is occurring instead of narrowing my perspective to only what is painful or uncomfortable. Changed attitudes/perspectives can aid my recovery. If I can't see any good, I return to my miracle journal to be reminded that I am always in the care of a loving Greater Power.

In this moment, I will shift my perspective from obsession to searching for miracles of ease and comfort.

I love that the *Declarations* are written as affirmative, positive statements about envisioning a life that is happy and worthwhile. They are about what can happen when I work the program. They are not necessarily statements that are true today; they remind me of what is possible for me through the gifts of my recovery.

When I first came to CPA, I couldn't imagine a life that was not isolated, filled with self-pity, focused on suffering, and steeped in resentment and blame. Yet as I worked the Steps and turned my will and life over to a Power greater than myself, I found my life was altered in profound and positive ways. I love sharing this opportunity for joy with others and letting them know that even if they are feeling miserable and stuck, there is hope.

In the *Declarations*, I learned that, even with my conditions, I am loveable, and I can love others. Even on my worst days, I am reminded there is something I can find to be grateful for. Even if my functioning is limited, I can give to others, and there is purpose to my life. Even if today looks bleak, I am never alone, and I have a Higher Power that will be there for me. My life will never be perfect. However, the *Declarations* tell me that my life can be one I love.

In this moment, I will reacquaint myself with the CPA Declarations. I am willing to experience all the tools of the program.

I made the decision this year to not visit my parents for the holidays. They live on the beach in a southern state, and we are in the Mid-Atlantic region. I am a summer girl, so why would I opt to turn down a beach vacation in mid-winter? My chronic pain makes traveling difficult for me in many ways (walking, sitting, trying to manage luggage), and I often pick up a bug from the close confines of the airplane. The bed at my parents' home is uncomfortable for me, and the humidity flares up my condition. For many of our visits, I have spent more time lying in bed than lounging on the beach. Looking at the cost and benefits of this journey, I didn't feel I could manage it.

The holidays are still difficult for me emotionally. I feel guilty not seeing my parents and sad about time passing by so quickly. I have learned in CPA that the emotional parts of my pain are something I can safely examine and be less afraid of/controlled by/ limited by. I worked with my Sponsor to let go of the negative feelings that came up from not seeing my folks. I hope I'm able to visit them in the spring (my pain is somewhat seasonal, with winters being the worst).

I make my best educated guess at what my body and my mind can handle at a given time, and I enjoy the ways I *can* be present. Surprisingly, I truly feel that I navigated the holidays in a manageable and pleasant way this year.

In this moment, I will honor my limitations realistically regardless of calendar norms and expectations.

In Step Six, I worked with my Sponsor to determine my list of character defects and character assets. I am changing the things I can and accepting the things I cannot change. I cannot control my feelings, but I can have control over my behaviors and actions. There is courage in being willing to choose, during difficult situations, how to act and behave. I try hard to keep my focus on the positives and fill my moments with the gratitude I feel. Each day, I turn my mind to what kind of positive day I would like to have and to letting my Higher Power do His job of removing my defects of character.

When I engage in regrettable behaviors and things start to become unmanageable, I realize this is due to my character defects. I can count on my Higher Power to give me strength so I can breathe and reflect on how to choose a peaceful way to unwind and to bring myself to a mindful place. Then I do my best not to act in ways that are harmful to myself and others.

Living in the solutions is actually easier than letting things get out of control. Being honest with myself and others helps me choose to take estimable actions. I feel so much better about myself when I do. I like myself much more. I'm able to let the part of me that feels guilty or ashamed be in my Higher Power's hands. I try to live in the moment, one day at a time, and focus on what really matters. For me, Step Six is an ongoing daily practice.

In this moment, I will pray and have faith and trust that my Higher Power will remove my character defects when the time is appropriate.

I enjoy being in the presence of people who are serene. My personal serenity surely waxes and wanes, but it generally correlates with my connection to my program and my Higher Power. In a recent meeting, we were joking around: "Wouldn't it be great if a doctor could prescribe a pill to help increase my serenity level?" Thinking about this later on, it clicked for me that I do have "medicine" that increases my serenity (and it is not in pill form). The medicine that unfailingly provides me with a healthy dose of serenity is CPA!

I have learned some powerful remedies for "serenity deficiency" from CPA members. I have learned to rely on a deep breath, the Serenity Prayer, a quiet meditation or guided imagery. I know the benefits of taking inventories (Fourth Step/Tenth Step) and listening to wise and trusted voices. I cry and laugh and share my truth while witnessing my friends navigate difficult circumstances with fortitude and grace. All these things have also helped me to identify "serenity antagonists" in my life, and I do my best to limit my doses of these.

Even at times of heightened pain and physical symptoms, I am able to use a program tool. My Higher Power gives me this strength, or He brings me someone who does. I trust that "this too shall pass," and sometimes, I can see that "pain is the touchstone of all spiritual growth." Thank you for sharing this prescription for serenity with me.

In this moment, I will gladly take the serenity that CPA offers.

Chronic pain and chronic illness brought extreme self-loathing to the forefront of my every experience. My diagnoses seemed to prove there was something innately wrong with me. I was sure I would be abandoned, that clearly I had created my health problems...I had failed at life. Death was the next logical course of action. I cried out to the heavens, and almost immediately, CPA entered my life. I clung to it. I worked the Steps in CPA, and awakening upon awakening occurred.

Through grace and my willingness to continue my Twelve Step journey, I am promised freedom. And freedom is what I now experience. The sinister inner critic has been removed. I now see life as an experiment: no harm, no foul. Self-acceptance, self-care, and self-love—once inconceivable—are now daily experiences. My fear has been replaced by courage and faith. I see the lighter side of situations. I am kind and compassionate with myself and others. My life has a renewed purpose and meaning as I open myself to new beginnings.

I will keep coming back to peel this onion that is me because with every layer revealed, more awakenings are promised.

In this moment, I will keep coming back for the awakening promised in Step Twelve.

"Fear will be replaced by courage, strength, and faith to rise and meet any challenges. We will even see challenges as opportunities for spiritual growth." — CPA Declarations

Until I had actually experienced this "promise" coming true in CPA, I had absolutely no idea what it would look like when these declarations became my reality. My entire journey in CPA has been that way, thus far. I cannot predict what my gifts will look like. I only strive to work the Step I am on, and I discover that how it works for me is beyond anything my imagination can come up with.

I now have a Higher Power (HP) who believes in me and gives me the miracles I need—in HP's time. I focus on *living with* my chronic pain and illness rather than putting my life on hold until I "feel better." I pace myself. I slow down. I practice gratitude. I've learned self-compassion and made friends who understand. My pain and illness no longer control my moods. By pacing myself according to what is acceptable to *me*, not to the healthy population, I actually accomplish *more*.

I actually had a *lot* of faith before I got sick, but it is the quality of faith that matters for facing my fears that come along with my chronic pain and illness. Before CPA, my faith and the way I worked the Steps were sufficient for where I was then and helped me recover from serious addiction. It took a different faith to recover from the effects of chronic illness and its symptoms. My HP provided that faith, and still does, through CPA.

In this moment, I will credit my daily peace, joy, and comfort to CPA and my Higher Power.

Appendix A

The CPA Preamble

CPA is a fellowship of people who share their experience, strength and hope with each other, so that they may solve their common problem and help others to recover from the disabling effects of chronic pain and chronic illness. We believe that changing attitudes can aid recovery. The only requirement for membership is a desire to recover from the emotional and spiritual debilitation of chronic pain or chronic illness. There are no dues or fees for CPA membership. We are self-supporting through our own contributions. CPA is not allied with any sect, denomination, politics, organization or institution; does not wish to engage in any controversy, neither endorses nor opposes any causes. Our primary purpose is to live our lives to the fullest by minimizing the effects of chronic pain and chronic illness in our lives and helping others to do the same. We do this by practicing the Twelve Steps, and welcoming and giving comfort and understanding to each other.

Appendix B

The Twelve Steps of CPA

1. We admitted we were powerless over pain and illness—that our lives had become unmanageable.

2. Came to believe that a Power greater than ourselves could restore us to sanity.

3. Made a decision to turn our will and our lives over to the care of God as we understood Him.

4. Made a searching and fearless moral inventory of ourselves.

5. Admitted to God, to ourselves, and to another human being the exact nature of our wrongs.

6. Were entirely ready to have God remove all these defects of character.

7. Humbly asked Him to remove our shortcomings.

8. Made a list of all persons we had harmed, and became willing to make amends to them all.

9. Made direct amends to such people wherever possible, except when to do so would injure them or others.

10. Continued to take personal inventory and when we were wrong promptly admitted it.

11. Sought through prayer and meditation to improve our conscious contact with God as we understood Him, praying only for knowledge of His will for us and the power to carry that out.

12. Having had a spiritual awakening as the result of these steps, we tried to carry this message to others with chronic pain and chronic illness, and to practice these principles in all our affairs.

Appendix C

The Twelve Traditions of CPA

1. Our common welfare should come first; personal recovery depends upon CPA unity.

2. For our group purpose there is but one ultimate authority – a loving God as He may express Himself in our group conscience. Our leaders are but trusted servants; they do not govern.

3. The only requirement for CPA membership is a desire to recover from the emotional and spiritual debilitation of chronic pain or chronic illness.

4. Each group should be autonomous, except in matters affecting other groups or CPA as a whole.

5. Each group has but one primary purpose – to carry its message to people living with chronic pain and chronic illness.

6. A CPA group ought never endorse, finance, or lend the CPA name to any outside enterprise, lest problems of money, property, and prestige divert us from our primary purpose.

7. Every CPA group ought to be fully self-supporting, declining outside contributions.

8. Chronic Pain Anonymous should remain forever nonprofessional, but our service centers may employ special workers.

9. CPA, as such, ought never be organized; but we may create service boards or committees directly responsible to those they serve.

10. Chronic Pain Anonymous has no opinion on outside

issues; hence the CPA name ought never be drawn into public controversy.

11. Our public relations policy is based on attraction rather than promotion; we need always maintain personal anonymity at the level of press, radio, television, film, and the Internet.

12. Anonymity is the spiritual foundation of all our traditions, ever reminding us to place principles before personalities.

Appendix D

Twelve Concepts of Service

1. The final responsibility and the ultimate authority for the CPA World Services should always reside in the collective conscience of our whole Fellowship.

2. The CPA groups delegate complete administrative and operational authority to their World Service Conference and its service arms.

3. As a traditional means of creating and maintaining a clearly defined working relationship among the groups, the World Service Conference, the Service Board of Trustees and its service corporation, staffs, and committees, and of thus ensuring their effective leadership, it is hereby suggested we endow each of these elements of World Service with a traditional "Right of Decision."

4. The "Right of Participation" ensures equality of opportunity for all in the decision-making process. Participation is the key to harmony.

5. Throughout our structure, a traditional "Right of Appeal" ought to prevail, so that minority opinion will be heard and personal grievances will receive careful consideration.

6. The World Service Conference recognizes the chief initiative and active responsibility in most world service matters can be exercised by the trustee members of the Conference acting as the Trustee Board.

7. The Trustees have legal rights while the rights of the Conference are traditional.

8. The Trustees are the principal planners and administrators of overall policy and finance. The Service Board of Trustees delegates full authority for routine management to its executive committees.

9. Good personal leadership at all service levels is a necessity. In the field of world service, the Service Board of Trustees assumes the primary leadership.

10. Every service responsibility should be matched by an equal service authority, with the scope of such authority well defined.

11. The General Service Virtual Office is composed of the Executive Director, selected committees, and staff members.

12. The Conference shall observe the spirit of CPA tradition, taking care that it never becomes the seat of perilous wealth or power; that sufficient operating funds and reserves be its prudent financial principle; that it place none of its members in a position of unqualified authority over others; that it reach all important decisions by discussion, vote, and whenever possible, substantial unanimity; that its actions never be personally punitive nor an incitement to public controversy; that it never perform authoritative acts of government; that, like the Fellowship it serves, it will always remain democratic in thought and action.

General Warranties of the Conferences

- Warranty One: "that it never becomes the seat of perilous wealth or power"

- Warranty Two: "that sufficient operating funds and reserves be its prudent financial principle"

- Warranty Three: "that it place none of its members in a position of unqualified authority over others"

- Warranty Four: "that it reach all important decisions by discussion, vote, and whenever possible, substantial unanimity"

- Warranty Five: "that its actions never be personally punitive nor an incitement to public controversy"

- Warranty Six: "that it never perform authoritative acts of government; that, like the Fellowship it serves, it will always remain democratic in thought and action"

Appendix E

The CPA Declarations

Some of us believe our problems are insurmountable. We have lived with pain and suffering for so long; we have given up hope for happiness. We believe any promises for positive change are only true for others, not for us.

The CPA program of recovery offers new attitudes and ways of thinking. We may start this journey with doubt, yet little by little, through our consistent efforts, we will discover a different way of life in which beneficial habits will begin to replace ones that once brought us misery.

Our spiritual recovery will be accomplished by being open to the experience, strength and hope shared by our friends in the fellowship. We will come to understand if we do what others have done, we will get what others have gotten. As we steadily work the Twelve Steps of CPA and engage in service, our relationship with chronic pain and chronic illness will no longer be adversarial. We will begin our day with gratitude and hope. Possibilities we never dreamed of will be part of our daily existence and we will begin to see that we can have a quality of life despite living with pain and illness.

So, with the little bit of faith and guidance that brought us to CPA, we begin. If we arerigorous in our endeavor, we will be astounded by the results.

1. Fellowship, rather than loneliness and isolation, will be present in our life.

2. We will enjoy connecting with other people.

3. We will be compassionate and kind to ourselves as well as consider the needs of others.

4. Fear will be replaced by courage, strength and faith to rise and meet any challenges. We will even see challenges as opportunities for spiritual growth.

5. We will forgive those whom we perceive have harmed us so we can be free from the chains of the past.

6. Remembering progress, not perfection, we will approach each day with a positive attitude. We will choose to focus on gratitude, placing our attention on all that is good.

7. Our pain and illness will no longer be the primary focus of our day. We will feel serenity and peace regardless of what condition our body is in. Our body will not determine the joy we experience in life.

8. We will laugh and see the lighter side of situations.

9. We will value ourselves and believe we have something to give to the world. Self-pity will be replaced by a belief our life has meaning and purpose.

10. We will be open to new beginnings and no longer cling to how things were in the past.

11. We will believe we deserve to love and to be loved.

12. We will have faith in a Higher Power which does for us what we cannot do for ourselves. This Power is the foundation that will support and guide us as we move through each moment. Our life will be far better than we ever imagined possible.

Appendix F

One Day At A Time

One Day At A Time – I will make an effort to participate in the world. I will reach out and connect with another person. I can pick up the phone and call a friend, greet someone on the street, or I can smile at the clerk in the store.

One Day At A Time – I will put my focus on promoting the well-being of someone besides myself. I will take the attention off of me and my issues, and place it on the needs of another being.

One Day At A Time – I will pace myself and trust my body to guide me. I will not push when my body tells me it's time to stop. I will do half of what I think I can Accomplish.

One Day At A Time – I will eat well and exercise in moderation. I will take an interest in my appearance and tend to my personal hygiene. I may dress comfortably, but I will try to look my very best.

One Day At A Time – I will ask for help when I need it. I will accept assistance graciously and be thankful. I will appreciate the people in my life who support me.

One Day At A Time – I will live each day to the best of my ability and take responsibility for my own happiness. I will notice the good in life and not dwell on the negative. I will count my blessings and enjoy all that I've been given.

One Day At A Time – I will remember that I am more than my pain or my illness. I will believe that I am perfect exactly as I am. I will accept whatever comes my way with an attitude of gratitude.

One Day At A Time – I will make an extra effort to be patient and gentle with myself and others when I am feeling irritable and frustrated. No blame, no shame. Just because I am in pain doesn't mean I have to be a pain.

One Day At A Time – I will create some quiet moments for

myself. I can use them for inner reflection, reviewing my day, or strengthening my spiritual connections. Taking this time each day is a rich and rewarding gift to myself.

One Day At A Time – I will enjoy something that is fun. I will engage my mind in creative activities. I will try something different and be open to new possibilities.

One Day At A Time – I accept the conditions of my life as they are this day. Within any condition I can contribute to myself, my family, and my community. I am a valuable member of society.

One Day At A Time – I will acknowledge feelings of fear and anxiety as they rise up. When they appear, I will remember to put my trust in a Power greater than myself. I will have hope in knowing that this, too, shall pass, and I will have faith that I can thrive through anything when I do it one moment at a time.

Appendix G

One Night At A Time

In CPA we learn to live in the solution and not in the problem. These *One Night At A Time* suggestions can guide us toward serenity. We can't take them all on at once. It helps to take one, study it, and apply it to our lives until we are familiar with it. Over time we will see how changing attitudes and actions can open the door to newfound happiness and a celebration of life.

One night at a time, I will honor my gratitude.Challenges and blessings happened today, and I am grateful for both. I have come to believe that my Higher Power is in charge and is working toward the greatest and highest good for myself and others—regardless of circumstances and appearances. This night, I choose an attitude of gratitude.

One night at a time, I will honor my willingness to surrender. I applaud my willingness to surrender that which no longer serves me or my Higher Power. I surrender my powerlessness and relax. I trust my Higher Power to change my relationship with myself, my body, and all that troubles me. Even in the depths of chronic pain and chronic illness, I am willing to change and be changed. This night, I choose to celebrate my growing faith.

One night at a time, I will honor my courage and my fears. I may have taken risks today, big or small. I may have asked for help and been willing to be of service. I may have felt frightened, may have been reactive, or may have felt hopeless—yet I faced another day with the help of my Higher Power. This night, I choose to acknowledge my courage and bravery when facing my fears.

One night at a time, I will honor myself exactly as I am in this moment. My body, mind and spirit have served me today. Perhaps not in the way I would have liked, but they have served me—and they have served my Higher Power. I remember to pray for Higher Power's will to be done—not my own. I release judgment and criticism. I accept my whole self in its limited functionality as beautiful in the eyes of my Higher Power. This night, I choose self-compassion and self-care.

One night at a time, I will honor self-acceptance. I am a work in progress, a perfectly imperfect human being just like everyone else. I choose to view positive and negative thoughts, sensations, emotions, and behaviors with kindness and gratitude. I release the need to label these experiences as good or bad. Each arrives with wisdom and clarity that Higher Power will reveal to me. This night, I choose self-love.

One night at a time, I will honor others just as they are. I may have felt anger, frustration, or disappointment with others today. I might have had expectations that were not met. These feelings signal my need to practice tolerance, acceptance, and unconditional kindness. In all my relationships, I release my resistance with compassionate self-awareness. This night, I choose to bless everyone in my life and wish them all a serene night.

One night at a time, I will greet all my feelings as valued friends. I may have felt rage, panic, irritability, jealousy, loneliness, or grief today. Although some feelings can be overwhelming and unpleasant, they all have something to teach me. I can acknowledge all my feelings and ask for Higher Power's guidance in processing (not suppressing) them. I do not have to let these feelings dictate the quality of my rest tonight or my actions tomorrow. This night, I will trust Higher Power to show me the wisdom in all of my feelings.

One night at a time, I will remind myself that nothing is required of me in this moment. My day is done, and tomorrow offers a new beginning. I am more open to Higher Power's guidance when I honor my need for rest. I do not need to plan, solve problems, or correct errors. In this present moment, I pray for a quiet mind and a contented heart. This night, I choose to turn over yesterday, today, and tomorrow to the care of my loving Higher Power.

I will rest now, safe in the knowledge of my Higher Power's love for me. I believe the help, guidance, and strength I need for tomorrow will be freely given to me as I continue to pray, "Thy will,

410

not mine, be done." I remember that my Higher Power dreams bigger than I do. I choose to rest in the loving care of my Higher Power.

Appendix H

CPA Suggested Meeting Format

1. Welcome to the _____ meeting of Chronic Pain Anonymous. My name is _____, and I live with chronic pain and chronic illness ("I am a grateful member;" location, etc.). Let's begin the meeting with a moment of silence, followed by the Serenity Prayer.

2. Would someone (or name) please read the Preamble?

   Would someone (or name) please read the Twelve Steps?

   Would someone (or name) please read the Twelve Traditions?

3. Let's introduce ourselves by our first names only. (Optional: People can introduce themselves with their location as well.) If you are new to the group, please let us know so we can welcome you.

4. Group Announcements:

- Our monthly business meeting is held the _____ of each month. Any group member may call a group conscience at any time.

- Are there any CPA-related announcements?

- Is anyone celebrating a CPA milestone?

5. Tradition Seven states, "Every CPA group ought to be fully self-supporting, declining outside contributions." While CPA has no dues or fees, we do have expenses. Our donations pay for services such as literature (professional edits, publishing, printing, and audio recordings), public information, website administration, and bookkeeping. Please give what you can. However, we need you more than we need your money. https://chronicpainanonymous.org/contributions/

6. This is a (topic, discussion, speaker, literature, step study, etc.) group. We will discuss the CPA Twelve Steps and Twelve Traditions, exploring ways to apply the program to living with chronic pain and chronic illness. (We are currently reading _____.)

7. Sharing Guidelines:

In CPA, we concentrate on our feelings and attitudes about our situation rather than on the details of the situation. We reflect on how chronic illness and chronic pain have affected our thinking and our behavior. We look at the part we play in our problems and how the Twelve Steps can guide us toward recovery from the obsession of our chronic illness and chronic pain. When we focus on ways to apply the principles of the program in our daily lives, we discover that our changed attitudes and actions can lead us to a meaningful life of peace and serenity.

Tradition Ten states, "Chronic Pain Anonymous has no opinion on outside issues; hence the CPA name ought never be drawn into public controversy." Therefore, in our meetings we avoid discussions about religion or specific diagnoses, medications, therapies, doctors, insurance providers, and healthcare systems. If referring to our own medical issues, we find it is best to keep to general terms. We do not give medical advice. When we share, we guard against crosstalk. When one person responds directly to another who has shared, this is crosstalk.

8. We come together to share our experience, strength, and hope freely without interruption. We listen to suffering individuals with compassion and understanding, to offer hope and support. We empower each other to be vulnerable by providing a nonjudgmental, safe meeting.

9. This meeting ends at _____ . (Optional: the top of the hour/the bottom of the hour, etc.)

CLOSING

In closing, I would like to remind everyone that the opinions expressed here were strictly those of the person who spoke. Take what you like and leave the rest. Everything that was shared here was done so in confidence. Please respect the anonymity of this group and its members. Discussing who was at a meeting or what they shared is a breach of anonymity. Let what you heard here, stay here. Tradition Twelve states, "Anonymity is the spiritual foundation of all our Traditions, ever reminding us to place principles before personalities."

If you are new to CPA, we encourage you to keep coming back. We have found that while our health challenges may differ, how they affect us is often similar. Although today we may be feeling at our worst, in CPA we see the best in each other. In time, with the love and support we have found here, we begin to see the best in ourselves.

If you have any questions, we invite you to stay after the meeting and talk with someone who is familiar with CPA and the Twelve Steps. Will all who care to, please join me in the Closing Prayer/Words.

Please see CPA's website under Member Resources > Meeting Materials > for more detailed information.

Index

A

Ability 17, 43, 55, 84, 96, 106, 111, 117, 125, 128, 143, 152, 153, 161, 213, 249, 254, 257, 259, 289, 298, 307, 325, 326, 328, 362, 371, 372, 375, 386, 387, 389, 407

Acceptance 9, 10, 13, 14, 25, 26, 30, 43, 48, 49, 54, 56, 65, 77, 78, 90, 93, 96, 104, 106, 108, 109, 111, 114, 115, 119, 122, 123, 128, 129, 130, 131, 138, 142, 143, 147, 150, 151, 152, 164, 165, 169, 171, 173, 176, 181, 182, 188, 190, 193, 196, 205, 217, 220, 222, 230, 235, 241, 244, 251, 265, 279, 301, 322, 325, 327, 331, 339, 345, 349, 389, 396, 410

Act as if 23, 213, 222, 227, 229

Action 15, 17, 22, 29, 39, 48, 49, 55, 61, 72, 78, 80, 87, 112, 115, 118, 125, 128, 129, 144, 148, 151, 156, 160, 164, 173, 176, 181, 196, 201, 204, 207, 216, 223, 224, 225, 229, 230, 241, 254, 270, 272, 273, 275, 284, 285, 292, 293, 312, 321, 322, 331, 337, 341, 353, 357, 362, 370, 376, 377, 379, 388, 396, 403, 404

Addiction ix, 301, 343, 397

Advice 62, 105, 192, 195, 277, 321, 323, 413

Aging 21

Alone. *See* Loneliness

Amends 13, 57, 89, 94, 103, 123, 124, 129, 141, 148, 149, 171, 242, 248, 254, 257, 271, 277, 290, 305, 315, 316, 379, 399

Anger/Angry ix, 3, 12, 23, 27, 28, 56, 81, 99, 103, 104, 106, 109, 110, 123, 124, 128, 137, 138, 158, 160, 162, 163, 171, 174, 175, 176, 187, 188, 193, 194, 211, 214, 217, 225, 230, 248, 257, 261, 265, 278, 292, 294, 304, 325, 327, 347, 357, 363, 386, 390, 410

Anonymity 3, 107, 121, 186, 194, 256, 367, 389, 401, 414

Anxiety 48, 59, 75, 90, 128, 144, 181, 188, 191, 197, 235, 265, 270, 274, 325, 363, 408

Appointment(s) 47, 81, 88, 108, 116, 117, 139, 225, 230, 306, 313, 328, 385, 391

Art 180, 205, 252

As it is 26, 38, 58, 77, 78, 95, 110, 122, 130, 142, 152, 169, 228, 279

Asking for help 14, 75, 135, 138

As we understood 356, 399

Attachment 383

Attitude 7, 16, 18, 19, 23, 31, 42, 47, 49, 52, 60, 61, 69, 78, 80, 106, 156, 195, 198, 202, 207, 221, 225, 227, 229, 236, 241, 242, 252, 253, 254, 257, 265, 271, 283, 290, 297, 301, 305, 309, 349, 360, 363, 367, 373, 383, 385, 388, 406, 407, 409

Authentic 76, 85, 123, 132, 245, 255, 298, 312, 415

G

H

I

M

N

O

P

U

V

W

Notes

Notes

Notes

Notes

Notes

Made in the USA
Las Vegas, NV
02 February 2024

85208164R00246